THE HERITAGE OF SYMBOLISM

THE HERITAGE
OF
SYMBOLISM

BY

C. M. BOWRA

LONDON
MACMILLAN & CO. LTD
1943

TO

L. v. W.

PRINTED IN GREAT BRITAIN
BY R. & R. CLARK, LIMITED, EDINBURGH

PREFACE

Some years ago I wrote, for my own satisfaction, and with no real intention to publish, a series of essays on some poets whose work meant much to me. I have at times showed them to friends, who have pressed me to make a book. They tell me that there is a general interest in these poets and that some account of them is needed. I have therefore rewritten my chapters and tried to make them into a whole. In Chapters III and V I have included parts of two essays already published, and I am grateful to Messrs. Sidgwick and Jackson and Messrs. Faber and Faber for allowing me to do so. This book makes no claim to learning or to scholarship or to be anything more than an attempt at explanation and criticism. Although two of the poets with whom it deals were known to me, I have abstained from biographical details except where they seemed relevant to my argument. I can make no pretence to have a good knowledge of Russian or even of German, and I may well have made mistakes. For these I ask forgiveness. I have been quite inconsistent in my treatment of foreign languages. I have assumed that all my readers will know French, will be willing to attempt German with the help of translations, and will be content not to have original texts in Russian. I am most grateful to Professor Oliver Elton for his translations from the Russian, to Mr. J. B. Leishman for revised versions of Rilke, and to Mr. Cyril Scott for pieces of George from his forthcoming book. These admirable versions do far more than anything I can say to show the excellences of the originals. Where they are lacking, I have in desperation made translations of my own, but I hope that the originals will not be judged by them.

C. M. B.

OXFORD
October 23, 1942

CONTENTS

	PAGE
I. INTRODUCTION	1
II. PAUL VALÉRY	17
III. RAINER MARIA RILKE . . .	56
IV. STEFAN GEORGE	98
V. ALEXANDER BLOK . . .	144
VI. WILLIAM BUTLER YEATS . .	180
VII. CONCLUSION	219
INDEX	231

I
INTRODUCTION

It is dangerous to speak of movements in literature. Inspiration blows with too wild a breath for its motions to be measured, and the poet's personality defeats our efforts to claim him for this or that party or to explain him as an example of a rule. But if we compare the poetry written in Europe after 1890 with what preceded it, we must admit that there was a change and that the newer poets had some common qualities which make them look like members of a movement. This similarity is not the result of an agreed programme or of an entirely conscious purpose. It cannot be compared with that of the members of the Pléiade or of the Lake School. But it recalls those writers who seemed sufficiently different to their contemporaries but are found by posterity to be all tinged with the characteristic colour of an epoch. Just as at the present day Byron, Pushkin and Hugo are seen to share qualities which have almost disappeared from poetry, so the poets of the generation which reached manhood about 1890 have other qualities which distinguish them from those who preceded and from those who are now at work. The movement with which we are concerned has already spent most of its force. Its most notable exponents are dead. Its ideas and its ideals are falling into disuse. It belongs to history. The peculiar character of its aims can be discerned and the value of its achievement assessed.

This movement may be regarded as a later development, a second wave, of those poetical activities which are variously known as Symbolist and Decadent. Neither name is exact, and attempts to demand precision from them usually fail. A poetical movement is recognised in its exponents, and the chief poets of Symbolism are Baudelaire, Verlaine and Mallarmé. Baudelaire was the first to exalt the value of symbols ; Verlaine used them instinctively, and Mallarmé erected a metaphysic to explain and justify them. In his theory and his practice Mallarmé was the conclusion and crown of the Symbolist Movement. When we speak of it, it is of him

I

primarily that we think, his ideas that we remember. But his work would have been impossible without Baudelaire and would hardly have found recognition but for the more popular form which Verlaine found for its principles. Despite their obvious differences these poets had a common view of life which marks them from their predecessors and accounts to a large degree for their influence. In spite of its many shapes Symbolism was united by a single creed which determined the character of its poetry. Its inheritors and successors, the men of the 'nineties, began by absorbing this creed. Some abandoned it ; others changed it into forms almost past recognition or moved through it to new forms of their own. All provide a commentary on the validity and vitality of the Symbolist doctrines, and their work shows what different results can be reached from a theory which might seem narrow and temporary. In other lands and in other languages a French doctrine has been put into practice. In the variety of their experiments and the success which has crowned them these poets show how important a theory may be in the arts so long as it is not treated theoretically but used as a basis for new performance.

Seen in retrospect the Symbolist Movement of the nine-teenth century in France was fundamentally mystical. It protested with noble eloquence against the scientific art of an age which had lost much of its belief in traditional religion and hoped to find a substitute in the search for truth. The characteristic figures of the time were novelists like Zola, who painted in ruthless detail large canvases of contemporary life, and poets like Heredia, who composed impersonal vignettes of past centuries and distant scenes. In this art mysticism had no place. The Realists had no use for that belief in a superior world above the senses which has been familiar in Europe since Augustine absorbed the doctrines of Neo-Platonism ; they had a stern conviction that what mattered was truth and that truth could be found empirically in this world. Orthodox Christianity, of course, continued to exist and to produce its own writers, but these were not representa-tive of their time. In the third quarter of the nineteenth century the Realists and the Parnassians held the field in France, and even in England something of the same spirit may be seen in the dramatic poems of Browning or those poems of Tennyson like the " short, sweet idyll " of *The*

Princess which are entirely objective in their account of men and things.

Against this scientific Realism the Symbolists protested, and their protest was mystical in that it was made on behalf of an ideal world which was, in their judgment, more real than that of the senses. It was not in any strict sense Christian. It is true that Verlaine had his days of simple unquestioning belief, that Baudelaire's diabolism was an inverted form of Catholicism, that Mallarmé derived much of his imaginative ritual from the ceremonies of the Church. The mystical character of Symbolism was less definitely Christian than any of these manifestations. It was a religion of Ideal Beauty, of " le Beau " and " l'Idéal ". This may be seen in Baudelaire's belief in that ideal beauty which he contrasted so poignantly with his own life, in Verlaine's attempt to write on parallel lines of soul and body, in the oracular and enigmatic utterances of Mallarmé. For Baudelaire the Ideal of the Beautiful gave force and purpose to his tortured and disordered soul; for Verlaine it justified the search for forbidden pleasure ; for Mallarmé it was all that mattered. The fabric of their Christian beliefs had been mutilated or undermined, and feeling a need for a gospel to take its place they found in the Beautiful something which unified their activities and gave a goal to their work. To this belief they clung with a conviction which can only be called mystical because of its intensity, its irrationality, its disregard for other beliefs and its reliance on a world beyond the senses.

Symbolism, then, was a mystical form of Aestheticism. Its counterpart in England was the Aesthetic Movement whose apostles were Rossetti and Pater and whose martyr was Wilde. Rossetti's poetry is infused with a belief in Ideal Beauty. It creates a strange view of love in his *House of Life* and it brings even religious subjects into his scope. The doctrine implicit in his art was made explicit in the famous last chapter of Pater's *Renaissance*, where art is proclaimed as the end of life because it gives " a quickened, multiplied consciousness ". Nor were the clamour and execration which greeted Wilde's downfall prompted simply by moral indignation at his offence. The massed forces of Philistinism saw that their enemy had fallen and rejoiced over him. He stood for a creed which they feared and hated, and his punishment meant not only that his own life was ruined but that the cause

3

of Aestheticism was routed. Because art had fallen into disrepute, the poets of the Edwardian age became an isolated sect, cut off from the main currents of contemporary thought and compelled to work in small cliques or in solitude. It was only with the Four Years' War that English poets again won something like their traditional place in national life.

English Aestheticism, however, was less exacting, less theoretical, less mystical than French. Neither Rossetti nor Pater developed their theories of the Beautiful with the desperate logic of Mallarmé. Knowing what they admired and finding in art an experience more vivid than any they found in religion or morality, they lived sincerely and naturally for it. Their convictions and their doctrine were indeed revolutionary, caused dismay among their contemporaries and altered the whole character of English culture. They were too in a sense religious in that they felt that the principle of the Beautiful unified life and gave meaning to it. But they were not mystical as Mallarmé was. Their theories were not so transcendental, so exacting, so complete as his. They were content with impressions as they met them and did not attempt to exalt them to an ideal world. The protestant English nature seems to refuse any complete surrender to mysticism or to metaphysics, and Pater's aestheticism had a subjective and experimental character. He arranged his experiences as they came to him and theorised about them ; but his conclusions were more practical than theoretical, and his influence was perhaps greater on conduct than on thought. His teaching created a new ideal for many who wished for something to believe, and he prepared the way for great changes. He certainly influenced the poets of the 'nineties such as Johnson and Dowson, but perhaps his greatest pupil was the Jesuit priest Gerard Hopkins, whose poetical life lay apart from any current, English or European. Pater gave dignity and honour to the arts in an age which tended to misunderstand or to undervalue them, but his views were never so complex or so mystical as those of Mallarmé.

For Mallarmé certainly created a new mysticism of art. He expressed it disjointedly in words of Heraclitean darkness and power. Indeed any attempt to epitomise his views must end in distorting them ; for he preferred to speak on particular issues in metaphor and simile. But his main tenets and his actual practice may be discerned, and in them the most

4

important doctrines of the Symbolists are contained. In his *Divagations* he says :

> Je dis une fleur ; et hors de l'oubli où ma voix relègue aucun contour en tant que quelque chose d'autre que les calices sus, musicalement se lève, idée même et suave, l'absente de tous bouquets.

This hermetic text is a central clue. The flower, evoked by the magic word, is the ideal flower which has in it the beauty of all flowers and is not one among them but something above them. Readers of Plato will see a resemblance between this " idée " and the Platonic εἶδος, or Form, which is both a universal principle and an ideal particular. And the comparison is justified so long as we remember that for Mallarmé the Absolute is not Being but the Beautiful. In this world of beautiful things he found a creating and sustaining principle in " les Idées " which are both beautiful in themselves and the cause of beauty in other things. In his *Prose pour des Esseintes* he expresses much the same doctrine in verse :

> Oui, dans une île que l'air charge
> De vue et non de visions
> Toute fleur s'étalait plus large
> Sans que nous en devisions
>
> Telles, immenses, que chacune
> Ordinairement se para
> D'un lucide contour lacune
> Qui des jardins la sépara.

The flower is the ideal flower. It belongs to pure sight, not to the senses.

A doctrine of this character has much in common with that of orthodox religious poets. Just as Mallarmé tried to capture in verse an ideal beauty, so Dante had tried to create a visible image of an invisible world. And just as Dante created his image by the accepted symbols of the Christian Heaven and Hell, so Mallarmé too had to use symbols. He and his followers are rightly called Symbolists, because they attempted to convey a supernatural experience in the language of visible things, and therefore almost every word is a symbol and is used not for its common purpose but for the associations which it evokes of a reality beyond the senses. His method was not new. It may be seen in the apocalyptic poems of William Blake, and mystical literature is almost inconceivable without it. But whereas most earlier Symbolists had been concerned with the facts of religious devotion, Mallarmé was concerned with a special aesthetic experience which he interpreted as a saint might his visions of God. In this too he had a forerunner ; for in his sonnet *Correspondances* Baudelaire saw nature as symbolical of another reality :

> La Nature est un temple où de vivants piliers
> Laissent parfois sortir de confuses paroles ;
> L'homme y passe à travers des forêts de symboles
> Qui l'observent avec des regards familiers.
>
> Comme de longs échos qui de loin se confondent
> Dans une ténébreuse et profonde unité,
> Vaste comme la nuit et comme la clarté,
> Les parfums, les couleurs et les sons se répondent.

For Baudelaire the visible and sensible world was full of symbols which fill man's heart with joy and sorrow and convey him through scent, colour and sound to raptures of the spirit.

The essence of Symbolism is its insistence on a world of ideal beauty, and its conviction that this is realised through art. The ecstasies which religion claims for the devout through prayer and contemplation are claimed by the Symbolist for the poet through the exercise of his craft. Nor is so proud a claim entirely unreasonable. For the undivided attention which the enraptured worshipper gives to the object of his prayers and the sense of timeless contentment which he finds through them are not entirely different from the pure aesthetic state which seems to obliterate distinctions of time and place, of self and not-self, of sorrow and joy. Nor is it easy to say whether the rapture which so entrances in the poetry of St. John of the Cross is really religious or aesthetic. It is far removed from the ratiocinative religion of Milton and it has much in common with the exaltation which is known to fill poets in the moment of creative vision. In certain characteristics aesthetic rapture may resemble religious devotion. It was not without reason that the Mediaeval Church considered the illumination of manuscripts to be a proper way of serving God. For those who believe in a world above the senses there may be more than one way of approach to it.

But the Symbolism of French poets differs from traditional Symbolism in one vital respect. The Church has its own symbols of august and splendid majesty, hallowed by time and familiar from centuries of religious art. The symbols of Christianity are rich in associations and easily recognised. But the poet who writes of his private exaltations has to find his own symbols, and it may be difficult for others to appreciate these at their full value. Baudelaire solved the problem by inverting the symbols of Catholicism and using them for his mistress or for himself. But Mallarmé had to find new symbols. He chose them from the varied field of his impressions, and though most may be understood from a careful study of his work, some remain in darkness and others cannot convey all that they meant to him. For this reason Mallarmé's poetry is more difficult than almost any other great poetry of the world. It requires for its appreciation a knowledge which it is almost impossible to obtain fully. But when the symbols are intelligible, as they often are, they convey, as no other method could, the transcendental joy which Mallarmé found in his poetical vision. Even if the outlines are blurred, the main colours stand out with great brightness, and experiences beyond the common lot are conveyed in words, although by their very nature they belong to categories of existence for which words hardly exist.

A peculiar intensity is what the Symbolists sought to give. In their loyalty to this aim they had to break with many familiar characteristics of poetry. Above all they avoided those public and political themes which were dear to the Romantics. Of course if it is sincere and strongly felt, political poetry has its own greatness. Its defects are not necessarily due to its subject. But for the Symbolist, absorbed in an ideal beauty, politics are an alien and hostile theme. Their clamour impinges on the serene silence of his contemplation and their vulgar emotions spoil the delicate concentration of his vision. The Symbolist was equally hostile to the realistic or scientific view of art because by its very nature it denies or destroys the ideal world which is the centre of his activities. Though they might have personal friends among the Parnassians, neither Verlaine nor Mallarmé was of their number. That art was too scientific for them. It aimed at reproducing scenes from the visible world, and they looked elsewhere. Mallarmé, it is true, published in *Le Parnasse Contemporain*, but it was soon plain that his real place was not there. That poetry appealed to the eye, but his to secret desires and

excitements, to the thrills of solitude and to the silent contemplative self.

The strength of the Symbolists lay in their devotion to an
ideal. It saved them from those failures of taste, even of
sincerity, which appal in Tennyson and Hugo. If their world
is narrow, it is undeniably rich ; for no limits may be set to
the unseen. It is therefore not surprising that their advent
was hailed as a revolution and that poets who hardly understood their purpose or their technique fought for a time under
their banner. Here was a poetry both exciting and sincere.
Here were no lapses into frigid rhetoric or trite morality, no
appeal to the crowd, no attempt to serve ends other than
the Beautiful. Moreover Symbolism brought back to poetry
qualities which had been lacking and were welcomed by all
who knew what poetry is. By a paradox they recovered that
subjective element which the Parnassians had excluded. It
is true that Mallarmé regarded art as impersonal, but since he
was concerned with his own remarkable visions, he showed
that the self was as rich a subject for poetry as Leconte de
Lisle's elephants or the submarine marvels of Heredia. When
he wrote

Nuit blanche de glaçons et de neige cruelle

he gave the austere magnificence of an Arctic or Alpine night
to his own thoughts, but when Heredia wrote

Le fond vermiculé du pâle madrépore

he simply described nature. The Symbolists showed that
poetry could be both decorative and personal. Younger poets,
full of their own excitements, saw a way to write about themselves. The new method, so suited to express every shade of
sensibility, taught them how to do it.

No less important was the regard which the Symbolists
had for the musical element in poetry. The great revelation
for their age was the music of Wagner. In it Mallarmé saw
" la cime menaçante de l'absolu ", and Verlaine praised it in
more than one sonnet. To their ears the music of Wagner, in
its grandeur and sonority, was something new. In it they
found an excitement which seemed to be just what they
wished to convey through their own poetry. Music became
a catchword, and Verlaine wrote :

8

De la musique encore et toujours !
Que ton vers soit la chose envolée
Qu'on sent qui fuit d'une âme en allée
Vers d'autres cieux à d'autres amours.

Que ton vers soit la bonne aventure
Éparse au vent crispé du matin
Qui va fleurant la menthe et le thym . . .
Et tout le reste est littérature.

This aim has been summarised by Valéry, who says that the chief task of Symbolism was to take back from music what poets had lost to it. In such an ideal there were undoubted difficulties and ambiguities. But for the moment there seemed a great promise and a great hope. To French poets at least this was a glorious task. To do with words what Wagner had done with musical notes seemed both possible and desirable. Even outside France, in England and in Germany, this seemed a new call, a return to lost traditions of song, to the very heart of poetry.

To this problem Mallarmé gave his prolonged and devoted attention. He set himself an ideal of what poetry ought to be and meditated on it :

Ouïr l'indiscutable rayon — comme les traits dorent et déchirent un méandre de mélodies : où la Musique rejoint le Vers pour former, depuis Wagner, la Poésie.

His theory, put briefly, is that poetry should not inform but suggest and evoke, not name things but create their atmosphere. This was not new. His great idol, Poe, had demanded " a suggestive indefiniteness of vague and therefore of spiritual effect ". To add mystery to poetry by suggestion was a noble ideal. In their own way most poets have done it, and Mallarmé's demand does not look very singular. But he pursued it with relentless consistency. His poetry grew progressively more obscure from the clarity of his early work to the half-mysterious splendours of *Hérodiade* to the strange last text of *Un Coup de Dés* where the size of the print and the arrangement of words on the page are almost more important than the words themselves. To convey all the mystery that he felt he reduced his punctuation, made new collocations of words, sometimes disregarded the rules of syntax. But these traits, which outraged the public, were of little importance in

B

comparison with his central aim of suggestion. For him what matters is the aroma, the air, of a thing, not the mere thing itself. He omits the old machinery of similes and comparisons and identifies a thing with what it resembles ; for after all this conveys it more fully than its name can. For instance, in one sonnet he considers the spectacle of the starry sky which many have believed to show the nothingness of man. This is not his view. For him the great abysses of nightly space are like a phantom palace whose ebony and garlands are simply falsehoods :

> Luxe, ô salle d'ébène, où, pour séduire un roi,
> Se tordent dans leur mort des guirlandes célèbres,
> Vous n'êtes qu'un orgueil menti par les ténèbres
> Aux yeux du solitaire ébloui de sa foi.

This is his highly individual way of saying that all the notions of the sky as the palace of God are merely the proud dreams of the anchorite. He does not name the sky or God. He conjures up instead this splendid palace with its dead garlands. The poetical gain is immense. All preliminaries, explanations, comparisons, are omitted. Only the essential points are given, and the gain in concentration and power is enormous. The poetry is fully packed. It has some of the direct appeal of music. There are no prosaic joints or interstices. Again and again Mallarmé brings off this success. No French poet has written lines of so indubitable and unmixed poetry. The author of

> Et l'avare silence et la massive nuit

or

> Un peu profond ruisseau calomnié la mort

had brought a concentrated richness to French verse such as it had never known before. So much at least the example of Wagner had done.

This method of suggestion brought one special advantage. There is much in the human consciousness for which plain statement is not inadequate but impossible. We all know fleeting, indefinite states of mind which have no clear outline or character and can hardly be expressed at all. They can, however, be suggested and conveyed in poetry by Mallarmé's method. For instance, in one poem he hints at an amorous adventure and closes with a note of triumph :

Dis si je suis pas joyeux
Tonnerre et rubis aux moyeux
De voir en l'air que ce feu troue

Avec des royaumes épars
Comme mourir pourpre la roue
Du seul vespéral de mes chars.

Attempts have been made to give a precise meaning to this. Some have thought that the poet goes for a drive in a carriage whose wheels are reddened by the setting sun, others that he refers to a kind of great Catherine-wheel at a show of fireworks. This is to ask for exactness where it does not exist. The splendid picture of the triumphal chariot in the evening conveys a state of mind, of joyful success and exaltation. This is what it is intended to do and what, with remarkable brilliance, it does.

But Mallarmé was not content merely to suggest. In music he found more than an analogy. He somehow believed that poetry was a kind of music, and by this he did not mean that its pleasure is comparable in kind and quality, though this follows from his belief. He had a mystical faith which means much more. He knew an Absolute of aesthetic joy which was outside and beyond thought and therefore beyond significant words. His ideal is " l'absence ", the perfection which is never actually present, the silence which is more musical than any song. It was this that he wished to capture. In *Sainte* the Saint in a stained-glass window touches an Angel's wing, and this wing becomes, as it were, a musical instrument, while the Saint, disdaining her own lute, becomes

Musicienne de silence.

Mallarmé dreamed of something like the music of the spheres, a harmony audible to the spiritual ear in forms of ideal beauty. For him a poem is like this :

De scintillations sitôt le septuor,

a septet of starry sounds, like the seven stars of the Great Bear. The unheard music, the silent word, were his symbols for the ecstasy and delight which meant much to him and whose glory he tried to convey to others. He believed that beyond any poetry that he might write was some ideal and absolute poetry, compared with which what was actually written, the ordinary matter of poetry, was

Un inutile gisement :
Nuit, désespoir et pierrerie.

Most will agree that in pure aesthetic pleasure there is some-times an absolute quality which seems to bear no intelligible relation to the actual work of art which provokes it, a pure joy which is not bound to any meaning in words and is for that reason like the pleasure that comes from music. Mallarmé knew this and made it the centre and the goal of his beliefs. He hoped so to purify poetry that it would produce an un-mixed ecstasy, an absolute joy which transcends the limitations which nature imposes upon words, and seems to belong to an ideal world.

Symbolism, then, was in origin a mystical kind of poetry whose technique depended on its metaphysics and whose first popularity was due to the importance that it gave to the poet's self and to the element of music in his art. It made converts and spread to many lands. But behind this golden promise lurked defects, not indeed fatal or fundamental but still insidious. By the simple act of cutting himself off from vulgar emotions and concentrating on private visions the Symbolist severed himself from a large part of life and his work became the activity of a cultivated few. Politically this might be explained as an aristocratic reaction against the insurgent tide of democratic opinions. Nor is such an explanation entirely untrue. Men like Villiers de l'Isle Adam liked to boast — without good reason, it seems, — of their high lineage, and the cult of Wagner was not always distinguishable from that of Ludwig II of Bavaria. The Symbolists hated the public as much as Flaubert hated it. For Mallarmé it was the hydra that had killed Poe. He saw his age as hostile because of its democratic character. But this isolation from life was really more that of the anchorite than of the dispossessed or threatened nobleman. It grew out of the demands which aesthetic sensibility makes of those who yield themselves to it. The true Aesthete who wishes to increase his impressions and to catch the most remote or fleeting sensations is barred from action and the cruder claims of life. The sincere pursuit of his aims demands a concentration and an isolation impossible for most men. This aesthetic withdrawal was idealised by the Symbolists and found its complete expression in des Esseintes, the hero of Huysmans' novel *A Rebours*, who wishes

" to hide himself away, far from the world, in some retreat, where he might deaden the sound of the loud rumbling of inflexible life as one covers the streets with straw for sick people ". The conclusion of such a view may be seen in Villiers' *Axël*, in which life is nothing and imaginative experience is everything. " Live ? " cries Axël. " Our servants will do that for us." Nor is such a spirit lacking in the English Aesthetes. Pater liked to let his fancy play on imaginary heroes who refused to commit themselves to life, and drew his picture of Sebastian van Storck with his " fastidious refusal to be or to do any limited thing ".

This fastidiousness drove a wedge between poetry and ordinary life. The public, finding itself despised and feeling that the new poetry was beyond its comprehension, turned to cruder authors. And the poets, cut off from the public, were forced back on themselves and deprived of the strength which may be found in streets and crowds. They spoke not for a country or for a generation but for themselves. If, like Wilde and Pater, the prophets attempted to make their gospel more popular, their gains were made at great cost to themselves. In his lifetime Pater was regarded with suspicion by many of his colleagues ; Wilde spoiled much of his art by his desire to win public applause. In France the Symbolists did not seek for popularity and liked to flout and mystify the bourgeoisie. They looked to posterity, but because they neglected their own times, their claim on posterity too is less ; for they often lack that vitality which comes from contact with life and survives the centuries because of its lasting human qualities. Nor is it easy for a poet to live in a small circle, however charmed it be. His inspiration may run dry ; he may feel that his work is unrecognised ; disappointment and disillusion may assail him. If he thinks too much about his art, he may find that after all he cannot practise it. Indeed Mallarmé's pathetic failure to produce his " œuvre pure ", the great work of which he had dreamed for more than twenty years, may be explained by the view that he had thought too long about it and dried up the springs of his strength. Remy de Gourmont was perhaps right when he said that Mallarmé had killed in himself " la spontanéité de l'être impressionnable ". He had so concentrated on the theory of poetry that he could think of nothing else, and when he should have been devising the details of a particular poem, he could only think what the ideal poem should be.

A second difficulty in Mallarmé's doctrine was the enormous importance that he attached to music. The vision of Wagner's achievement obsessed him, and he sought by many means to equal its effects in verse. Nor was he alone in this. When Pater said that " All art constantly aspires to the condition of music ", he said in his plainer English way what Mallarmé often said. Neither should be taken too literally. Both saw that there is in poetry an obstinate element because words have meanings, and this prevents poetry from producing so purely an aesthetic effect as music. But Mallarmé was certainly deluded by the analogy of music. He believed that in poetry he might produce an effect so absolutely aesthetic that the understanding would almost be in abeyance. The sounds and associations would do all the work ; the mere meaning of the words would not matter. But words are concerned with ideas, and poetry is made of words. It can never have the unlimited breadth of pure vision. Mallarmé was haunted by an absolute beauty which meant everything to him. He symbolised it in many forms, in the azure sky, in the dawn, in glaciers, and each symbol shows that it was impersonal, static, remote. To convey these qualities he dreamed of finding " la parole sous la figure du silence ", and he could give a hint of its nature in

L'insensibilité de l'azur et des pierres.

But to write a complete poem on such a state is almost impossible. Words are limited by their meanings. The most melodious and associative poetry cannot hope to snatch his honours from the musician. Attempts have been made to justify Mallarmé's belief, but the facts are against him. His own confession " Mon art est une impasse ", his failure to write his great poem, the failure of his apologists to show that poetry can achieve effects comparable to those of music, the unalterable truth that words cannot be divorced from their meanings, all these show that his doctrine was faulty.

These two weaknesses, the severance from common life and the belief that music is the end of poetry, are revealed above all in Mallarmé's career. Perhaps too they account for the fact that after his death the Symbolists failed in France and that the true successor of Mallarmé is a poet who faced both difficulties and saw their meaning, — Paul Valéry.

14

They had, we may admit, a positive side. The first brought an enlivened sensibility, the second a proper regard for the sound of poetry. And perhaps these are the most lasting contributions of Symbolism to the modern world. But there are difficulties in both, and the successors of the Symbolists have been largely concerned with them. Indeed the poets who wrote in this tradition after 1890 were usually compelled to abandon their elaborate styles and to leave their ivory towers for the life of the crowd. They have widened the sphere of Ideal Beauty and in the process have been forced to change their technique and their notions of what a poem ought to be. In these changes and adaptations their special interest lies. For poetry lives by change. Once a style has been perfected, it must be thrown aside; for there is nothing which resembles a great style so little as its imitations. The successors of the Symbolists began with a conviction that Mallarmé's doctrines were right, but all have in some way or other abandoned them. This is no comment on Mallarmé himself. A poet's theories about his art must not be judged by their universal truth but by the vitality which they bring to the creation of poetry. If Mallarmé's theories are now as disproved as those of Horace or Du Bellay or Wordsworth, he is not to be blamed. He is to be praised, because these very theories inflamed strong imaginations to work and did not hamper them from developing on lines which favoured their special inclinations.

The successors began by accepting the ideas of Symbolism. They represent the shift from an age which was content to regard art as a private mystical experience to one which regards it more as a public and social activity. As such they are, curiously enough, the true inheritors of Mallarmé, who said, " Je pense que le monde sera sauvé par une meilleure littérature ". If their transference is incomplete, it is because the age through which they lived has also been incomplete in its changes. But their effort to see the world with a new vision and to interpret its movements entitles them to be called representative. Few of them have stayed in a single place or remained faithful to a single style, but in the very divergence of their efforts lies their peculiar interest. For they show how the competing claims of a complex age affect men of great sincerity and sensibility. Here is no case of unrecognised and isolated singing like that of Blake or Hopkins. These men are the poets of an age singularly rich in imaginative experience, of Bonnard and Matisse in painting, of Maillol and Mestrovic in sculpture, of Ravel and Stravinsky in music. The age is finished, but its great exponents in the arts have other than historical interest for posterity. By their own merits they have won a permanent place.

II

PAUL VALÉRY

1871–

When Mallarmé died in 1898, the movement of which he was the high priest and the foremost practitioner seemed to die with him. In the next few years French poetry found distinguished exponents in Jean Moréas, Francis Jammes, Henri de Regnier and Paul Claudel, but not one of these was really a Symbolist or, if he owed anything to Mallarmé, owed more than a high respect for poetry and for craftsmanship. In 1900 it looked as if the master who had devoted many years of subtle thought to finding a true view of poetry had succeeded only in defining his own attitude towards it. But in one friend and disciple Mallarmé had planted seeds of growth and development. Paul Valéry had as a young man known and revered him, written poems under his influence and then retired from poetry to studies more exact and more analytical. Between 1898 and 1917 he published no poetry, but in 1917 *La Jeune Parque* appeared and showed that in the intervening years Valéry had not forgotten his first lessons or his youthful ideals. The spiritual movement which had seemed so full of promise in the last decades of the nineteenth century and then waned and faded, came again to life. *La Jeune Parque* shows many signs of a highly individual talent, but it could not have existed if Valéry had not mastered the principles of Mallarmé's art. It is composed on the master's methods and is unintelligible to those who do not understand what they are.

Valéry had not wasted the years between 1898 and 1917. Even if in them he wrote no poetry, his mind was at work in a way that was to help him to find his own manner. In them he gained that distance from his master which is necessary to every artist who wishes to be himself. In his first work the methods of Mallarmé are manifest in such a poem as *Profusion du Soir*, where the colours and shapes of a sunset are treated as the poet's own thoughts, where no distinction is made between fact and feeling and what matters is the poet's interior state. In this poem there is much charm, but its whole method is derivative. The young writer has not emancipated himself from his schooling. Even in the much maturer *Air de Sémiramis* there is still something of the same kind. In the dramatisation of the pure lust for power in a single female character the influence of Mallarmé is still strong and we doubt if the poet has yet found the new self which he must find to deserve his name or if he has decided what poetry means in his scheme of things. We feel that Valéry is still uncertain of his direction. But when *La Jeune Parque* appeared, it was clear that he had found a way and that it was his own. By turning his mind to subjects other than the composition of poetry he had strengthened and clarified his ideas about it and found where his own tastes and talents lay.

For many years Valéry has for his private satisfaction kept note-books in which he has jotted down his thoughts. Some of these have been published and show the process by which he has disciplined himself and found his own view of life. In them Valéry seems to do what other great French writers have done before him, to present acute comments on life in condensed maxims. The apparently easy and simple thoughts surprise by an insight which is often dissimulated under wit, irony and paradox. On a second reading we see how much there is in them, how serious they are. In such works we look, with justification, for a unifying principle, a theory which connects the disparate pieces together. The older writers had such principles,— self-esteem in La Rochefoucauld, benevolence in La Bruyère, the Christian religion in Pascal. In Valéry too there is a principle. But it is different. It is simply the conviction that things are what they are and must be accepted as such, that no general rule will tell us what they are or explain them, that each phenomenon must be examined in itself and stated as it really is. Such a theory sounds simple, but, like most theories, it becomes interesting when it is applied with consistency and integrity. Few dare to go so far this way as Valéry does, to subject to close analysis so many accepted ideas, to be absolutely scientific in matters which are commonly reserved for faith or for that unquestioning accept-ance which is often its substitute. Such a philosophy, — and it deserves the name, — is the last that we should expect from a poet. The endless examination of things as they are, the bold criticism of matters so sacred that professed philosophers shrink from them, the wit and irony which make the discoveries palatable to the many, might all seem to be hostile to poetry, which seems usually to require an uncritical trust at least in all matters that concern itself. In his acceptance of things as they are Valéry has been compared to Lucretius, and in some ways the comparison is apt. But Lucretius built his whole view of existence on a scientific theory and gave to it his absolute uncritical devotion. Valéry shows no such devotion. With gay courage he examines all that comes in his way. The marvel is that from such activities and with such interests he should have returned to poetry liberated and strengthened.

From the beginning poetry had been foremost among Valéry's interests. It had engaged much of his critical attention. The " given " in his case was his undoubted love of it, his feeling that it is something of great importance, his knowledge that he himself is a poet. These convictions were strengthened at an early age by his intercourse with Mallarmé, in whom he saw " l'extrême pureté de la foi en matière de poésie ". But he could not rest in this devotion without examining it, and on examination he found that poetry was not in reality all that it was said to be. The poet claims to be inspired, to perform a special and superior duty, to have a peculiar insight into the nature of things, to create in his own way through his own powers. But Valéry found that the facts did not correspond with these beliefs, that inspiration is a mere hypothesis which reduces the author to the position of an observer, that the poet writes of subjects because for some obscure reason they suit him, that some of the finest poetry is in no sense clairvoyant but almost nonsense, that the process of creation is largely haphazard and determined by quite trivial matters such as the choice of a special kind of stanza. He knows the craft too well and is too honest to acquiesce in common views of it. An attitude so careful and so critical is fraught with dangers for a poet. In examining the roots of his work he may cease to believe in its importance ; his complex and conflicting thoughts may hamper the concentration which he requires for creation ; his close analysis of facts may lead him to limit the sphere of poetry until there is almost nothing left of it.

In Valéry's approach to poetry there was a discord between his instinctive sense of its importance and his intellectual analysis of its nature. That he was to some degree conscious of this may be seen from his *La Soirée avec Monsieur Teste*, first published in 1906. In his monstrous hero who acts entirely through the intellect Valéry has dramatised one side of himself. Even in 1896 he had written his first essay on Leonardo da Vinci and presented him as a man who tried to understand everything. The other side of Valéry's nature remains unexplained and unfathomed. Philosophy and poetry have always been uneasily wedded; the first may depress and destroy the second. When he meditated on his Leonardo and created Monsieur Teste, something of this seemed to have happened in Valéry. Conscious of the struggle in himself, he gave his powers to describing the analytical side, with which poetry can have no relations. But something flowered in him. Poetry triumphed, not ultimately at the expense of thought but by taking thought into partnership. The process was gradual, and the alliance took time to form. It is not complete in *La Jeune Parque* but it is in *Charmes* (1922). Faced by the modern problem of relating poetry to life, Valéry has found an answer which denies the importance neither of poetry nor of science. He has not retired to an irrational world of his own but found in the existing world a place for his art. In this he has achieved something which Mallarmé never desired and never attempted. Valéry has no quarrel with the universe, no complaint of the poet's place in it. Experience continues to engage his attention, to excite his comments, to demand analysis. In all this he is candidly, even ruthlessly, scientific. But he remains a poet.

The problem which faced Valéry as an artist faced him also as a man. Just as his purely intellectual activities were hard to reconcile with his poetic, so in himself there was a division between the thinker, withdrawn, independent, impersonal, analytical, and the man with all the claims that manhood makes on the emotions and on the flesh. It is therefore not surprising that when he returned to poetry with *La Jeune Parque*, it was such a conflict as this that seems to have prompted him. For though it is impossible and certainly uncritical to define the subject of *La Jeune Parque* with any exactness, it still displays a conflict which is most easily grasped if we approach it with some such formula in mind. It is not a record of a struggle, but a symbolical poem based on different movements of consciousness. In its ebb and flow, its hesitations and decisions, its contrasts between states of calm withdrawal and activity and emotion, it may be regarded as a poem of the poet's own conflicts. It comes to no clear conclusion, has no autobiographical reference, touches on no precise issue ; it is not a dramatic poem, not a narrative, but a symbolical poem in which a nebulous myth serves to give a form to what is ultimately a highly personal experience.

La Jeune Parque has been acclaimed as the most obscure poem in French. It has been variously interpreted as the monologue of a Young Fate who has to choose between celestial seclusion and earthly responsibilities, as the revery of the poet lying in bed, as a voyage of the human consciousness through vast issues of life and death. It is all these things, and none of them. Valéry's subject cannot be stated with precision ; for by its very nature it is formless and indefinable. The poem does not state a thesis but makes an effect. It might be said to record a series of states of mind, but these melt into one another, and the contour of each is dim. It is natural to compare it with Mallarmé's *Hérodiade*. Just as Mallarmé found a subject in the human instinct which desires remoteness and coldness and found a centre for his symbols in the ice-cold virgin Hérodiade, so Valéry, it might be thought, makes his symbolical Young Fate the mouthpiece of a conflict between desires for an active life and for independent, passionless contemplation. There is truth in this, but it is not the whole truth. Mallarmé's dramatic method, with its contrast between Hérodiade and the Nurse, serves to emphasise two sides of a struggle which may ultimately be his own. Valéry has no drama, and with reason. In the movements of his poem the issues are not clearly cut. The uniting thread is of a half-dreaming consciousness, in which what counts is not contrast but continuity. It begins and ends without any marked event. It is a section of a complex poetical experience. To appreciate it we need not so much a vigilant intelligence as a receptive sensibility which marks symbols for their associative and imaginative worth and responds to the subtle changes of atmosphere which pass across the dreaming landscape. In reading *La Jeune Parque* we may forget the character who holds it together ; we may even feel that the poet forgets her. In both cases we are right. For in the last analysis the poet deals with matters for which even his central symbol is inadequate, with feelings so little definable that they resist attempts to arrange them in a system or to relate them to ordered thought. Mallarmé's pupil has gone beyond his master's method. In interpreting *Hérodiade* we need not look beyond the two characters ; with the Young Fate we are compelled to grasp an order of things in which even she has faded into something vaguer and larger.

This essential indefiniteness marks the poem from its start. The opening words :

> Qui pleure là, sinon le vent simple, à cette heure
> Seule avec diamants extrêmes ? . . . Mais qui pleure,
> Si proche de moi-même au moment de pleurer ?

suggest that the poet speaks in the first person. But from this, without hint or warning, we advance to the indubitable monologue of the Young Fate, who has arrived in a world that is strange to her. The poet passes into her ; his words become hers. She is the vehicle of his meditations, the personification of something in him. Even when she has begun to speak, we are not always sure that it is she. It is easy to think that it is the poet who speaks when he helps with brackets in

> (La porte basse c'est une bague . . . où la gaze
> Passe. . . . Tout meurt, tout rit dans la gorge qui jase . . .)

but without such aids we suspect his presence in other places. When he writes

> Délicieux linceuls, mon désordre tiède,
> Couche où je me répands, m'interroge et me cède,
> Où j'allai de mon cœur noyer les battements,
> Presque tombeau vivant dans mes appartements . . .

all fits the Young Fate until the last word, and with that we are back with the poet. The poet and his symbol are not ultimately distinguished or distinguishable. Mallarmé's Hérodiade may symbolise part of his nature, but she has always her own strange personality, a law which rules her being ; the Young Fate, creature of semi-consciousness, emerges from the poet only to fade into him again.

This ambiguity pervades the poem. Many of its lines are applicable both to the poet and to the Young Fate :

Dors, ma sagesse, dors. Forme-toi cette absence ;
Retourne dans le germe et la sombre innocence,
Abandonne-toi vive aux serpents, aux trésors . . .
Dors toujours ! Descends, dors toujours ! Descends, dors, dors !

They are quite relevant to the Young Fate who is torn between heaven and earth and wishes to stay with the latter where the serpent has bitten her. They are no less relevant to the poet who abandons his struggle with the waking consciousness and relapses into the confused but vivid experience of dream. In such passages, and they are many, we must not distinguish between the poet and his symbol. We must appreciate and enjoy an effect, a something which we cannot quite understand but which we can none the less grasp with pleasure through the sensibility. *La Jeune Parque* does not convey information ; it produces a result, a state of mind ; it provides an experience. It illustrates what Valéry has said elsewhere, " La poésie n'a pas le moins du monde pour objet de communiquer à quelqu'un quelque notion déterminée ". What matter are the words and their rhythm, the images they provide, the associations they evoke, the experience which somehow they create. If the poem were less ambiguous, if the narrative were more emphatic, if we could distinguish more clearly between the poet and the Young Fate, something essential would be lost, the creation in us of the state which the poet intends to create.

It does not matter how difficult poetry is, provided that in the end we can relate it to ourselves and grasp it as an experience akin to our own. And this happens with *La Jeune Parque*. It conveys something of the state between dreaming and waking, when images of peculiar significance and brightness melt into an undifferentiated and nebulous background, when at moments we seem to have a peculiar understanding of matters of great import only to sink back into the half-unconscious confusion of dream. Such a state is familiar enough, but it has seldom provided matter for poetry. Yet its claims are obvious. Both its mistiness and its moments of clarity are well fitted for imaginative presentation ; for neither can be adequately expressed in prose or even with classic clarity in verse. Compared with such a state, that of pure dreaming is easily conveyed. Its violent emotions, its vivid, if irrational, images, fall naturally into the art of Vergil or Racine. But this intermediate state in which sleep and consciousness struggle in the scales, and the subject of them passes nearer now to the one, now to the other, is better suited to the method of the Symbolists. The art of *La Jeune Parque* lies in an evocation of atmosphere in which some things are seen with unusual clearness, others fade into mist and lose their contours. In so far as it does this, it does its special task. It can do more than this, and it does. But this is its first and essential characteristic.

In this half-dreaming state the mind sees matters of great importance in a special way. Images that rise before it seem to have a remarkable significance, to be symbolical of things far greater than themselves. In such a mood we may well see ourselves in a new light, as figures of cosmic import. And this happens in *La Jeune Parque*. The poet transposes the movements of his consciousness into a strange *milieu*. He sees himself as a divine figure who has left a serene supra-terrestrial dwelling for the chances and passions of mortal life. So may a man dramatise himself who is torn between his thoughts and his actions. In this state the ordinary limits set to our powers seem not to exist. We feel that we are the centre, if not of the universe, at least of some enormous scheme, and that anything we do or that happens to us is pregnant with huge issues. This kind of experience *La Jeune Parque* evokes in such lines as

> Tout l'univers chancelle et tremble sur ma tige

and

> Tous les corps radieux tremblent dans mon essence.

Each slight change of tone or symbol indicates that a new horizon has opened, and that new possibilities of pleasure and pain are revealed, each of which is somehow not personal but cosmic. The poet is no longer the centre of a private universe but transmuted into something large outside himself. It is as if a Copernican revolution had taken place in the metaphysics of Symbolism. Its subjective idealism has been replaced by an absolutism in which the thoughts of a single soul are the thoughts of the Whole.

In the half-dreaming state which pervades *La Jeune Parque* what counts most is the sustained tone. In this lies its chief poetry. But this tone varies as the thoughts of a man vary in trance-like meditation. Half the pleasure lies in the delicate adjustment of tone, in the transition from one shade to

another.   Though the whole pattern is made of subdued
colours, it has many strands and patterns.   To isolate one
or the other is necessarily an artificial process which may
damage our appreciation of the whole.   But it is perhaps
legitimate to note some of the extremes.   For they set, as it
were, the limits to what is said and what passes between them.
The Young Fate pauses between heaven and earth, as the poet
pauses between thought and passion.   At the one extreme is
active life with all its claims and its hopes, its movements
and its promises :

> Les arbres regonflés et recouverts d'écailles
> Chargés de tant de bras et de trop d'horizons,
> Meuvent sur le soleil leurs tonnantes toisons,
> Montent dans l'air amer avec toutes leurs ailes
> De feuilles par milliers qu'ils se sentent nouvelles.

The whole prospect of human life is seen as a forest, but it is
no ordinary forest.   It has its relations to life — " tant de
bras ",— to movements of the spirit — " toutes leurs
ailes ",— to the consciousness of all in it — " ils se sentent ".
Such a vision may sometimes be given to us, and even if it is
unfamiliar, the poet creates it for us.   At the other extreme
are the words in which the Young Fate seems to record her
desire to return from this world :

> Je renouvelle en moi mes énigmes, mes dieux,
> Mes pas interrompus de paroles aux cieux,
> Mes pauses, sur le pied portant la rêverie,
> Qui suit au miroir d'aile un oiseau qui varie.

The words are apt for her celestial state, and apt too for the
poet who turns with desire to his dispassionate riddles and
speculations.   The lines provide a contrast with those just
quoted and show the extremes between which the poem moves.
Between these limits there can be no agreement or harmony.
The Young Fate must choose, and she chooses heaven.   At
one moment she feels a horror for terrestrial life and the
flesh :

> Non ! l'horreur m'illumine, exécrable harmonie !
> Chaque baiser présage une neuve agonie. . . .
> Je vois, je vois flotter, fuyant l'honneur des chairs
> Des mânes impuissants les millions amers. . . .

This strong repulsion decides the Young Fate to go back to her home. Her conflict is settled by her disgust at the failure of so much human life. Through these passages we see the sphere in which the poet works. He presents his feelings about two extremes of consciousness ; between these his poetry moves. And these feelings are in some degree common to all men. What the poet does is to present their colour and significance, to give them a highly individual form. His poetry may be difficult but it is not confined to a narrow experience.

The extremes of feeling which Valéry presents in *La Jeune Parque* are easily related to his own divided mentality, to the antithesis between his thinking and his poetical selves. In so far as he has made this conflict into a poem he has for the moment solved it. What might have been an obstacle to his creative activity has actually become its inspiration. But his success in producing a poem from his inner strife does not mean that he has solved another related problem, the place which poetry is to have in a life which accepts the rule of the intellect and insists on seeing things as they are. The difficulty for Valéry, as for many other modern poets, is to relate poetry to common experience, to find subjects which are neither unreal nor impossibly esoteric, to fuse the findings of the intellect with the visions of the imagination. In so far as *La Jeune Parque* can be related to known experience, it avoids the errors of the Romantics, who too often looked outside reality for their themes. But it is akin to the work of the Symbolists in that it is a poem for the few, not merely in its manner but in its matter. Its last subtleties can be appreciated only by those who know this conflict and what it means. Valéry has not quite brought his poetry into touch with reality, or rather, has brought it into touch only with reality of a special kind. The half-consciousness which permeates *La Jeune Parque* is certainly fit matter for poetry, especially for a poet whose analytical intelligence has closed the way to many themes. But this dream-world is only part of his self. There remains much outside it no less important, no less adaptable to poetry. Valéry is still a divided personality in so far as his poetic activity lies outside the sphere of his ranging intelligence. This is no criticism of it as poetry. It is still a triumph in a peculiarly difficult kind of art. But until Valéry puts more of himself into his verse we feel that his success is not complete, that he has not mastered all the material at his disposal.

In *Charmes* he has done this. At first sight it is clear that his whole manner has changed from that of *La Jeune Parque*. A series of poems composed in a wide range of metres show that he has found a new way to express himself, an adaptation of the Symbolist method which is his own. The dreaming atmosphere of *La Jeune Parque* has given place to something much clearer, much more readily grasped by the intelligence. Instead of a tone he presents a series of themes, sometimes stated in such a title as *Poésie*, usually clear enough on reading. The ambiguity has disappeared. Each poem has its own temper and atmosphere, but in the sum of them there is much variety and divergence. The deliberately mixed metaphors which contribute so much to the effect of *La Jeune Parque* have almost gone. Their place has been taken by a new art in which a single figure or symbol is elaborated throughout a whole poem, gives consistency to it and holds it together. In *Palme* all that matters is the tree that promises a rich harvest of fruit, in *Les Pas* the feet of the beloved that hesitate. Such a tree and such feet have a special significance ; they are symbols of no common importance. But because they are sustained through whole poems, they make it easier to appreciate an abstract and impalpable experience, and add to the force of the poetry by this very consistency. A defect in the Symbolist method was that in its concentration on a single point and the mixture of symbols which it used to secure this it sometimes lacked exactness in presenting, not thoughts, which do not matter, but states of imaginative experience, which do. This defect is not altogether absent from *La Jeune Parque*. In the delicate and subtle presentation of special states it does not always yield a full and satisfying effect. No doubt this matters less in a poem which is concerned with a half-conscious condition. But when the poet advances into the daylight of consciousness this vagueness of outline may impede him. With his poet's instinct Valéry saw this, and in *Charmes* his symbols are either strictly self-consistent or else chosen in such a way that we know what each one means and does.

This advance in method is accompanied by what look like concessions to the common reader. Valéry is now more ready to explain what he means, to give hints in his titles and elsewhere about a poem's subject, to make statements of fact which are not in the spirit of Mallarmé. A title like *Poésie* is in the best classical tradition ; *Ode Secrète* at least warns us that we may fail to understand the contents ; *Cantique des Colonnes* is what it claims to be ; a quotation from Pindar at the beginning of *Le Cimetière Marin* is a useful clue. So too in the poems themselves those lines of explanation which Mallarmé abhorred are not wanting. Not all are so clear as the end of *La Pythie* with its emphatic statement of fact, but with rare exceptions these poems have definable subjects to which the poet leads by different means. Nor is this method merely or truly a concession to our desire to understand. It is dictated by a more reputable and more artistic motive. In *Charmes* Valéry writes about matters on which clear thought is in some degree possible. This is not to say that he writes didactic or explanatory verse. He writes indubitably as a poet. But since his subjects are those about which thought is possible, then thought has its part in poetry about them. To present these themes in the manner of *La Jeune Parque* would be to mutilate or falsify them. In so far as they arise from the poet's conscious meditation and have their place in it, it is right to maintain this element of thought, even of explanation. For Mallarmé such a situation hardly existed. The aesthetic state of which he wrote is divorced from ordinary analytical thought. Prose cannot describe it except in the language of poetry. But Valéry is concerned with other matters, more mundane perhaps but not less poetical. He is therefore entitled to make himself clear to the intellect as well as to create an effect through the imagination.

The title *Charmes* is itself significant and almost a comment on the contents. The notion that poetry is a kind of magic and that the poet knows secrets and has powers not shared by other men is deeply rooted in the human race. The Latin *vates* was both a prophet and a poet ; the Romantic poets were equally prophets. To this conception of poetry Mallarmé implicitly gave his support when he formed his ideal of the Word which liberates a man from his ordinary trammels. In his view poetry is a kind of incantation, a force released by the poet on the world, which sooner or later yields to its power. With such a view we should hardly expect Valéry to agree. The critic who says " La poésie a pour devoir de faire du langage d'une nation quelques applications parfaites ", who has explained his own manner of composition as dictated largely by the choice of a certain kind of verse and by the need to write once he has pen and ink before him, who thinks it possible that poetry may disappear from the world as geomancy, heraldry and falconry have disappeared, would hardly seem to think that it is a kind of magic. Yet the title *Charmes* suggests that he does. It is certainly not an imposture, not ironical. If Valéry calls his book by this name, we may be sure that he knows what he is doing. For him poetry is still a creative act, the creation of an effect. This effect is produced through means so mysterious that even the poet himself hardly understands them. He works as he will, but the result is outside his vision and beyond his intention. The title *Charmes* is justified. For this book is made of poems which are intended to produce effects, not to convey information. The poet is a magician in so far as he can work on the souls and sensibilities of others by means which he does not fully understand and of which he is only partially the master.

The mere fact of poetry is enough to excite enquiry in the critic and wonder in the poet. In Valéry it excites both. His mind is drawn irresistibly to the whole business of poetry, its creation, its worth, its reputation. On these subjects he has written well and wisely. But in his prose he cannot state what he really feels about poetry, what he wishes others to feel. Such a task poetry alone can do for itself. Valéry is, as no other poet, the poet of poetry, in the sense that he tells what it means to those who are deeply engaged in it. Others have presented their ideal states of song, but neither Shelley's skylark nor Coleridge's Abyssinian maid take us to the heart of their creative process. They are symbols of unimpeded activity, ideals which can hardly be reached in this world. Valéry explores the obscurities and faces the bright lights of the poet's inmost life. His special success is that on this subject he is both true to experience and radiantly expressive. His careful and precise observation of fact has been transmuted into song, and song is greatly the gainer. Behind the rapture and the excitement we see the original experience, the firm foundation of fact. Poetry, as Valéry portrays it, is no ideal but a reality. He is concerned not with the poet's ideal poem, or with his position in the world, or with his hopes of glory, but with his work and what it means to him. Unlike

Shelley or Baudelaire or Mallarmé, he is interested not in the poet's desires but in his task and in the spirit which informs it. Of this he presents in different poems a picture at once complex and complete. Each treats the subject from a different angle, but when we have read all, we have seen a view of poetry from its first appearances in the poet to his feelings about it when he looks at it from without. Such poems are of course autobiographical, but they are more than that. They give a poet's account of something which the world still values though it may have little knowledge of how it comes into being.

To convey these mysterious and elusive processes Valéry has found a means both adequate and delightful. His poems are not usually meditative ; they are more like songs and are often lyrical. His task in them is twofold. He must make intelligible the difficult subject of which he writes and he must place this in the special light that it has for him. The method and his success in it can be seen in *Les Pas* :

> Tes pas, enfants de mon silence,
> Saintement, lentement placés,
> Vers le lit de ma vigilance
> Procèdent muets et glacés.
>
> Personne pure, ombre divine,
> Qu'ils sont doux, tes pas retenus !
> Dieux ! . . . tous les dons que je devine
> Viennent à moi sur ces pieds nus !
>
> Si, de tes lèvres avancées
> Tu prépares pour l'apaiser,
> À l'habitant de mes pensées
> La nourriture d'un baiser,
>
> Ne hâte pas cet acte tendre,
> Douceur d'être et de n'être pas,
> Car j'ai vécu de vous attendre,
> Et mon cœur n'était que vos pas.

At a first glance this might seem to be no more than an account of the poet waiting for his mistress who is coming to him. But if this is right, the poet speaks in an oblique and stilted way. Why is his bed " le lit de ma vigilance " as if it were an abstraction ? Who is " l'habitant de mes pensées ", and why are his beloved's steps " enfants de mon silence " ? In so careful a writer as Valéry such phrases are not used without reason. The answer, clear soon enough, is that the steps belong not to a human mistress but to poetry, the poetic impulse, for which the poet waits. Then the phrases fall into their place. The steps are " enfants de mon silence " because the new sense of creative power has been matured in a time of inactivity ; " le lit de ma vigilance " is the waiting expectant self who will receive the visitant ; " l'habitant de mes pensées " is the creative self which dwells among habitual thoughts. The poem gives the mood of concentrated, confident, joyful expectation before creative activity begins. The symbols are entirely consistent and harmonious. This waiting for poetry is like waiting for a mistress, is waiting for a mistress. Shakespeare classes the lover and the poet together ; Valéry makes them one. The mood of the expectant poet is that of the expectant lover. Each is serenely confident of the joy which awaits him, so confident indeed that the actual delay and suspense are themselves delightful, that he feels no call for haste. In this moment the poet collects himself before the surrender which poetical creation demands of him, the

Douceur d'être et de n'être pas

in which he gives himself up and yet remains himself, just as the lover gives himself up to the beloved. The moment is the climax almost of a lifetime. The long period of waiting and preparation is about to end. The poet faces what is coming with rapture and yet without impatience.

In *Les Pas* Valéry suggests that when his beloved comes and kisses him he will both be and not be. The paradox is instructive. The old view of poetic inspiration was that the poet was a vehicle for some divine power which spoke through him. Homer conforms to this when he bids his Muse tell of the wrath of Achilles, but it is too simple, too unscientific for Valéry. He has told us his objection to it. On the text " The Spirit bloweth where it listeth ", he comments " Il incombe au spiritualisme et aux amateurs d'inspiration de nous expliquer pourquoi cet esprit ne souffle pas dans les bêtes et souffle si mal dans les sots ". The notion of untrammelled inspiration, of an external power which works through the poet unaided, does not agree with his observation of the facts. With typical insight he sees that the poetic process works otherwise, and he tells us what it is. It is quite

THE HERITAGE OF SYMBOLISM

simple : " Il y a des vers qu'on *trouve*. Les autres, on les *fait*." A. E. Housman said much the same when he told how lines and even stanzas came into his mind without effort and for no accountable reason ; then he had to settle down to the hard task of completing a poem by deliberate toil. This is the double nature of composition which Valéry recognises. The second task is easy to understand, but the first is still a mystery. How do these lines come, and why ? Psychology may perhaps be able to explain, but its explanation will be inadequate. For it can only ascribe a cause, not explain the peculiar joy and strength which such a process brings with it. It is fit matter for poetry ; it is mysterious and evokes emotions which can only be expressed in verse. If he can convey what this process means, the poet has done something difficult and well worth doing.

In *Aurore*, the first poem of *Charmes*, Valéry tells from another angle how he begins to compose. His spirit awakens with the dawn and proceeds to its normal and delightful task of thought. But these thoughts, these riddles, have nothing to do with poetry. Though his ideas weave silken suns for him, the poet breaks their web and looks elsewhere for his subjects of song :

> Leur toile spirituelle,
> Je la brise, et vais cherchant
> Dans ma forêt sensuelle
> Les oracles de mon chant.

This intellectual poet is not a poet of ideas but of the body. Again we recall Housman,— " Poetry indeed seems to me more physical than intellectual ". Valéry, true to the tradition of " la poésie pure ", discards ideas as alien and finds his material in sensations. And it is sensations that he goes on to recount in the joyful, confident struggle which is his as he gets to work. Before him lies a vineyard full of fruit, and everything that he can pick from this is pure gain :

> Tout m'est pulpe, tout amande,
> Tout calice me demande
> Que j'attende pour son fruit.

In the world of sensations everything can be turned to poetry. This is the confidence that carries the poet joyfully through his task. Therefore he does not fear the thorns and the pains of his work :

PAUL VALÉRY

Il n'est pour ravir un monde
De blessure si profonde
Qui ne soit au ravisseur
Une féconde blessure,
Et son propre sang l'assure
D'être le vrai possesseur.

Each check is profitable to him, and we know what he means. No poet who composes knows exactly what he is going to say. His meaning changes and grows richer with each effort that he makes, each obstacle that he meets. As he overcomes his difficulties, he feels that he has added something to himself and mastered something new. In all this he is kept confident and active by his certain hope that great results await him. He does not know what the end is, but he knows that something is there, and Valéry symbolises this as " Espérance " which floats in a clear fountain. He knows that his trust will be rewarded, that all will come to him in the end.

In the poet's activity there is an element of what looks like pure chance. He begins with one intention, but, as he works, he finds that his purpose and his performance change. Mallarmé recognised this and summarised it in his doctrine that " un coup de dés jamais n'abolira le hasard ". By " le hasard " he meant the absolute uncertainty which always faces the poet. He can make a lucky throw and find some kind of success, but he is still faced by the unforeseeable and incalculable nature of his material. Valéry knew this idea and it must lie behind his *Le Vin Perdu* :

J'ai, quelque jour, dans l'Océan,
(Mais je ne sais plus sous quels cieux)
Jeté, comme offrande au néant,
Tout un peu de vin précieux. . .

Qui voulut ta perte, ô liqueur ?
J'obéis peut-être au devin ?
Peut-être au souci de mon cœur,
Songeant au sang, versant le vin

Sa transparence accoutumée
Après une rose fumée
Reprit aussi pure la mer. . . .

Perdu ce vin, ivres les ondes ! . .
J'ai vu bondir dans l'air amer
Les figures les plus profondes. . . .

33

The theme is clear. The poet, for some little understood reason, makes a libation and is rewarded by a miracle, a rosy smoke on the sea and vague figures stretching out into the distance. A single, unpremeditated act leads to wonderful consequences. Such, we may believe, is the experience of many poets. A casual impulse produces magnificent results. But this poem has a special interest because in it Valéry uses some of Mallarmé's own symbols and uses them differently. The offering is made " au néant ". For Mallarmé this is the Absolute, the reality into which the poet finally enters and loses himself. But for Valéry it is simply Nothing. His libation is made without any ulterior purpose ; it is quite casual. Again, the Ocean for Mallarmé is also a symbol of " le hasard ", of the vast Indefinite which confronts the poet. For Valéry it is simply existence, unknown and uncharted, but certainly real. He takes the Master's symbols and reduces them to a logical, unmystical scheme. For him the creation of a poem may simply be a matter of chance.

These poems are concerned with the preliminaries of poetic creation. They do not touch on its actual character except by implication. But even from this central subject Valéry does not shrink. In *Poésie* he takes us to its heart. The poem purports to be written when the creative activity has ceased but is still vivid in the mind. It describes the activity and its sudden end. The imagery is that of a child feeding at the breast. In this state he has known an incomparable contentment :

> Dieu perdu dans son essence,
> Et délicieusement
> Docile à la connaissance
> Du suprême apaisement,
>
> Je touchais à la nuit pure,
> Je ne savais plus mourir,
> Car un fleuve sans coupure
> Me semblait me parcourir. . . .

So long as he imbibes his celestial food, the poet feels himself a god and immortal. Once again he uses a symbol from Mallarmé. " La nuit pure " is for the older poet the protecting cover of the Absolute which surrounds the dead poet in his glory. But here it is reduced to its place in a terrestrial order. It suggests many associations, but it serves a single purpose in showing the poet's absolute contentment while his blessed state lasts. But something has come between and cut off the stream of divine nourishment :

> Le silence au vol de cygne
> Entre nous ne règne plus.

The breast which fed him has become as hard as stone. And in the last verse we know why. The Source tells the child that he has bitten so hard that her heart has stopped. The abrupt surprise of the finale, the simplicity of its language, bring us up with a jerk. The rapturous memories of lost delights fade before this plain fact, and the change of tone marks the change of condition. We are moved violently from a world of visionary joy to reality, to the recognisable and even familiar experience that when we ask too much of our gifts they are denied to us. The last verse brings the rare moments of poetic creation into contact with common life. This strange and splendid state is seen to have connections with more ordinary things and to be governed by intelligible rules. The mystical view of poetry provides Valéry with imagery but with no more. Poetic joy is what it is and nothing else. He presents it as it is and accepts it.

This poem takes us closer than any other to Valéry's actual feelings when he creates, to that state which as a young man he described : " Je m'abandonne à l'adorable allure : lire, vivre où mènent les mots ". But such high moments are rare. In the intervals the poet must wait, and it is while he waits that he asks what place poetry has in his life, what he feels about it. This is the subject of *Palme*. The peculiarly special place of poetry is revealed by the angel who appears at the beginning and tells the poet to wait calm and trustful. The angel is another symbol from Mallarmé, the absolute of peace and beauty. The poem is concerned with what the angel's command means, the trust that the poet must feel in his calling. " A man ", said Shelley, " cannot say ' I will compose poetry '. Even the greatest poet cannot say it." This being so, the poet may spend long periods of emptiness and apparent impotence. The theme of *Palme* is that in these delays something is always happening and in due time poetry will come :

> Ces jours qui te semblent vides
> Et perdus pour l'univers
> Ont des racines avides
> Qui travaillent les déserts.

35

The secret powers are at work invisibly. Therefore the poet must wait and hope that sooner or later he will be rewarded and that something will fall to him :

Patience, patience,
Patience dans l'azur !
Chaque atome de silence
Est la chance d'un fruit mûr !
Viendra l'heureuse surprise :
Une colombe, la brise,
L'ébranlement le plus doux,
Une femme qui s'appuie,
Feront tomber cette pluie
Où l'on se jette à genoux !

What may seem the merest accident will provide the poet with a sudden creative impulse and strength. Before this fact he must wait in hope and patience. It is useless to force the pace or to complain. These things cannot be secured at will. But when the impulse comes, it atones for all delays and its effects are enhanced by waiting. The thoughts which the poet has matured in his mind, the associations which he has unconsciously collected, the images which have passed into his memory and ripened there, all these may, when the time comes, suddenly pass into poetry and help to enrich it. *Palme* is true to fact. It is even a record of fact, though it is much more. It is the record of a poet's trust in his capacities and of his conviction that even in these incalculable movements of the spirit there is a reason and a system.

In these poems Valéry nearly always distinguishes, as he does in prose, between what is " given " to a poet and what he " makes ", between the unexplained strength which comes to him and the effort he must make to reduce it to art and order. He emphasises now one side, now the other. In *Source* he stresses the "given", in *Aurore* the "made". So far as making poetry is concerned, the excitement is of action. It has such mystery as belongs to any concentrated rapturous action. But the " given " is more mysterious. We may invent hypotheses for it in the Muse, in Mallarmé's Absolute, in Milton's Holy Spirit. But they are only hypotheses. They add nothing to our appreciation of the actual thing. And this is what excites and interests Valéry. But on one point he commits himself. He says more than once that poetry comes not from ideas but from the flesh, which we may translate

36

crudely and prosaically as " sensations ". The instances of
Palme confirm this. The dove, the breeze, the woman, are
objects of the senses who suddenly summon poetry to work.
Valéry's mere belief that this is so is important. It shows that
he makes no artificial distinction between the poet and the
world, and claims no ideal sphere for his activity.

The " given " in the poet's task is certainly mysterious,
but is it any more mysterious than the coming and going of
our thoughts ? This is a question which Valéry seems to pose.
If " idées " are alien to poetry, " pensées " are not. The
distinction is legitimate. The dry abstractions of philosophy
are not suited to poetry, but the casual thoughts of our minds
are. And when we examine this " pensée ", whence and how
does it come ? Valéry is surely right when he calls it " cette
parole intérieure sans personne et sans origine ". The
thoughts which feed poetry are, after all, of this kind. They
come as mysteriously and are as hard to control as our
ordinary thoughts. They merely come more vividly and more
insistently, demanding to be stated in a permanent form.
And this strange phenomenon may excite poetry about itself.
Such is *Le Sylphe* :

> Ni vu ni connu
> Je suis le parfum
> Vivant et défunt
> Dans le vent venu !
>
> Ni vu ni connu,
> Hasard ou génie ?
> A peine venu
> La tâche est finie !
>
> Ni lu ni compris ?
> Aux meilleurs esprits
> Que d'erreurs promises !
>
> Ni vu ni connu,
> Le temps d'un sein nu
> Entre deux chemises !

The thought that comes on the wind is scarcely formed and
certainly momentary. It is at a low level of reason. But it is
none the less real and productive of hopes. The delicate
movement of this song gives its diaphanous nature. But this
thought is provoked by the senses. The last line, which
shocks and distresses, is meant to do so. It is such moments

37

THE HERITAGE OF SYMBOLISM

as this that provoke thoughts beyond our control and open vistas of illusory promises. This little poem shows the intimate connection between our minds and our bodies and forbids us to make any absolute distinction between them.

The process which may start from such casual or humble beginnings may end in great glory, in achievement which excites a peculiar wonder and pleasure. Such seems to be the theme of *Ode Secrète*. The title may warn us against any full understanding, but it is possible to find a clear meaning. The poem describes the ease and contentment which follow a victory. Then it continues :

> Mais touché par le Crépuscule,
> Ce grand corps qui fit tant de choses,
> Qui dansait, qui rompit Hercule,
> N'est plus qu'une masse de roses !
>
> Dormez, sous les pas sidéraux,
> Vainqueur lentement désuni,
> Car l'Hydre inhérente au héros
> S'est éployée à l'infini. . . .
>
> Ô quel Taureau, quel Chien, quelle Ourse,
> Quels objets de victoire énorme,
> Quand elle entre aux temps sans ressource
> L'âme impose à l'espace informe !
>
> Fin suprême, étincellement
> Qui par les monstres et les dieux
> Proclame universellement
> Les grands actes qui sont aux Cieux !

The poet is the heroic conqueror. The constellations of Bull and Dog and Bear are imposed by him on the starry skies. They are the permanent signs of his effort. The idea comes from Mallarmé who in *Un Coup de Dés* wrote :

> Rien n'aura eu lieu
>   excepté
>   peut-être
>   une constellation.

For Valéry this triumph owes something to the body. The monsters and gods show the paradoxical nature of his achievement. Even the Hydra that was in him is translated to the stars. Out of his own disorder the poet creates a starry order. The symbols of Mallarmé are used to a new purpose. The Hydra, who tries to destroy the poet, is absorbed in his success. The starry places are not the Absolute but the scene of the poet's victory. The space into which the poet enters is not hostile but the place of his work and artistry. The picture is of an infinite celestial satisfaction to which he is reduced. And this success lies in the use which the poet has made of his body and its struggles. After the fight he himself may hardly exist as a person, but his performance is visible in the starlit hemisphere. This is the song of his triumph.

The mystery of poetic creation involves many dark questions about the human soul. In *La Pythie* Valéry touches on some of these. It may even be called philosophical ; for it advances a problem and comes to an explicit, even gnomic, conclusion. The title explains the subject. The Pythian Priestess, through whom Apollo speaks, has a likeness to the poet through whom words come without any known reason. Of this process she presents a special aspect, its pains and its despair, its horror and its humiliation and its final unexpected deliverance. This is the reverse of the creative bliss in *Poésie* and the confident activity in *Aurore*. Whereas these poems are purely personal, *La Pythie* is more general in its intention, more instructive. Its subject is not so much what the poet endures as what all endure who use language in a certain way. It is both dramatic and philosophical. The Pythian Priestess is a kind of character ; her sufferings are her own, though they are also typical and symbolical. There is no ambiguity, no direct reference to the poet. The Priestess is an extreme example of a special case. She suffers in a violent form what all suffer who go through the pangs of creation. In her person she sets the tone, provides the agonies and the crisis. What happens takes place in her. Through twenty-one stanzas the poet gives her struggles and excitements, then in one stanza her deliverance and in another his conclusion. The balance between the agony and the conclusion is marked by the deliberately quiet tone of the last verse. But despite this proportion of the parts, the end is as important as what precedes it. It is the explanation of what has happened, as well as its climax.

The drama of *La Pythie* is of a virginal woman who finds herself invaded by an external power. This invasion is a kind of rape, painful, revolting, humiliating. As she writhes and groans and cries, she curses the god who torments her. He is " Maître immonde " ; she is like a victim decked for sacrifice. In her a fearful struggle takes place as she resists

39

the god who forces himself into her being. The words convey the internal struggle in the Priestess, the gradual appeasement and the final deliverance. The Pythian Priestess is not normally an object of horror or of pity, and her circumstances are not usually thought of as painful. Valéry presents her in this way because she is a symbol of an important spiritual process, the transformation into ordered speech of contending divine and human powers. The god works through her, and her human nature resists him. In a sense her struggle is that of the poet in whom the divine instinct to create an order in words has to work on the shapeless passions and instincts of the body. The body resists because its independence, its sense of security, its happy sloth, are invaded. The poet even feels that in this act it is not he who is at work but some power outside himself, and that this power is too much for him and almost unendurable. And this struggle of the Priestess or the poet is an example of a wider kind of struggle in which the simple soul comes to grips with life and innocence is lost in the effort to adapt itself to existence. It is even Valéry's own struggle between the intellect and the heart, between abstract thought and poetry. The conflict is acute and hard to bear, but slowly its pains are abated and at last a solution is found in the creative act of speech. We may legitimately read all these meanings into *La Pythie*. Yet it remains a unity. The Priestess suffers what she suffers ; it is for us to see what relevance her situation has to our own.

The Priestess feels humiliated, shamed and violated because her intellectual and spiritual fastnesses have been invaded. This is not the life of which she once dreamed. She imagines an ideal world in which there is no movement and no life, in which she would be a kind of Medusa's head by which everyone and everything are turned to stone :

> Alors, par cette vagabonde
> Morte, errante, et lune à jamais,
> Soit l'eau des mers surprise, et l'onde
> Astreinte à d'éternels sommets !
> Que soient les humains faits statues,
> Les cœurs figés, les âmes tues,
> Et par les glaces de mon œil,
> Puisse un peuple de leurs paroles
> Durcir en un peuple d'idoles
> Muet de sottise et d'orgueil !

The pride of innocence and independence could go no
further. It is Hérodiade applying her desires for herself to
the whole world, the artist wishing to reduce the whole of
experience to a final, irrefragable order, the human spirit
trying to create its private universe from the common
universe of other men. The Priestess typifies all these.
Through her the poet has extended an experience learned
through the creative activity to other and wider spheres.
Speech, which is his special concern, is after all the concern of
the whole human race, though in it he is an expert practitioner. The ideal innocence of the Priestess is a denial of life:

> Dieu ! Je ne me connais de crime
> Que d'avoir à peine vécu ! . . .

and it is no solution to wish for a virginal remoteness and
power. The god who invades her breaks down her ideals,
her longings, her self-contained existence. The struggle is
naturally painful, as is any such struggle for those who are
forced to abandon their dreams for common life.

The paradox is that this struggle is fought through the
flesh. Just as the poet finds his material for poetry in his
body, so the Priestess is made conscious of her body in this
struggle. The body is after all what all men have in common.
Its needs, its appetites, its satisfactions are the accepted base
of human life. Speech is a physical thing. By enforcing his
will and his words on her the god reduces the Priestess to
order and makes her one with humankind. As the poem
advances, the struggle becomes less painful. The hideous
humiliation begins to show promise of better things. There
is a breath of relief, even of hope. The effort may not after
all have been in vain ; victory may still be found in submis-
sion to the invader :

> Entends, mon âme, entends ces fleuves !
> Quelles cavernes sont ici ?
> Est-ce mon sang ? . . . Sont-ce les neuves
> Rumeurs des ondes sans merci ?
> Mes secrets sonnent leurs aurores !
> Tristes airains, tempes sonores,
> Que dites-vous de l'avenir !
> Frappez, frappez, dans une roche,
> Abattez l'heure la plus proche. . . .
> Mes deux natures vont s'unir !

The Priestess sees what is happening. Her two natures, intellectual and physical, private and public, are about to join. The struggle is leading to a harmony, a solution. In isolation neither part is sufficient. Just as the poet knows the struggle between the thinker and the poet in himself, so the Priestess knows a struggle between her virginal thoughts and her physical passions. In *La Pythie* Valéry displays the need that these two sides of human nature have of each other. Without the body the mind lives in an abstract unreal world ; without the mind the body is a turmoil of indeterminate emotions. The union of the two is the work of a god.

When at last the prophetic voice comes, it comes quickly and is despatched in a single verse. It is an act and almost beyond poetry. The short shrift which it gets makes the right contrast with the agonies that have preceded it. After it comes a postscript, so alien in its didactic tone to the rest of Valéry's poetry that it has caused surprise. It brings the particular events of the poem into their universal setting, tells in general terms what the poem means. Its method is far from the ideals of " la poésie pure ". Yet it has an aesthetic function. The wild ravings of the Priestess have been closed with the prophetic utterance. Yet something else is required to still the excitement which she arouses, and this is provided by something essentially reasonable and rational. The last verse displays the peace which comes once the deliverance has taken place. It is a poetry of reason, of order. Yet even here Valéry keeps a small surprise for us : .

> Honneur des Hommes, Saint LANGAGE,
> Discours prophétique et paré,
> Belles chaînes en qui s'engage
> Le dieu dans la chair égaré,
> Illumination, largesse !
> Voici parler une Sagesse
> Et sonner cette auguste Voix
> Qui se connaît quand elle sonne
> N'être plus la voix de personne
> Tant que des ondes et des bois !

The last line is indeed unexpected. We do not anticipate that the philosophical Valéry will put forward a theory of language which looks almost Wordsworthian. He is surely not one to believe that

the forms
Of Nature have a passion in themselves
That intermingles with those works of man
To which she summons them.

The voice that speaks in the Pythia is not the voice of woods and waves, but it bears some resemblance to them. It is a natural portent in the same sense that they are. And it is not an individual voice but shared by all. The mere act of speech, the fact that it can be understood, is a denial of the ultimate separateness of human souls. The conclusion of *La Pythie* is that speech or poetry is an act which brings the individual into closer touch with life and breaks down the limits of personality. The pupil of Mallarmé denies that poetry exists only in the Absolute, and shows that even though its pains are great, it must come into relation with ordinary existence.

These poems do not present a theory of poetry. Nothing could be further from Valéry's intention. But they present views of the poet's activity which are consistent with what Valéry says about it in prose. And they do what prose cannot do. They show what poetry means to the poet, how it affects and engages his spirit. In them he recreates the strain and the stress, the long waiting and the unforeseen rewards, the moments of concentrated felicity and timeless ecstasy which are his in his art. But since the poet is also a thinker and his poetry has roots in his thoughts, these poems are consistent with each other and imply a philosophical outlook which is the poet's own. In *Charmes* Valéry has moved from the special experience of *La Jeune Parque* to a state nearer to conscious awareness. If poetry is his chief theme, it is not his only theme. It suggests considerations which are not confined to itself, and opens up avenues which the poet feels himself driven to explore. In all his work Valéry illustrates the truth of Yeats' words, " we make . . . out of the quarrel with ourselves poetry ". His quarrel is between the thinker and the human being, between the mind and the flesh. Poetry is a special battlefield for this struggle and has naturally provided him with many subjects. But the struggle extends elsewhere and may be seen in other fields. In his analysis of himself Valéry finds discords and contrasts which can be expressed in cold prose, but are of such interest to him that they demand poetry for their full expression. They engage and excite him, and the excitement must be conveyed in verse. *Charmes* covers more than one department of the human spirit, but everything in it seems to follow from some discord or struggle in the poet's self.

Valéry accepts the universe, accepts the discord in himself between analysis and poetry, thought and sensation. This discord is an example of something more general and may be represented theologically as a struggle of the soul with the flesh. In *Ébauche d'un Serpent* Valéry takes his symbols and his subject from theology. The Serpent who tempted Eve is one of the most ancient attempts to frame the problem of evil. In this myth the primal innocence of man is lost when he tastes of the Tree of Knowledge. The meaning of this loss can be differently assessed, and Valéry has his own view of it. His Serpent is his own. It is in the tradition of the nineteenth century, which more than once felt the charm and even the justice of what is usually thought to be the Spirit of Evil. In his Mephistopheles Goethe created his witty and delightful " Geist, der stets verneint " spirit who always denies, and put into him much that was real and vital in himself. In *Les Litanies de Satan* Baudelaire depicted the real god of his devotion, the protector of the drunkard and the defeated, the keeper of dark secrets and healer of human anguish. In his *À Satana* Carducci invoked a spirit of intelligence and joy, the companion of the Olympian gods, the enemy of popes and kings. For these poets the Spirit of Evil was almost a spirit of good, active and intelligent, the enemy of dark customs and clogging emotions. He symbolises a side of the human spirit which is valued in an age of science and discovery. Valéry sees his Serpent differently. Free from the religious and political controversies of the nineteenth century, he feels no impulse to idolise the enemy of God. His Serpent symbolises something in every man. It is nearly all belly, a creature of sensuality and bodily appetite. It is therefore as much an enemy of light as Goethe's Mephistopheles :

> Grand soleil, qui sonnes l'éveil
> A l'être, et de feux l'accompagnes,
> Toi qui l'enfermes d'un sommeil
> Trompeusement peint de campagnes,
> Fauteur des fantômes joyeux
> Qui rendent sujette des yeux
> La présence obscure de l'âme,

44

Toujours le mensonge m'a plu
Que tu répands sur l'absolu
Ô Roi des ombres fait de flamme !

Valéry's Serpent is the incarnation of instincts which are none other than bodily appetites. As such it hates the orderliness of the Universe and would like to destroy it. It too is " der Geist, der stets verneint ". It takes a pleasure in confounding God's reverent servants and likes to insert its poisoned thoughts into their minds. But its message is almost entirely sensual. What it wants to take from Eve is her innocence. It hates the sight of her perfection and would like to destroy it :

Cette parfaite m'apparut,
Son flanc vaste et d'or parcouru
Ne craignant le soleil ni l'homme ;
Tout offerte aux regards de l'air,
L'âme encore stupide, et comme
Interdite au seuil de la chair.

It whispers in her delicate ear and tells her how beautiful this knowledge is. In time she yields to its temptations, and then it feels that it has succeeded because it has spread despair, disorder and death.

To this exciting story Valéry brings different and delightful arts. He conveys by many suggestions the sultry air of the Garden where the temptation takes place. He conveys too the sensual appeal which Eve makes to the Serpent in her body and its movements. His Serpent is wise. It knows that its prey is not easily caught, that simplicity is guarded by other forces than its own innocence.

Sottise, orgueil, félicité,
Gardent bien la belle cité !

Half the art of the poem lies in its suggestion of sexuality, in the joy which the Serpent takes in breaking down Eve's innocence. And this joy has its own metaphysics. The Serpent advances reasons which carry weight. But what really matters is its cold calculating nature. Valéry achieves a poetry of sensuality which is free from illusion and sentimentality. Goethe's Mephistopheles has something of this quality when he enjoys the night on the Brocken or refuses to respect Faust's love for Gretchen. But Mephistopheles' attitude towards sex is simply that of the man of pleasure who is not going to be disturbed by sentimental complications. The Serpent is deeper and wiser ; for it knows that the body has its own claims and its own glory. It adds variety and colour to life ; it breaks up the monotony of a too well ordered universe.

The Serpent is all body, all appetites, and the poet stresses this :

> Et je sentais frémir le nombre,
> Tout le long de mon fouet subtil.

But the body has its powers. The Serpent's triumph over Eve is that of knowledge over ignorance, and knowledge is the great claim that it makes for itself. For it the Tree of Knowledge pushes desirable dark branches into the eternal morning ; knowledge alone exalts it to the power of real being. The intimate association of sensuality and knowledge is the central paradox of the poem, and Valéry means a good deal by it. His Serpent is wise because it is all body and because the body, even more than the soul, has its own wisdom and can cast an iridescent glamour over the objects of desire. The appetites which Dante saw as destroying beyond recovery a man's whole nature are seen by Valéry as contributing largely to the variety and glamour of life. It is they, and not the pure light of reason, that give a meaning to most things and events in the visible world. In *La Pythie* and *Aurore* the senses provide the poet with his material ; here they have a far wider scope. The Serpent corrupts because it will, and finds thereby a satisfaction for its misery :

> Le triomphe de ma tristesse.

The body's satisfaction is not all pleasant, and herein lies the dignity of the victories which it wins over the soul. Its chaotic and purposeless activities, its essential " Not-being ", are as necessary to the Whole as the dispassionate, absolute, undifferentiated activities of the spirit. Human life passes between the extremes of spirit and flesh and owes its character to their interpenetration. The Serpent is as necessary as the Lord of Light.

The Serpent represents one side of Valéry's view of life, the side which he also displayed, with disagreeable thoroughness, in the amorous activities of his Monsieur Teste. But there is another side. The spirit too has its poetry, its glamour. In Valéry there is little between these two extremes. He is hardly a poet of the tenderer and commoner emotions. Even poems like *La Dormeuse* and *La Fausse Morte*, which are inspired by a kind of love, are curiously detached. But he sometimes writes poetry of an almost pure aesthetic state in which an object is seen so clearly that there is no other thought in the mind. The poet needs nothing outside or beyond it, and in it emotions seem, and are, out of place. Few have attempted to convey just this state, and we can understand why. Poetry makes its effects through a series of words ; it normally describes something which has duration and change and variety. In this it differs from painting and sculpture, which are concerned with an instantaneous moment or even with a timeless reality. They may hint at movement, but they cannot convey it. But Valéry's aesthetic state is at times akin to that of the painter or the sculptor, and sometimes he does in words what is normally done through the visual arts. He presents a state of mind in which there are no distinctions between past and present, no development and no climax. Other poets have done something like this in describing inanimate objects ; Valéry applies their method to certain states in the self. His success is unquestionable. He creates an effect of motionless permanence, of timeless joy.

Just as the mathematician finds a rapturous delight in figures, or the architect in the balance of material bodies and planes, so Valéry finds a source of poetry and a pleasure hardly less intellectual than these in certain inanimate things which both please the senses and, through them, the mind. Such is *Cantique des Colonnes*. Pillars, broken or unbroken, have long played their part in landscape and in painting. T. S. Eliot has found a peculiar symbol in his

Sunlight on a broken column.

Valéry goes further and writes the poetry of all columns as such, of ideal columns. In it he passes from the visible to the mental, from the eye to the mind. At the start his columns are such as we all have seen, and are described with all the pleasure of delighted sight :

Si froides et dorées
Nous fûmes de nos lits
Par le ciseau tirées
Pour devenir ces lys !

47

De nos lits de cristal
Nous fûmes éveillées,
Des griffes de métal
Nous ont appareillées.

Pour affronter la lune,
La lune et le soleil,
On nous polit chacune
Comme l'ongle de l'orteil !

So far all is sight and touch. But imperceptibly the columns become subjective and metaphysical. They embody a principle which appeals to the mind as well as to the eye ; they are the embodiment of a mathematical beauty :

Filles des nombres d'or,
Fortes des lois du ciel,
Sur nous tombe et s'endort
Un dieu couleur de miel.

In the poet's mind the visible columns are merged with the principles that make them what they are. Their beauty is intellectual ; they awake a special aesthetic delight in which the pleasure of the eye is sustained and strengthened by an invisible harmony and order which appeal to the mind.

In the rarefied joy of *Cantique des Colonnes* and in the strange, sensual atmosphere of *Ébauche d'un Serpent* Valéry's art is at home. He understands the intellect and the body, but of a whole intermediate range of sentiment he seems, as a poet, to be ignorant. The spectacle of ordinary human life, with its emotions and efforts, seems alien both to the metaphysical columns and to the crafty Serpent. Yet once or twice Valéry has written poetry, not indeed about ordinary life, but about his relation to it. In *Fragments du Narcisse* he takes a Greek symbol and adapts it to an intimate situation in his own experience. The old story of the beautiful boy who fell in love with his own reflection in the water and was drowned can be interpreted in many ways. It may originally have meant no more than that those who think too much of themselves are punished for it. For Valéry it means something quite different. As a young man he was puzzled by the problem of the self's place in a world among other selves, and all through his life he has at intervals sought a complete detachment in which, like his own imaginary Leonardo, he will be able to understand everything and to be a master of all rules.

Such an ideal is almost solipsist in its concentration on the self. Philosophically such a position is hardly tenable, but poetry may well try to convey both what such a desire means and what conflicts or failures it involves. This is what *Fragments du Narcisse* does. Through the symbol of Narcisse the poet presents facts about himself, his desire to find a complete satisfaction in himself, undisturbed by exterior forces, and the extreme difficulty, if not impossibility, of finding it.

The foundation of the poem is the scene in which Narcisse in the silence of dusk looks at his own image in a still pool. The atmosphere is of unbroken peace. Surely at such a time, if ever, Narcisse will find the complete communion with himself that he desires. All nature helps him :

> La voix des sources change, et me parle du soir ;
> Un grand calme m'écoute, où j'écoute l'espoir.
> J'entends l'herbe des nuits croître dans l'ombre sainte,
> Et la lune perfide élève son miroir
> Jusque dans les secrets de la fontaine éteinte. . . .
> Jusque dans les secrets que je crains de savoir,
> Jusque dans le repli de l'amour de soi-même,
> Rien ne peut échapper au silence du soir. . . .

What counts is the atmosphere, the silence and dusk which seem to welcome Narcisse to his strange task. This is certainly symbolical. It stands for that special frame of mind in which a man, believing himself at last alone, is ready to examine and to know himself. In such a state the merest echo or hint of an echo from outside is disturbing. Narcisse does not find the satisfaction he desires. He seems near to it. He sees his reflection

> Délicieux démon désirable et glacé !

but there is no action. Nothing happens. The mood is expectant, willing, hopeful, but no more. We see a hint that no man can ever know himself as he would wish.

The pool is a symbol of the world as the self-contained soul sees it. It is of most importance to Narcisse because it reflects himself. But somehow it contains elements outside himself. Narcisse imagines that it is pure and undefiled, that others have never tasted of it :

> A cette onde jamais ne burent les troupeaux !

but he soon knows that it has its own secrets :

> L'oiseau mort, le fruit mûr, lentement descendus,
> Et les rares lueurs des clairs anneaux perdus,
> Tu consommes en toi leur perte solennelle.

So when a man examines himself, he may find hidden things of which he has been unconscious and yet which seem to belong to him. His other self may be impenetrable with its store of undiscoverable riches, its accumulated relics of the past. And more than this, this other self may seem to have some relation to an outer world which the thinking self denies and rejects. The pool has seen much before Narcisse came to it. It has known

> Astres, roses, saisons, les corps et leurs amours !

The last is the most disturbing. Narcisse is troubled by the thought of other men who have been there, especially of lovers, with their ignorance, their illusions, their weakness. He feels that they are unreal, and yet the thought of them troubles him. So the thought of men's emotions may disturb and perplex the man who thinks that he is beyond them. Valéry himself with his desire for an absolute of thought may well have suffered so himself, but as a poet he cannot but feel what these human actors mean and describe them in touching and penetrating words :

> La caresse et le meurtre hésitent dans leurs mains,
> Leur cœur, qui croit se rompre au détour des chemins,
> Lutte, et retient à soi son espérance étreinte.

That is the other side of the picture, the reality which breaks in upon the contemplation of the self.

Narcisse's desire is unattainable. He cannot realise his desire to be alone with his image. Even in the first magical hour of dusk he finds that he has no satisfaction :

> Pour l'inquiet Narcisse, il n'est ici qu'ennui.

His image refuses to speak to him, and in the end disappears. The self is not self-sufficient. We all may imagine a kind of contemplative state in which there are no other persons, no experience which is not really our own. As an ideal this has its charm, and the poetry of it is given in the picture of

Narcisse by the pool. But the ideal is not to be realised. The other self is itself an illusion. It is less real than the phantoms of men and women who intrude from outside and may have their own illusions :

> Rien ne peut dissiper leurs songes absolus,

but at least they have voices, desires and presence. *Fragments du Narcisse* shows the impossibility of finding this complete satisfaction alone with oneself. It is a poem of frustrated desire, of failure. It draws no conclusion and ends abruptly, but we may draw our own conclusions from it. In the poetry there is more strength and reality, more power, in the description of the deluded human lovers than in Narcisse's dreams about himself. Whatever Valéry's intellectual ambitions may be, when it comes to poetry he finds more sustenance in this common spectacle than in any ideal self-realisation. It is as if he had set out fairly the two sides of his nature and found in the end that what count are the pathos and variety of the human scene.

To this poem *Le Cimetière Marin* provides a kind of complement. In place of mythology Valéry provides a meditative poem in the first person. This is his own crisis as he knows it, his own conflict and conclusion. His style and his mannerisms, his method and his peculiar gifts, combine to give his most pondered, most deeply felt poem. He finds himself in a cemetery by the sea, and the moment of his presence there is one of lull in his life. He is open to the impressions which the sea, the sun and the tombs make on him. Because he is in this receptive mood, he conveys not this or that external aspect of the scene but the whole as it affects him and passes into him. What begins with being description becomes a symbol in his mind. The roof on which he seems to be, with doves walking on it, becomes an " édifice dans l'âme " and the doves are his thoughts. The tombs of the cemetery become quiet objects in his mind, matters that his intellect has settled. The sunlight which flames on the sea becomes his own intellectual detachment. There is a correspondence between the scene and his own spiritual condition, a correspondence so close that the elements in the one become imperceptibly elements in the other. The natural objects take on a new meaning as symbols of his life. The impartial sunlight, " Midi le juste ", gives the setting.

51

In it the poet finds a kind of absolute content after his intellectual labours, and feels sure of himself :

> Le Temps scintille et le Songe est savoir.

For the first seven stanzas this state of mind is presented in all its strength and brilliance. Then comes the crisis. The poet pays his homage to the light. It is his first object of veneration :

> Mais rendre la lumière
> Suppose d'ombre une morne moitié.

This other side gradually forces itself on him in the second half of the poem. From his detached intellectual illumination he is driven to think of his earthly state and to accept it. In this process lie the main movement of the poem and its intense beauty.

The moment is of crisis in the poet's life. He has been rapt in thought, and the thought is finished. It is the kind of moment at which he may turn to poetry ; for he feels a need in himself :

> J'attends l'écho de ma grandeur interne,
> Amère, sombre et sonore citerne,
> Sonnant dans l'âme un creux toujours futur !

From this he turns to the nature around him, the light and shadows of the graveyard, the insect buzzing in the dry air, and in contemplating them he finds a sweet bitterness and a clear spirit. Then under the motionless noon he thinks of the dead lying in their tombs, and his verses about them are the most tender and most touching that he has ever written :

> Ils ont fondu dans une absence épaisse,
> L'argile rouge a bu la blanche espèce,
> Le don de vivre a passé dans les fleurs !
> Où sont des morts les phrases familières,
> L'art personnel, les âmes singulières ?
> La larve file où se formaient les pleurs.

> Les cris aigus des filles chatouillées,
> Les yeux, les dents, les paupières mouillées,
> Le sein charmant qui joue avec le feu,
> Le sang qui brille aux lèvres qui se rendent,
> Les derniers dons, les doigts qui les défendent,
> Tout va sous terre et rentre dans le jeu !

The contrast between life and death, the complete severance between the living and the dead, could not be more nobly or more touchingly stated than in these lines where the common circumstances of life, its pathetic or pleasing activities, are consigned to the hazardous impartiality of the grave.

This vivid poignant experience determines the course of the poem. The poet must face the issues raised by the dead. Valéry does not draw the common and unsatisfactory lesson that mortality makes all men equally unimportant. Still less does he conceive any life in or beyond the grave. The dead are indeed immortal, but there is no consolation in that :

> Maigre immortalité noire et dorée,
> Consolatrice affreusement laurée.

It is not they but the living who are devoured by worms. The dead under the earth are as remote from life as is the absolute of thought itself. Turning from his ideal sunlight to the grave, the poet finds himself confronted with an order of things no less inhuman and no less remote. The dead remind him of his mortality, not by his likeness to them, but by his unlikeness. They are of no use to him :

> Qui ne connaît, et qui ne les refuse,
> Ce crâne vide et ce rire éternel !

In meditation on them he knows that he is what he is, a man. The abstract timelessness of contemplation is an unreal dream. The paradox of Zeno that nothing really moves is untrue. The arrow has pierced the poet ; he is an Achilles pursued by the shadow of a tortoise. From this conclusion he turns to life, to the activities of living, to the new birth which comes from the wind and to the freshening sea. These give him back his soul :

> Le vent se lève ! . . . Il faut tenter de vivre !

He closes his book, and summons the waves to break the stillness of the remote place where he is.

In this magnificent poem Valéry again confronts the problems raised by his divided self, but this time he comes to an emphatic decision. It is life that counts. Against the call of action the immortality of the dead and the abstract aloofness of meditation fail to make their claim. But the poem is much more than a victory of action over thought. In it

Valéry gives much more than delicate tones and exquisite sensations. It states his relation to life and shows that he has his own poetical vision of it. The bounds which Mallarmé set between the poet and the public are broken. Something of its old empire is given back to poetry. The process which began in *La Jeune Parque* here reaches its conclusion. The discord between intellect and sensation is settled when the poet accepts life, and enters into its activities with an undivided being. In the process nothing has been lost. *Le Cimetière Marin* gives its full due to the intellectual pleasures of the mind and displays them with a peculiar brilliance. But it relates them to a place in the scheme of things. They are not all that count. Indeed the poem is all the richer for the contrast between

> Midi là-haut, Midi sans mouvement

and

> Mes repentirs, mes doutes, mes contraintes.

These extremes come from the poet's whole nature. His poetry is no longer the product of one department of it.

In *Le Cimetière Marin*, and indeed in most of *Charmes*, Valéry has moved far from Mallarmé. He may use some of the same symbols — " l'azur ", " l'ange ", " l'hydre ",— but the intention and the effect are different. The mystical view of poetry has been replaced by the acceptance of it as a fact like other facts. The special place of the poet in society is not mentioned. Indeed the poet moves nearer to other men as his art finds its capacities. The desire for " pure poetry " is tempered by a realisation that in poetry the intellect must have its place and that poetry may gain by admitting elements of reason and almost of argument. The difficulties of Mallarmé's grammar, the abrupt breaks in syntax, the deliberate obscurities, are not to be found in Valéry. His poetry is difficult. His symbols are not always easy to grasp. But the grammar and the sense are there. On the other hand, Valéry's debt to Mallarmé remains incalculable. His poetry is intensely personal. It is also extremely poetical, in the sense that subjects proper to prose are excluded from it and that it aims not at instruction but at creating an effect. The poet has found his relation to life, but on the whole he lives in a rare and special atmosphere. He writes for the few. Such poetry is only possible when there exists a cultivated society able to face its difficulties and to understand its subtleties. Above all it is the poetry of an extremely intelligent man, who knows what things are and is not afraid to see them in their true nature. It demands the sacrifice of many false or romantic notions. It needs a considerable adjustment of mind before its full strength is revealed. As such it is representative of the age in which it was written, scientific and sceptical of transcendental hypotheses but willing to admit that in the varied pattern of life there is much that calls for wonder.

III

RAINER MARIA RILKE

1875–1926

All the great achievements of French civilisation have
been European in character and in influence. In the Middle
Ages, in the *Grand Siècle*, in the nineteenth century, French
painting, sculpture, architecture and poetry were accepted as
examples of what such arts ought to be and copied in many
countries. The peculiar French genius has been to find forms
which suit the mass of civilised men and are in no sense
local or provincial. To this rule Symbolism was no exception.
It spread abroad and affected literatures quite unlike the
French. In its denial of politics and its cult of the Beautiful
it was essentially international. Its tenets could be accepted
by Germans and English alike. Moreover, in so far as it represented the protest of art against the commercial material-
ism of the age, it was equally valid in every European
country. Transferred to foreign climes, it changed its character till it became almost unrecognisable. In England the
native traditions of song and a tendency to make all poetry
lyrical prevented the element of music from making such an
appeal as it made to the French with their centuries of correct
statement in classical verse. Yet even in England it was
important. In Germany with its traditions of transcendental
philosophy and its groping search for mysteries Symbolism
was obviously more at home. But its most emphatic manifestation was in a man who was the most international of all poets
in his time, who seems to have no local roots and few racial
affinities, an artist whose only country was Europe.

Rainer Maria Rilke was born in Prague, wrote in German
and found his inspiration in a cosmopolitan aestheticism.
He tried to get away from life into himself, to be independent
of everything except the Beautiful, to live entirely for his
art. No one, not even Mallarmé, treated his art more seriously ; few sacrificed more to it. He was a martyr to his
ideal. His life was a long struggle to wring out of himself
every drop of poetry. For this he endured long months of

56

melancholy solitude and unremitting, often unrewarded, labour. He organised his life to be a poet. He belonged to no clique and had no place in contemporary movements. He did not listen to criticism or believe in its value. He made changes in his manner of writing, but each followed some change in himself; and when he found what seemed to him adequate, he exhausted himself in it and spent his last years in a wasting sense of emptiness. He is a representative figure of his time because he is the most considerable poet in it who gave himself up to Aestheticism as such. He was a deliberate and uncompromising aesthete. The Beautiful was his only goal; he interpreted it in an exacting sense. By nature he responded strongly to sights and ideas, and in these responses he found the material of his poetry and his theory of it. He was completely dependent on his sensibility. For it, and on it, he lived.

Rilke's poetical career, and he had hardly any other, may be seen as a series of attempts to give full expression to his sensibility, to translate into permanent form all that he felt. He took time to find what his feelings were and how best to convey them. But his later works were written on principles of his own discovery. In *Neue Gedichte* (*New Poems*), 1907, and the volumes that followed, he set out with a definite aim and achieved it. His work was the inevitable development of his own nature. But because he lived when he did, he illustrates the movements of his time. His career is almost a commentary on Symbolism in that he moved from Romanticism to Aestheticism and from Aestheticism to a peculiar kind of mysticism. It is as if he had been intended by nature to be a Symbolist but had expended his energies on other kinds of poetry until he found himself forced into a Symbolism of his own creation. No doubt he was influenced by the example of other men. His Aestheticism owed a great deal to Rodin; his latest manner was confirmed by his discovery of Paul Valéry. But these examples served mainly to strengthen impulses which were already at work in him and to give sanction to opinions which he had already formed for himself. His career shows how natural the ideals and methods of the Symbolists were to a poet whose religious nature had lost its moorings and needed a new faith. The belief in Art and the Beautiful made Rilke what he was.

Rilke's early poetry belongs to the last wave of Romanti-

E

cism. It has some charm and too much sweetness. It conveys his longings, his unsatisfied desires, his attempts to dramatise himself as a young girl or a Russian monk. His aim is quite clear :

> Ich möchte werden wie die ganz Geheimen :
> Nicht auf der Stirne die Gedanken denken,
> Nur eine Sehnsucht reichen in den Reimen.[1]

In the denial of the reason and the emphasis on " Sehnsucht " we see the old German spirit, the desire for something beyond the frontiers of being, the belief that poetry is a kind of dream. Rilke is deliberately and consciously anti-intellectual :

> Du musst das Leben nicht verstehen,
> Dann wird es werden wie ein Fest.[2]

This poetry has the virtues of its kind. It is melodious in an obvious way, touching, sensitive, true perhaps to the frustrated longings of youth, but too remote from life, too dream-laden and too derivative. It tells of Rilke's longings but not really of himself. He has not found out what he can do or where his real self lies. Even as the poetry of youthful sensibility it is much inferior to that of Hugo von Hofmannsthal, whose precocious talent made Stefan George say, " If he had died at twenty, what a genius we should have lost ". Rilke took time to free himself from his origins, to assert his real creative personality. The change came gradually and was complete when he published *Neue Gedichte*. After *Das Stunden-Buch* (*The Book of Hours*) Rilke seems to have felt that he had written enough about his feelings. He turned to a different kind of poetry, to something more objective, more sincere, less personal and in some senses less intimate. But in it he found the real range of his gifts. His earlier books seem to have been a preparation for it. They taught him his craft and showed him what he could and could not do. At last he wrote poetry that no one else could have written.

The causes and character of this change are complex.

---

[1] Like very secret people I would be,
  Not to be thinking thoughts out with the brain,
  Nothing but longing in my rhymes to see.

[2] Life is not for your understanding ;
  Then will it be just like a feast.

Rilke seems to have felt that he had said all that he could about his feelings, that to continue writing as he had written must mean the repetition of what he had already done. From this his artistic conscience revolted. He needed a new outlet, and he found it in France. The direction which he now took was largely determined by his admiration for Rodin. Rodin's belief that art must follow nature dispelled the last traces of Rilke's belief that it dealt with " Sehnsucht ". He was naturally interested in sculpture, and in Rodin he saw a creative genius who towered above his contemporaries by the strength and independence of his work. The close contact that he found in Rodin's house with another art than his own affected him strongly. He saw that Rodin's sculpture was the fruit of a great tradition, and to the masterpieces of this tradition, Greek or Mediaeval, Rilke brought his studious, perceptive and devoted attention. Instead of among dreams, he lived among works of visual art until he wished to make his own poems like them,— self-sufficient, perfectly wrought and rich in content. Of this process *Neue Gedichte* was the result. Its special character does not lie in its being more objective than Rilke's earlier work but in its being written with a different conception of poetry. These poems move to a different rhythm ; they are more concentrated, more vivid, more visual. And, what is more remarkable, they are largely written in accordance with a theory. This theory makes its public appearance in Rilke's novel, *Malte Laurids Brigge* (1910), where he says " Verses are not, as people imagine, simply feelings (these we have soon enough) : they are experiences ". And in *Requiem* he wrote :

> O alter Fluch der Dichter,
> Die sich beklagen, wo sie sagen sollten,
> Die immer urteiln über ihr Gefühl
> Statt es zu bilden.[1]

Rilke had finished with his notion that poetry is concerned with feelings. He essayed something else, the patient, passive, absorbing state of the aesthete, who waits for impressions to come to him, collects them, ponders them, until " in a most

[1]   O ancient curse of poets,
    Lamenting their own lot and telling nothing,
    For ever passing judgment on their feeling
    Instead of shaping it.
                            (Trs. J. B. Leishman)

rare hour the first word of a poem arises in their midst and goes forth from them ". But the mere collection of impressions and sensations was not all that Rilke demanded. They must be reduced to order and turned into art. He saw himself as the mediaeval stone-mason who transformed his feelings into the permanent shape of a cathedral. The poet's many experiences must be transmuted into something independent and complete, something which stands in its own right and needs for its understanding no reference to the poet's life or thought or feelings.

At first sight this doctrine might seem to bear a close relation to that of the Parnassians. They had not aimed, like Victor Hugo, at creating a poetic personality whose every poem was but an incident in a single career and intelligible largely through what had preceded it. They aimed rather at creating poems which stood by themselves, needed neither preface nor comment and said nothing about the poet. In poems like Leconte de Lisle's *Les Éléphants* there is no philosophy, no moralising, no personal revelation. It describes an occasion, an event ; its appeal is to the inner eye ; it says nothing to the heart or to the conscience. It exists through its vivid details and the design to which they are subordinated. It comments neither on the universe nor on the poet. But independence of this kind was not what Rilke achieved, nor what he desired. His poems were much more than pictures in words ; much more went to their making than what he had seen. However independent he wished his poetry to be, its independence would not be of the impersonal, pictorial, Parnassian kind. He started with an act of faith that every experience would ultimately become part of himself and that out of this enriched self poetry would emerge. But he also felt that when the poetry came, it would not be personal and subjective like his earlier work but self-sufficient and complete like a masterpiece of the visual arts.

Rilke's purpose might be regarded as an attempt to harmonise and combine two different kinds of poetry. On the one hand, it demanded the fullness which comes from living in the imagination, from yielding to every impression, and in this it recalls the Romantics with their eager quest of sensations and their belief in the unique nature of the poet's calling. On the other hand, it recalls Mallarmé's conception of the ideal poem as something absolute in itself and free from anything that might be called the private tastes of its maker. The two views are not easily reconciled ; for the one asserts the importance of everything that the poet feels, the other demands that his individuality must be omitted from the actual poem, which exists in its own world of pure art. But Rilke's attempt to combine the two views is intelligible in the light both of his time and of his own development. He saw, as others saw, that the Romantic personality was in many ways destructive of poetry while the impersonal art of the Parnassians omitted too much, and he himself had known both the ardours of an intense inner life and the majesty of works of art. In his last years he turned again to the poetry of self-revelation, but before that he passed through a period in which he deliberately tried to lose himself in impressions, hoping that out of them he would create an objective and self-sufficient art. In this task his temperament helped him. He had a most unusual, almost an incomparable, sensibility. He was often overwhelmed by what he saw. A casual sight might occupy and dominate his mind to the exclusion of almost everything else. He knew the state of pure receptivity, the true aesthetic condition, and when something was given to him on these terms, it stayed with him until it became a part of him. From such moments he made his poetry, and naturally he sought them, expected new excitements to come, and derived a strange strength when they came. In his search for them he looked all about him, in the life of large cities like Paris, in the monuments of the past, in the unfamiliar sights of foreign places, in sculpture and painting and architecture. He passed much of his life in solitude that his impressions might not be sullied or shaken by the impacts of personal relations or the stress of living. He regarded his aesthetic task as all-important, and faced it with unrelaxed determination.

A purpose of this kind is unusual in a poet. It might even be thought impossible. The creative faculty is usually accompanied by a strong sense of independence and refuses to wait for events to dictate to it. Even those who live on their emotions do not expect them to be imposed from without. But Rilke was a true child and apostle of the Aesthetic Movement. Where others found a unifying principle in religion or morality or truth, Rilke found his in the search for impressions and in the hope that they could be transmuted into poetry. To this task he gave his religious fervour, his moral earnestness, his intellectual integrity. For him what mattered was Art. To make Art as such the source of his inspiration is extremely exacting for a poet. Even when he is not concerned with the absolute of the Beautiful but contents himself with individual works of art, his task is not easy. It is hard to write poetry about other poems and only less hard to write about pictures and statues. In such work there is almost inevitably something second-hand ; it seems to have no independent vision and to add nothing new to experience. But Rilke felt no qualms. His concern with the arts was so single-minded that he tried to recapture through aesthetic appreciation the power and the vision which had gone to the making of masterpieces. The extraordinary thing is that he succeeded and found sources of original poetry in the works of other men.

Many of the *Neue Gedichte* are concerned with works of art. They vary greatly in manner and in quality, and, on the whole, it seems true that the further Rilke gets from a purely receptive state, the more striking his work is. So long as his poetry is dominated by the impression which a masterpiece makes on him, he is more a critic than a poet. He conveys his impression and makes us feel that what he sees is worth seeing, but his poem is still second-hand. It is the inspiring masterpiece that matters. This is true even of poems like *Früher Apollo* (*Early Apollo*) and *Die Fensterrose* (*The Rose Window*), which are far from being merely descriptive. In both the object seen is so important that Rilke can only weave fancies round it. His poem is a criticism, a commentary. The statue and the window remain more important than what is said about them. Sometimes this approach degenerates into what is hardly even poetry and is infused not with real delight but with a dry historical interest or a feeling for the quaint. In *Der König von Münster* (*The King of Munster*), for instance, or *Der aussätzige König* (*The Leprous King*), Rilke takes old legends which might have a human interest, but he presents them as oddities, not entirely agreeable, and leaves them at that. Even in *Auferstehung* (*Resurrection*) his feelings are in a very minor key and hardly amount to more than a pleasure in the curious. In such cases Rilke's pleasure was not strong enough to inspire poetry. He remained the mere aesthete.

Such failures, however, are not to be attributed to Rilke's

aestheticism. In them he was not the true lover of the beautiful but the sightseer, the man who likes the unusual but remains at a distance from it. Actually the more Rilke lost himself in aesthetic contemplation, the more in the end he found. When a sight ravished his senses and occupied his mind, he came to a new vision of what lay behind it, and from this he made poetry. The process and its results may be seen in *Eva* (*Eve*). The given is the statue at Chartres, and the first part of the poem is almost purely appreciative. The beauty of the statue has caught Rilke, and he describes what he sees :

> Einfach steht sie an der Kathedrale
> Grossem Aufstieg, nah der Fensterrose,
> Mit dem Apfel in der Apfelpose,
> Schuldlos-schuldig ein für alle Male
>
> An dem Wachsenden, das sie gebar,
> Seit sie aus dem Kreis der Ewigkeiten
> Liebend fortging, um sich durchzustreiten
> Durch die Erde, wie ein junges Jahr.[1]

So far the appeal is to the eye. The stance and the look of Eve have passed into his words. He sees her as the sculptor may have seen her. But the second part of the poem deepens and widens its meaning :

> Ach, sie hätte gern in jenem Land
> Noch ein wenig weilen mögen, achtend
> Auf der Tiere Eintracht und Verstand.
>
> Doch da sie den Mann entschlossen fand,
> Ging sie mit ihm, nach dem Tode trachtend,
> Und sie hatte Gott noch kaum gekannt.[2]

[1] Simple, where the great cathedral climbs
Upward, stands she, by the window-rose,
With the apple in the apple-pose,
Guiltless-guilty, now and for all times,

Of the growing, she who gave them birth,
When the circle of eternities
She abandoned for long enterprise,
Loving,— like a young year through the earth.

[2] Ah, she would have gladly in that land
Stayed a little longer and have learned
How the beasts agree and understand ;

But she found her master's purpose set,
And with him in search of death she turned,
Though of God she scarcely knew as yet.

In this Rilke passes beyond his delighted enjoyment of the statue to an appreciation of the mood which inspired its sculptor. By entering into this mediaeval world through his poet's insight, he creates something new. Through his interpretation Eve becomes a type of innocence and grace, of motherhood and wifehood, who appeals directly to the affections. Such perhaps she was for the Middle Ages ; so at least Rilke sees and presents her.

An experience captured in this way need not, of course, be historically correct. To history the poet has no obligations. Nor was Rilke always so respectful of the past as in *Eva*. More usually he looked at a work of art from a peculiarly personal standpoint and found new meanings in themes which had been largely fixed by the conventions of centuries. The great events of the Gospels are a dangerous subject for any poet. Hallowed by the long tradition of Christian art they might seem ill suited to Rilke who did not accept their sanctity. But in *Der Ölbaumgarten* (*The Olive Garden*) and in *Pietà* he extracted a new pathos from the most tragic episodes in the old story. In both his inspiration was not in the plain story of the Gospel but in the masterpieces of Italian artists. The hopeless despair of his Christ belongs more to Mantegna than to St. John. He is a purely human figure, abandoned and hopeless, and he turns with his complaint to God :

> Ich finde Dich nicht mehr. Nicht in mir, nein.
> Nicht in den andern. Nicht in diesem Stein.
> Ich finde Dich nicht mehr. Ich bin allein.
>
> Ich bin allein mit aller Menschen Gram,
> Den ich durch Dich zu lindern unternahm,
> Der Du nicht bist. O namenlose Scham. . . .[1]

The quivering sorrow, the pathetic complaint, of these lines are not so grand as the few words of the Gospel, but they are true to the heart and to life. Rilke's Christ is like all who have

[1] No more I find thee. In myself no tone
Of thee ; nor in the others ; nor in this stone.
I can find thee no more. I am alone.

I am alone with all men sorrow name,
Which to relieve through thee was still my claim,
Thee whom I cannot find. O nameless shame. . . .

(Trs. J. B. Leishman)

attempted a splendid task and found themselves betrayed and abandoned. In *Pietà* also Rilke was inspired by Italian art. The washing of Christ's body by the women who had loved him was a theme which drew from Titian and Michaelangelo some of their grandest work. Into their vision of the scene they inevitably put a sense of tragic longing for the dead, and depicted it in the sorrow-stricken figures of the Virgin and the Magdalene. It is this which Rilke makes the centre of his poem. His Magdalene speaks in the language of passionate desire, and the climax comes when she says :

> Nun bist du müde, und dein müder Mund
> Hat keine Lust zu meinem wehen Munde —.
> O Jesus, Jesus, wann war unsre Stunde ?
> Wie gehn wir beide wunderlich zugrund.[1]

What moves Rilke is the element of frustrated love. In this he finds a poignant pathos. By concentrating on it he makes his poem a new thing, though its subject is ancient and familiar. He does what the painters had done but no poet had quite done before him. His art is not derivative in any derogatory sense.

Yet despite his aestheticism and his reliance on works of art Rilke could not fail at times to insinuate into his poetry his own peculiar ideas. He does so with full right. For he does not teach or preach but recreates stories to fit his own convictions. He saw, for instance, the Prodigal Son as an example of a difficulty which he himself felt deeply, and this gives so strange a power to *Der Auszug des verlorenen Sohnes* (*The Departure of the Prodigal Son*). Rilke finds a new meaning for the parable. For him it is " the legend of one who did not wish to be loved ". The poem depicts a man who desires at all costs to free himself from the potent bonds of familiar life, to find a new existence far away from all that he knows :

> Aus Drang, aus Artung,
> Aus Ungeduld, aus dunkeler Erwartung,
> Aus Unverständlichkeit und Unverstand :
> Dies alles auf sich nehmen und vergebens

[1] Now art thou tired, and no delight has thy
Tired mouth in my mouth, and my mouth is sad.
Jesus, Jesus, when was the hour we had ?
How strangely both of us go down to die.

Vielleicht Gehaltnes fallen lassen, um
Allein zu sterben, wissend nicht warum —
Ist das der Eingang eines neuen Lebens ? [1]

The significance which Rilke discovers is certainly not that intended by the Bible. His own intense desire for escape seizes on the story as a means to express itself. The poem is almost a confession and is certainly based on Rilke's own longings. The Prodigal Son has become his symbol. So too in *Der Auferstandene* (*The Risen One*) the familiar theme of the Resurrection is seen from a new personal angle and presents the idea of " love without the beloved ". Rilke sees the Magdalene as one whom the Crucifixion makes to love Christ without wishing to be loved in return. He marks the contrast between her appearance at the foot of the Cross and after the Resurrection :

Sie begriff es erst in ihrer Höhle,
Wie er ihr, gestärkt durch seinen Tod,
Endlich das Erleichternde der Öle
Und des Rührens Vorgefühl verbot,

Um aus ihr die Liebende zu formen,
Die sich nicht mehr zum Geliebten neigt,
Weil sie, hingerissen von enormen
Stürmen, seine Stimme übersteigt. [2]

The idea here is more mysterious, more the poet's own. It gives an entirely new character to the episode and frees the poem from its sources. Rilke's individual views pass into poetry.

[1]
Impulse, generation,
Impatience, obscure hope, and desperation
Not to be understood or understand :
To take all this upon you, and in strife
To lose, perhaps, all that you had, to die
Alone and destitute, not knowing why —

Is this the entrance into some new life ?
(Trs. J. B. Leishman)

[2] She only comprehended later, hidden
Within her cave, how, fortified by death,
The gratefulness of oil he had forbidden
And the presentiment of touch and breath,

Meaning to form from her at last the lover
Who hangs no more on a beloved's choice,
Since, yielding to enormous storms above her,
She mounts in ecstasy beyond his voice.
(Trs. J. B. Leishman)

Many of *Neue Gedichte* treat of what Rilke saw about him in his own world. He followed his sensibility and wrote of whatever touched or moved him. Here he was hampered by no dependence on the arts or ancient traditions. Sometimes he was struck by quite trivial sights which could hardly be exalted into great poetry. In *Die Flamingos* (*The Flamingoes*), for instance, or *Persisches Heliotrop* (*Persian Heliotrope*) he appeals only to the eye. Such subjects might have been treated with all the delight of the eye by the Impressionist painters ; they might have inspired Heredia to glittering and sonorous lines. But they were not really suited to Rilke's gifts. He failed to catch the play of light and colour which is their chief claim. But such failures are exceptional. Rilke's sensibility was much more than of the eye. Certain sights awoke in him a deep pity from which he could escape only by translating it into poetry. The things that so moved him were not always the accepted objects of pity. Sometimes they affected him so vividly that they seemed to contain all the pathos of the world. In a caged panther, a revolving merry-go-round, a bachelor alone in his room, a woman at a tea-party who is going blind, an old woman who has had in her distant youth a glorious moment of success, he saw something at once enthralling and extremely poignant. In this respect he resembled Thomas Hardy, who felt a similar overmastering pathos in a blinded bird or a diseased man or a giant at a fair. But for Hardy, who was half a philosopher, these sights were instances of a general disorder and cruelty in the universe. From them he drew philosophical conclusions. But for Rilke they indicated nothing metaphysical. They are what he feels them to be, although his feelings are not described and may be discerned only from the general tone. In *Der Panther* (*The Panther*) he writes about a caged beast. There is no direct appeal for sympathy, but the poem is almost an assault on the emotions :

> Sein Blick ist vom Vorübergehn der Stäbe
> So müd geworden, dass er nichts mehr hält.
> Ihm ist, als ob es tausend Stäbe gäbe
> Und hinter tausend Stäben keine Welt.[1]

---

[1] His glance, so tired from traversing his cage's
Repeated railings, can hold nothing more.
He feels as though there were a thousand cages,
And no more world behind them than before.
(Trs. J. B. Leishman)

Rilke's primary emotion about the caged panther is not unlike that which inspired Hardy to write *The Blinded Bird*, but whereas Hardy breaks into impassioned denunciation of the order which allows such things to be, Rilke passes no judgment and closes his poem with the panther opening his eyes and seeing something which transfixes his whole frame. He draws the animal as it paces to and fro, and his words have the minute and loving attention of one who has felt the helpless pathos of a strong beast reduced to impotence. But all else is unsaid. We may draw what conclusions we like. The poet states what he has seen and felt, but he does not think it necessary to point a moral.

The same method may be seen in *Das Karussell* (*The Roundabout*). The subject is a merry-go-round with its painted animals and the living children who ride on them. The beginning is gay and happy. Then it concludes :

> Und das geht hin und eilt sich, dass es endet,
> Und kreist und dreht sich nur und hat kein Ziel.
> Ein Rot, ein Grün, ein Grau vorbeigesendet,
> Ein kleines kaum begonnenes Profil.
> Und manchesmal ein Lächeln, hergewendet,
> Ein seliges, das blendet und verschwendet
> An dieses atemlose blinde Spiel.[1]

It is almost impossible to read this without feeling that the merry-go-round with its mechanical rhythm, its purposelessness, its innocent happy riders, is an emblem of life. But of this Rilke says nothing, and there is no warrant for assuming that he intends it. It might be truer to say that he makes the merry-go-round significant by attributing to it qualities which are sometimes attributed to life. His poem is transparently clear ; it needs neither addition nor explanation. But it produces its effect largely because of the associations which it awakens and the hold which its details take on the reader.

Rilke, however, had his own peculiar notions, and even in this objective art they could hardly fail to force themselves sometimes to the front. He was always occupied with the

[1] And that goes on and hurries to its ending,
And only spins and turns and has no aim,
A red, a green, a grey before us sending ;
Or tiny, scarce begun, a profile's frame.
And now and then a smile comes outward tending,
A holy thing that blinds the eyes, and blending
Vanishes in this blind and breathless game.

subject of death. He believed that it was an enlargement
of life and a return to its sources. In *Der Tod des Dichters*
(*The Death of the Poet*) the dead poet is one who returns to
physical nature and shows his oneness with it in his face :

> Die, so ihn leben sahen, wussten nicht
> Wie sehr er *eines* war mit allem diesen,
> Denn dieses : diese Tiefen, diese Wiesen
> Und diese Wasser waren sein Gesicht.[1]

In *Todeserfahrung* (*Death Experienced*) he contrasts the uncertainty of our lives here with the reality of the existence
beyond :

> Doch als du gingst, da brach in diese Bühne
> Ein Streifen Wirklichkeit durch jenen Spalt,
> Durch den du hingingst : Grün wirklicher Grüne,
> Wirklicher Sonnenschein, wirklicher Wald.[2]

These poems express ideas, but so personally and concretely
that they are in no sense abstract. In *Orpheus Eurydike Hermes*
the same view of death gives power and strangeness to an old
story. Inspired by a Greek bronze group at Naples, it treats
of a myth by which the Greeks and Romans symbolised the
impassable gulf between the living and the dead. The sweet
singer, Orpheus, almost succeeds in bringing his wife back
from the realms of death, but when, overcome by longing, he
turns back to look at her, he loses her for ever. In this tragic
story the Greeks symbolised how song may almost recall the
dead but cannot make us see them face to face. Rilke was
not concerned with the traditional interpretation of the myth.
He did not, like Vergil, emphasise the appalling sense of loss
which his mistake brings to Orpheus, nor, like Valery Bryusov
in modern times, dwell on the ghostly faintness of Eurydice.
He saw the myth through his own view of death. For him the
dead have passed into the earth and become a part of the life-
giving process which comes from it. The pathos and the

---

[1] Those who had seen him living saw no trace
Of his deep unity with all that passes,
For these : these shadowy hills and waving grasses
And streams of running water were his face.
                                    (Trs. J. B. Leishman)

[2] Yet when you went, there broke upon this scene
A streak of something real and understood,
In through the crack you disappeared through : green
Of real green, real sunshine, real wood.
                                    (Trs. J. B. Leishman)

power of his version are that Eurydice is no longer a woman but something deeply rooted in the nature of things. So when Orpheus turns round, she fails to recognise him ; she is no longer his, no longer a woman or a wife :

> Sie war schon aufgelöst wie langes Haar
> Und hingegeben wie gefallner Regen
> Und ausgeteilt wie hundertfacher Vorrat.
>
> Sie war schon Wurzel.
> Und als plötzlich jäh
> Der Gott sie anhielt und mit Schmerz im Ausruf
> Die Worte sprach : Er hat sich umgewendet—,
> Begriff sie nichts und sagte leise : Wer ? [1]

The story is completely transformed by Rilke's interpretation. It has become a myth of his own thoughts about death.

Rilke's rich effects were the reward of his patient aestheticism. But they would not have been granted to him if he had not possessed a singularly receptive and sensitive temperament. His great gifts, however, had a weakness, not inevitable perhaps, yet to be expected. Despite his training among masterpieces and his unwavering devotion to the Beautiful, Rilke had not an absolutely impeccable taste. Sometimes he seems to allow a trivial or disagreeable image to mar an otherwise noble conception. In *Klage um Jonathan* (*Lament for Jonathan*), for instance, he gave his own version of David's lament and breathed a new softness into it. But in speaking of the pang of bereavement he says :

> Denn da und da, an meinen scheusten Orten,
> Bist du mir ausgerissen wie das Haar,
> Das in den Achselhöhlen wächst.[2]

The image of the hair pulled from the arm-pit is disgusting in itself and quite inadequate to the sense of loss which pervades

---

[1] She was already loosened like long hair,
And given far and wide like fallen rain,
And dealt out like a manifold supply.

She was mere root.
And when, abruptly swift,
The god laid hold of her, and, with an anguished
Cry, uttered the words : He has turned round ! —
She took in nothing, and said softly : Who ?
(Trs. J. B. Leishman)

[2] For here and there in my most timid places
Have you been plucked out from me like the hair
That grows inside the arm-pits.

the rest of the poem. It may have meant more to Rilke than to us ; for his sensitiveness may have been more shocked and shaken by such a deprivation. But it is hard not to ascribe this failure in taste to his very sensibility. Because of it he felt things more strongly than most men do, and he was liable to attach significance to some facts which are by common consent trivial. His slips recall the way in which Keats' sensuous appreciation of life sometimes led him into vulgarity. Both poets paid for depending on their impressions. The poet who lives entirely for sensations is at their mercy. If they dominate him, they may sometimes spoil his art.

The *Neue Gedichte* were Rilke's first completely mature poetry. But they pointed to something else. The strange imaginative ideas which occasionally inform them were capable of development ; the symbols suggested might well be used for poetry more self-revealing. And no poet can write in this way for ever. The most receptive of minds may be dulled and cease to absorb any more. The most aesthetic of poets may wish sooner or later to assert fully his private ideas. This happened to Rilke. His aesthetic period came to an abrupt end. " Spain ", he wrote later, " was the last impression. Hitherto my life had been beaten out from within (*travail repoussé*) so strongly and so constantly that it could be impressed no more." The experience is easy to understand and needs no comment. For Rilke it was a question which concerned his whole life. For years he had relied on his impressions. Now the source had dried up. He must look elsewhere, find a new method and a new manner. For the time being he was paralysed. His whole life must find a new direction. He found it, with labour and sorrow. It began in the winter of 1911–12 when he lived at the castle of Duino in Istria. With fearful delays and days of impotent despair it lasted until the beginning of 1922. The result was his greatest, most original work, the *Duineser Elegien* (*Duino Elegies*), published in 1923. Between this and *Neue Gedichte* lies a great gulf. The objectivity, the search for impressions, the simplicity of presentation, have disappeared. In their place we find a highly personal, symbolical, difficult poetry, unrhymed and in the strictest sense unmetrical. The poet who had subordinated his personality to the impacts of art now reasserted himself.

Rilke was fully conscious of all that the change meant.

In *Wendung* (*Turning*), written in 1914, he spoke of it :

> Denn des Anschauns, siehe, ist eine Grenze,
> Und die geschautere Welt
> Will in der Liebe gedeihn.
> Werk des Gesichts ist getan,
> Tue nun Herzwerk
> An Bildern in dir, jenen gefangenen.[1]

He knew that his many experiences had coalesced in his mind, that out of many faces he could make a single face, out of many women a single woman. His imaginative life had at last come to exist on its own and to be the object of his love. Phenomena had now no importance except as part of himself. The change was both psychological and metaphysical. The patient aesthete had ceased to wait ; he had enough inner resources to sustain him. The man who had given himself up to impressions now mastered them and ordered them. He saw that a high degree of self-analysis and self-absorption was demanded of him and that he must alter his views of the world. With characteristic thoroughness he put through the reforms demanded of him. He knew what the change meant :

> Durch alle Wesen reicht der eine Raum :
> Weltinnenraum. Die Vögel fliegen still
> Durch uns hindurch. O, der ich wachsen will,
> Ich seh hinaus, und in mir wächst der Baum.[2]

Rilke has found that all he has are his sensations and that these are his own and in him. The idea is old enough in philosophy, but it was new to poetry. Rilke, solitary by nature and habit, had formed a philosophy of solitude which was also a philosophy of art. He saw that what mattered was himself, his inner experience, his collected impressions. What had been missing in his objective poetry was precisely this. He had seen, admired, remembered, but he had not loved. His new

---

[1] For indeed there comes in time a limit to looking,
The looked and looked-at world
Longs to bear fruit in love.
Work of sight is achieved,
Now for some heart-work,
On those many pictures, those prisoned creatures within you.
(Trs. J. B. Leishman)

[2] A single space spreads through all things that be,
World's inner space. The birds are flying still
Through us, and through across. O, I that will
Grow, I look out, and in me grows the tree.

task was to create a poetry out of himself in which love was a power to illuminate and to make real.

Rilke regarded the Elegies as the crown of his achievement. We can understand why. He worked at them, on and off, from 1911 to 1923. The war hampered his creation, but he held to his purpose and was at long last rewarded. Small wonder that he wrote in ecstatic joy to proclaim their completion : " At last, the blessed, how blessed day, on which I can announce to you the conclusion ". Here, far more than before, his poetry seemed to be given to him as by some power outside himself. The work began when, standing in a storm and looking over the sea, he seemed to hear a voice which gave the first line of the First Elegy :

> Wer, wenn ich schriee, hörte mich denn aus der Engel
> Ordnungen ? [1]

and the last Elegy, the Tenth, was finished eleven years later in similar circumstances. As Rilke wrote, " All in a few days, there was a nameless storm, a hurricane in the mind (like that time in Duino), everything in the way of fibre and web in me split,— eating was not to be thought of, God knows who fed me ". The Elegies are a signal example of inspiration in the most literal sense. The poet almost felt that he had no part in their creation. Coming in this way the Elegies meant everything to Rilke. They expressed ideas which he had pondered for years. They seemed to be the reward of long waiting, the justification of his trust that in time his silence would be turned into song. It is therefore not surprising that in letters he wrote freely about them and even explained their meaning. His commentary is invaluable for the light that it throws on him. But the poems need not necessarily be read by it. Rilke might well find meanings in his poems after he had written them, but his imaginative temperament, his desire to avoid misunderstanding, may have led him into overstating his case, into making the poems say more than they do. The Elegies must be taken as they are. They provide answers to most questions that they raise. In reading his comments it is well to remember Valéry's words : " Quand l'ouvrage a paru, son interprétation par l'auteur n'a pas plus de valeur que toute autre par qui que ce soit ".

[1] Who, if I cried, would hear me among the angelic Orders ?
(Trs. J. B. Leishman and S. Spender)

F

In the Elegies Rilke used a new form. With the exception of the Fourth and the Eighth, which are written in the German equivalent of English blank verse, they are written in *vers libre*. The rhythm is predominantly, though by no means invariably, dactylic, and this gives a more regular tone than is usual in *vers libre*. The staccato effect which seems almost inevitable to the form is avoided by the construction of large paragraphs, the use of *enjambement*, the way in which images are sometimes sustained through a long passage, the prevailing sombreness of tone. The absence of rhyme, of stanzas, of regular rhythm, contributes to the effect in a remarkable way. The element of song is entirely lacking. Its place is taken not by quiet meditation but by nervous, excited, discursive thought in which sensibility plays a large part. It is hard to find a label for this kind of poetry. It is undeniably full of thought, even of argument, but it does not prove a thesis or move to a regular plan or appeal directly to the understanding. It appeals to the nerves and the emotions. Rilke almost anticipates the psychological sequence which T. S. Eliot used in *The Waste Land*, but he does not change with such leaps and jerks from one subject to another and he still keeps a poem, more or less, to a single theme. He even makes his intricate movements a little clearer by a certain amount of unpoetical matter. There are moments when he seems near to prose. Yet even then it is not argument that appears but thought that has not quite been raised to an imaginative level. The Elegies may be regarded as poems of nervous brooding. Their mood is that of a man who has withdrawn into himself and lived for long with his sensations and thoughts, until they have passed into himself. Such poetry would be inconceivable in anyone not deeply absorbed in himself. Everything passes into him, registers its impression on his sensibility, and becomes part of a metaphysical scheme which he creates to cover what is given to him. What before were exterior objects are now symbols of great issues. They are even more. They exist only in the poet and get their importance from what he feels about them. He seems to have abandoned his belief in an external world and to have replaced it by a system in which there is nothing but sensations existing in the mind. It is obvious that for such a system a special kind of verse is needed. The *vers libre* of the Elegies is well fitted to express the subtle and sinuous movements of a soul communing with itself.

The ten Elegies were conceived as a whole. Before the Angel spoke to him Rilke had in his mind a plan, and despite their variations they present a kind of unity in manner, temper and subject. Themes announced in the First Elegy appear for fuller attention later. The fear of the Angels with which it begins is answered at the opening of the Tenth with its note of hope and confidence :

> Dass ich dereinst, an dem Ausgang der grimmigen Einsicht,
> Jubel und Ruhm aufsinge zustimmenden Engeln.[1]

The familiar symbols,— children, animals, birds, puppets, the early dead,— emerge at intervals. The unity is poetical, not philosophical. The design covers many variations of temper and imaginative thought. We should not try to extract a close system of beliefs from what is essentially poetry ; still less should we complain of contradictions and inconsistencies. The Fourth Elegy, for instance, is notably more pessimistic than the Seventh. But Rilke writes as a poet who attacks his subject from different angles and in different moods. The unity is in the poet himself and in the field of his experience. To define it precisely is to mutilate its contours. When we read the poems, we see the kind of experience they reflect, and that is enough. Once we have made this reservation, the Elegies are seen to record a chapter of spiritual history. Sometimes the symbols are hard to understand. It is not everyone who knows about Gaspara Stampa or the inscriptions of Santa Maria Formosa in Venice. To Rilke these were familiar. He had lived long with the memory of them. For others they need interpretation. But such difficulties are few, and scholarship has unravelled them. The real difficulty of the Elegies is that they record a very special frame of mind and are the product of highly unusual thought.

It is hard to say what the main subject of the Elegies is. It might be said to be man's place in the world, and this is to some extent true. But the Elegies may be read at two levels, almost in two different ways. They are in the first place the record of the poet's own hard struggles to be a poet, of his efforts to come to terms with his inspiration, to find an answer to his own private problems. And in the second place they

[1] Some day emerging from this terrifying vision
May I burst into jubilant praise to assenting Angels !
(Trs. J. B. Leishman and S. Spender)

are the poetry of all men who struggle and are beset by doubt and despondency. The poet moves from his own struggles and his solution for them to the assumption that others are like him and that what is true of him is true also of them. As a poet he speaks for humanity. Their lot is his, though he sees it more clearly and feels it more acutely. In this Rilke does what others have done before him. The sorrows of the poet have commonly been presented as the sorrows of mankind and regarded as typical of the common lot. But in Rilke's case the ambiguity is greater because his experience was of a special kind. His Angels stand for the absolute of poetic inspiration, for the power which he courted in long years of barren silence, then encountered unexpectedly, only to find that it was almost too much for him to bear. So long as the poet speaks for himself, we know well what he means,— his feeling that if an Angel were to press him to his heart, he would fade in the strength of that stronger existence ; that if an Angel were to appear, he would find his heart beating too fast for him ; that if he could only join in the angelic choir, all his miseries would be turned to joy. All this is easily understood of the poet who struggles to find the absolute of inspiration, who shrinks from it only to find that in the end it is a boundless joy and strength. But it is not the usual experience of common men, and when Rilke viewed life from this position, he came to an uncommon conclusion.

Rilke knew that his own life passed between extremes. On the one side were the rare, rapturous, perilous, appalling moments when poetry came to him. These, following Mallarmé's precedent, he symbolised by Angels. There were other moments which he had known in his childhood when life seemed complete and rounded. The first moments were rare, the second had passed beyond recall. Rilke spent much of his time waiting for the one and regretting the other. This intermediate condition was largely one of " Angst ", of acute and unsolved apprehension. It was from this that he strove to deliver himself ; it is this which permeates the Elegies and sets so much of their tone. Rilke longed for an Absolute, for sustained rapture in creation. He found instead that he was at the mercy of his instincts, his doubts, his uncertainties, his inability to feel at home anywhere for long. To sustain himself he clung to those hours which remained brightest in his memory and in which he seemed nearest to his ideal. In certain trees and old-established customs, in the night and the spring, he caught echoes of his ideal. He saw examples of it in the hero, in the perfect lover, Gaspara Stampa, in moments he had known in churches at Rome and Naples. But these were only echoes. The real ideal was the Angel. In his Angels Rilke goes to the centre of his inspiration. Naturally he speaks in metaphor about what is itself a symbol. The actual power that inspired him was beyond words. Only some of its aspects could be told. In the Second Elegy Rilke addresses the Angels :

> Frühe Geglückte, ihr Verwöhnten der Schöpfung,
> Höhenzüge, morgenrötliche Grate
> Aller Erschaffung,— Pollen der blühenden Gottheit,
> Gelenken des Lichtes, Gänge, Treppen, Throne,
> Räume aus Wesen, Schilde aus Wonne, Tumulte
> Stürmisch entzückten Gefühls und plötzlich, einzeln,
> Spiegel : die die entströmte eigene Schönheit
> Wiederschöpfen zurück in das eigene Antlitz.[1]

The series of stark images, unadorned and unexplained, severe and remote, reveal especially the power of these mysterious forces to initiate and to create, but also their brightness, their gift of joy, the tumults which they awake, their incalculable appearances and disappearances. To them Rilke applies the language of mystical vision. The light and the height, the stairways and the thrones, the sense of space, are familiar from religious rapture. For the poet these powers are what God is to the saint, objects of absolute veneration yet so remote and so fearful that even the most devoted shrinks from them. The process of drawing near to them is almost too much for mortal man. They are

> Fast tödliche Vögel der Seele.[2]

Rilke contrasts angels as he knows them with what they once were, and the contrast is also between his present sense of this

[1] Early successes, Creation's pampered darlings,
Ranges, summits, dawn-red ridges
Of all beginning,— pollen of blossoming godhead,
Hinges of light, corridors, stairways, thrones,
Spaces of being, shields of felicity, tumults
Of stormily-rapturous feeling, and suddenly, separate,
Mirrors, drawing up their own
Outstreamed beauty into their faces again.
(Trs. J. B. Leishman and S. Spender)

[2] Almost deadly birds of the soul.

power and his old aestheticism. When he says

> Wohin sind die Tage Tobiae,
> Da der Strahlendsten einer stand an der einfachen Haustür,
> Zur Reise ein wenig verkleidet, und schon nicht mehr furchtbar ;
> (Jüngling dem Jüngling, wie er neugierig hinaussah),[1]

we cannot fail to contrast the terrible frightening Angels with the friendly Angel of Italian art who accompanies Tobias. We know what this art once meant to Rilke ; we see how much more its symbols mean to him now, how they have accumulated meanings in his long meditation over them, how he himself now encounters the dread facts from which his aestheticism protected him.

Rilke also finds symbols of completeness and harmony in animals. They are free of " Angst " and live entirely in the present. There is a regular rhythm in their existence. Their gaze on life is steady. He finds this in wild beasts :

> Und irgendwo gehn Löwen noch und wissen,
> Solang sie herrlich sind, von keiner Ohnmacht,[2]

and in insects :

> O Seligkeit der kleinen Kreatur,
> Die immer bleibt im Schoosse, der sie austrug.[3]

What the psychologists call the desire for the womb was natural to Rilke. He saw its claims and knew what it meant. He felt it because he was harassed by his anxieties and not at home in the world. Such a peace and even such absorption in another being were for him much preferable to the uncertain, shifting, fading cares of living. He contrasted it with his most mordant symbols of human life, the half-filled masks that are men, the acrobats leaping up and down on a carpet that gets gradually thinner, the passing of our appearances from us like dew from the morning grass or heat from a

---

[1]   O, where are the days of Tobias,
When one of the shining-most stood on the simple threshold,
A little disguised for the journey, no longer appalling ;
(A youth to the youth as he curiously peered outside).
                    (Trs. J. B. Leishman and S. Spender)

[2] And somewhere lions still roam, all unaware,
In being magnificent, of any weakness.
                    (Trs. J. B. Leishman and S. Spender)

[3] Oh, bliss of tiny creatures that remain
For ever in the womb that brought them forth.
                    (Trs. J. B. Leishman and S. Spender)

smoking dish. In his ordinary state, emptied of his rapturous angelic moments and haunted by memories of childhood's innocence, he felt this disorder dominating him. His sensibility found images easily to display it, and when images failed, he was ready with clear statement. At times he bursts past imagery into a stark account of facts. This kind of poetry is not song. It needs the intellect to grasp it, and plain statement often suits its tone.

The absolute of inspiration, the sense of strength, harmony and completeness symbolised by the Angel, comes as it will and is not to be wooed. Yet there are moments when something like it occurs and seems to be an approximation to it. In children and in lovers Rilke found examples of this. He felt that in them he saw principles of being which were somehow the equivalent of what the Angel was for him. He had long meditated upon childhood and often written about it. In the Fourth Elegy he contrasts it with the discordant state of ordinary existence. He knows that children live completely in the present, in a kind of timelessness because they are not concerned about the future :

> O Stunden in der Kindheit,
> Da hinter den Figuren mehr als nur
> Vergangnes war und vor uns nicht die Zukunft.[1]

So long as they are alone, children have a rounded self-contained life of their own. But their state has a fatal flaw and cannot last. It is all too soon broken by the impact of grown-ups. On this Rilke bursts into fierce denunciation as if he wished the state of childhood " between world and toy " to last for ever. The end of the Fourth Elegy denounces those who show a child what it is, who give it a choking core instead of a sweet apple, a death even before life begins. This is worse than murder, is beyond description. Images of similar pathos are presented in the Fifth Elegy where the figures of the boy and the girl from Picasso's picture " Les Saltimbanques " show children at the mercy of their elders. The boy, tossed again and again in the air, smiles pathetically at his mother, gets no response and continues to smile ; the

[1] O hours of childhood,
Hours when behind the figures there was more
Than the mere past, and when what lay before us
Was not the future.
(Trs. J. B. Leishman and S. Spender)

girl, in her frills and green silk, in all her serenity, is exhibited to public view on the shoulders of the troupe. The contrast between the children, absorbed in their private joys, and the ceaseless useless acrobatics of those who juggle with them, symbolises the place of children in the world. Their completeness is only temporary. Before long the world breaks it.

Of lovers Rilke has more to say. In the First Elegy he draws attention to his ideal lover, Gaspara Stampa. What he admires in her is her sacrifice of all wish to be loved in return. He asks if it is not time to be freed like her of the beloved, to spring like an arrow from the string and to become more than oneself. The love of which he dreams is a kind of self-realisation through self-denial. In ordinary love he finds something unsatisfactory. For lovers are never wholly lost in one another ; they are still tied up in themselves. In the Second Elegy the theme is developed. Rilke asks the lovers who seem satisfied with each other, and grasp each other, if their hopes are really fulfilled,— do they not lose something when they kiss, and does not every kiss miss something ? He contrasts them with figures of Attic sculpture :

> Erstaunte euch nicht auf attischen Stelen die Vorsicht
> Menschlicher Geste ? war nicht Liebe und Abschied
> So leicht auf die Schultern gelegt, als wär es aus anderm
> Stoffe gemacht als bei uns ? Gedenkt euch der Hände,
> Wie sie drucklos beruhen, obwohl in den Torsen die Kraft steht.[1]

Unlike ordinary lovers, these Greeks were sure of themselves and in control of themselves. Their embraces were not a price too heavy for them to pay. They still had something left afterwards. Rilke feels that all lovers should be like this and imagines some ideal secluded existence, a strip of orchard between river and rock, where this would be possible. Both in old and in new lovers there is abundance of heart, but to the new this brings dissatisfaction in the end. In the " Angst " of modern life there is a source of doubt and a failure of confidence, even for those who have the strongest claim to be thought satisfied. Rilke sets this against the Attic

---

[1] On Attic steles, did not the circumspection
Of human gesture amaze you ? Were not love and farewell
So lightly laid upon shoulders, they seemed to be made
Of other stuff than with us ? Oh, think of the hands,
How they rest without pressure, though power is there in the torsos.
(Trs. J. B. Leishman)

security and sense of strength. His modern lovers are hardly even an approximation to his ideal. They promise much, but the promise is never quite fulfilled. In the Third Elegy lovers are seen from a different angle. Uglier, darker doubts obtrude. In this remarkable poem the discoveries of psycho-analysis provide matter for intimate and piercing poetry. The main theme is that when a young man falls in love dark ancestral desires are awoken in him. The " Neptune in the blood " is aroused and fills the night with his uproar. These dark powers have always been in him. His mother's tender care for him has merely hidden them and soothed him. Behind the furniture his destiny has been there. But once his desire has been stirred, the powers come into action. The lover sinks into himself, into the depths of his being, and loves this primaeval forest in himself :

> Liebend
> Stieg er hinab in das ältere Blut, in die Schluchten,
> Wo das Furchtbare lag, noch satt von den Vätern. Und jedes
> Schreckliche kannte ihn, blinzelte, war wie verständigt.
> Ja, das Entsetzliche lächelte. . . .[1]

His love for this monster is older and stronger than his love for his mother. And against these powers his beloved must fight, against the women in him who hate her, the sinister men in his veins, the dead children trying to reach her. The poem shows how complex is the whole awakening of love. What looks like love for a single woman is really the awakening of unknown lusts in the blood. The woman's task is to protect her lover from these, to guide him gently and confidently. Rilke shows how far removed love really is from the ideal state of the Angel. It looks self-contained and complete, but it is insecure and based on foundations of which we know nothing.

A more satisfactory approximation to the ideal is the Hero. For Rilke he is not what he usually is in German poetry. What matters is not his fame, nor even the greatness of his achievement, but the inevitable certainty of his growth, like the fig-tree which bursts into fruit almost without flowering.

[1]   Descended
Lovingly, into the older blood, the ravines,
Where Frightfulness lurked, still gorged with his fathers. And every
Terror knew him, and winked, and quite understood.
Yes, Horror smiled at him. . . .
(Trs. J. B. Leishman and S. Spender)

No matter what awaits him, he is still himself and, true to himself, faces his dangers. He has his own destiny :

> Das uns finster verschweigt, das plötzlich begeisterte Schicksal
> Singt ihn hinein in den Sturm seiner aufrauschenden Welt.[1]

The direct course which a few superior beings follow in the life of action, its certainty and fated fullness, are for Rilke a symbol of the strength which he misses in most life and in his own. The noise of such a career strikes on the hesitant poet like a storm in the air. It was no doubt in this way that he would have wished to work, to know where he was going, to be certain of the next step and of the end. He traces back the hero to the womb where the unborn Samson is already shattering columns as he breaks into the world. The hero is a type of purposefulness and self-assurance, of someone in complete harmony with life. Therefore even love has little meaning for him. Each time that he is loved, he rises beyond it and smiles back on the past. His goal lies elsewhere. But he is too much for the ordinary man, who shrinks from him. In his way he is almost as remote as the Angel.

Against these extremes of the Angel and the Hero, against even such approximations to them as children and lovers, Rilke sets ordinary life. With this most of the Elegies are concerned. Its miseries, its incompleteness, its uncertainty, receive most of the poet's attention. The general effect is undoubtedly melancholy. This is a poetry of insufficiency. For Rilke life seems to be a contrast between high moments of hope and confidence and far longer, far drearier periods of ineffective anxiety and impatience. The futility of it all is conveyed with bitterness in the Fifth Elegy, where life is shown as an acrobatic show. The actors are swung up and down by a purposeless, never contented will. Each time that they descend, the carpet on which they fall gets thinner. There is pathos in these victims, in the elder man shrivelled in his skin, the youngster full of muscles, the children exhibited in public display. But stronger than the pathos is the sense of futility, of effort without reason or end. The whole is summed up in an extraordinary image :

[1]
> Fate
> Who deals so darkly with us, enraptured all of a sudden,
> Sings him into the storm of her roaring world.
> (Trs. J. B. Leishman and S. Spender)

Plätze, o Platz in Paris, unendlicher Schauplatz,
Wo die Modistin, Madame Lamort,
Die ruhlosen Wege der Erde, endlose Bänder,
Schlingt und windet und neue aus ihnen
Schleifen erfindet, Rüschen, Blumen, Kokarden, künstliche Früchte,
— alle
Unwahr gefärbt,— für die billigen
Winterhüte des Schicksals.[1]

Such men have no real destiny, and their death has no significance. They are, we can see, the antithesis of the hero. And
they are typical of the human state as Rilke sees it. For him
most men are too hampered, too limited, to see things as they
really are. To this defect he returns in the Eighth Elegy,
where the special flaw described is the sense of otherness, of
distance and separation, that we feel between ourselves and
others. We are never lost in something larger than ourselves,
as children may be, as animals almost are. Rilke contrasts
" Welt ", the world in which we live, with " Raum ", the
space in which we ought to be :

> Wir haben nie, nicht einen einzigen Tag,
> Den reinen Raum vor uns, in den die Blumen
> Unendlich aufgehn.[2]

For him this is the fundamental defect. He knows from his
own experience moments of rapture in which he has lost himself in some vaster power. He feels that this is pure Space,
the right field for activity. The question is how to find it.

It is clear that the question so posed was natural for Rilke.
As a poet he knew the uncommon strength which came to him
in times of creative energy, the conviction that he then had
of losing himself only to find himself vastly enriched and
strengthened, the entry into another kind of existence which

---

[1] Squares, O square in Paris, infinite show-place,
  Where the modiste, Madame Lamort,
  Winds and binds the restless ways of the world,
  Those endless ribbons, to ever-new
  Creations of bow, frill, flower, cockade and fruit,
  All falsely coloured to deck
  The cheap winter-hats of fate.
                    (Trs. J. B. Leishman and S. Spender)

[2] We've never, no, not for a single day,
  Pure space before us, such as that which flowers
  Endlessly open into.
                    (Trs. J. B. Leishman and S. Spender)

lacked distinctions of past and present, of subject and object, of self and not-self. Like other poets, he saw his own problem as typical of the world at large and transposed it to a wider sphere. The discords in himself between the ideal and the actual were in his view characteristic of everyone. Therefore he does not always or often distinguish between himself and others ; his " I " disappears easily into " we ", and even when he says " you " he may half be speaking of himself. This ambiguity is natural. It makes no difference to the poetry and only becomes important when we try to say what Rilke's view of life was and to extract a message from his poetry. In fact Rilke's view of life was so intertwined with his own special experience that any such abstraction is artificial, if not misleading. His poetry is often ambiguous because he saw and interpreted humanity through himself. The judgments which he passes on others, his pity or contempt for them, are reflections of what he felt about himself. The child, the lover, the animal, are different symbols for his own desires. He assumes that because they are in him, they are also in others. Even the hero, so unlike the hesitant, divided poet, is a vision of himself as he would wish to be and as at times he felt that he was. This highly confessional poetry spreads beyond its origins and becomes symbolical of life, because the poet finds his own struggles characteristic of the human state and proposes a solution which had served him well and should serve to cure similar troubles in other hearts.

The evil of life lies in its incompleteness. That is the problem as Rilke sees it. But it is not all that he has to say. As the Elegies advance, they become more hopeful and consoling. In the Seventh the tone and the message have changed. The sense of failure is replaced by an affirmation :

Hiersein ist herrlich.[1]

In the Ninth the tone of confidence ends on a note of great hope :

Siehe, ich lebe. . . . Woraus ? Weder Kindheit noch Zukunft
Werden weniger. . . . Überzähliges Dasein
Entspringt mir im Herzen.[2]

---

[1] Life here is glorious.

[2] Look, I am living. . . . On what ? neither childhood nor future
Are growing less. . . . Supernumerous existence
Wells up in my heart.

(Trs. J. B. Leishman and S. Spender)

84

In the Tenth a final solution of the problems and paradoxes is offered. From irony, defeat, despair he turns to joyful trust. His method must not be misunderstood. The later Elegies do not contradict the earlier in the sense that one argument contradicts another. They are later stages in a voyage of discovery, riper knowledge which succeeds incomplete acquaintance with the mysteries of living. What is said in the earlier Elegies is true so far as it goes, but it is not the whole truth. Man is indeed a creature of extremes, torn between opposing destinies, and from this arises much of his futility. But behind this there is a reason. In the universe all is right, and those who think enough will see this clearly. The solution which Rilke propounds appeals to the heart as well as to the intellect. It comforts as well as satisfies. But to give it its full force he has first to state all the difficulties in all their drabness and darkness. The solution is only satisfactory if we have really felt what it is meant to solve.

Rilke's solution turns on two fundamental ideas, related in his scheme of life, but ultimately distinct and distinguishable. They are Transformation and Death. The first is the theme of the Seventh Elegy, where Rilke proclaims that life is glorious because it provides the material for something more permanent and more important. He gives his doctrine in simple words :

> Nirgends, Geliebte, wird Welt sein, als innen. Unser
> Leben geht hin mit Verwandlung. Und immer geringer
> Schwindet das Aussen.[1]

The spirit transforms what is given to it by the outer world and makes it much more valuable in an inner spiritual world. He might have put this differently and said that what is seen and felt becomes spiritual only when we have absorbed it and given it a new existence. This is certainly true of the poet. Only when his impressions have passed into him and been coloured and shaped by him do they become more than impressions. The process is almost indispensable for all art. It is what Rilke himself had learned when he turned his collected impressions into the symbols of a metaphysical poetry. His houses, his lovers, his birds, his nights, are no

---

[1] Nowhere, beloved, can world exist but within.
Life passes in transformation. And ever diminishing
Vanishes what's outside.

(Trs. J. B. Leishman and S. Spender)

longer what ordinary men mean by them ; they are his own, his transformations. Once this has been done, these images belong to a different order of things. Rilke gave an account of this to his Polish translator in 1925 and seemed then to think that this transformation is necessary to preserve the visible world : " Our task is to stamp this provisional, perishing earth into ourselves so deeply, so painfully and passionately, that its being may rise again ' invisibly ' in us ". Rilke believed this and justified his art by it. He saw himself not as a creator but as a transformer. What came to him, the " given " and " perceived ", must be reshaped into a permanent form through his nature and his art. Through them the fleeting appearances of the visible world are made permanent and enriched with understanding and imagination. What counts is not this house or this tree, but the house and the tree that the poet has known and loved and made part of himself. The process gives life to the inanimate, worth to the otherwise worthless.

Such a view invites questions. We might argue that though the transformation was obviously real and vital for Rilke and must occur in any poet, it need not be of like importance for the average man. But Rilke claims that it is. Even in the lives of girls who seek a livelihood in abandoned and vile streets he sees an example of it :

> Denn eine Stunde war jeder, vielleicht nicht
> Ganz eine Stunde, ein mit den Massen der Zeit kaum
> Messliches zwischen zwei Weilen, da sie ein Dasein
> Hatte. Alles. Die Adern voll Dasein.[1]

For a moment they have really been alive, have had their veins full of existence. Rilke believed that what meant so much to him must mean no less to others. It was his answer to the transitory and unsatisfying character of life. He proclaims in his own way that the real is the spiritual, that what counts most is what has been absorbed in us and enriches our inner lives. Through his own experience and by his own ways Rilke came to a doctrine not unlike Pater's " experience itself is the end ". Sensations come from the sensible world, and

---

[1] For to each was granted an hour,— perhaps not quite
So much as an hour — some span that could scarcely be measured
By measures of time, in between two whiles, when she really
Possessed an existence. All. Veins full of existence.
(Trs. J. B. Leishman and S. Spender)

it is this which is caught, transformed and preserved. So Rilke's doctrine is not other-worldly. It is not a withdrawal into dreams, or an escape from life, but an attempt to love life by raising it to a level at which love can work more freely and thought with full consciousness of what is worth having. This belief explains Rilke's insistence on animals and children. For after all it is they who most transform experience and most enrich themselves with what they feel and see. The poet's belief has its validity for others. For it proclaims the true worth of what at times they think most valuable and says that this is permanent.

Another difficulty is Rilke's assumption that anything so transformed belongs to the real world, that " the earth has no other refuge except to become invisible ". The Seventh Elegy implies this and the Ninth says that things

> Wollen, wir sollen sie ganz im unsichtbarn Herzen verwandeln
> In — o unendlich — in uns ! wer wir am Ende auch seien.[1]

Phenomena clamour for Transformation. Rilke believes that this invisible state is real and lasting. As a philosophy of art this is easy to understand. All art is a kind of answer to Faust's wish :

> Verweile doch, du bist so schön.

Only through such Transformation as the artist gives are the disparate, changing phenomena of life exalted into art. But as a philosophy of life Rilke's doctrine is more difficult. Through the process which he describes each man creates and enriches his private universe, but we may ask how these different universes are one. The answer comes not from argument but from mystical belief. What counts for Rilke is the inner world, and he assumes that this can be shared by everyone. The assumption, granted his beliefs, is not unwarrantable. Rilke believed that the world of his creative vision was the real world, and assumed that it did not belong to himself alone but to all who enjoy the secrets of the imagination and the enhanced excitements of a full life. From this it was a bold but not inconsequent step to believe that this transformation is actually demanded by the world of phenomena :

[1] Want us to change them entirely, within our invisible hearts,
Into — oh endlessly — into ourselves ; whosoever we are.
(Trs. J. B. Leishman and S. Spender)

Erde, ist es nicht dies, was du willst : unsichtbar
In uns erstehn ? Ist es dein Traum nicht,
Einmal unsichtbar zu sein ? Erde ! unsichtbar ! [1]

So fine and bold a belief unites the opposing worlds of fact
and vision, of "Welt" and "Raum", whose discord Rilke
felt so acutely. His system has its own compulsive logic. It
assumes that things are after all a Whole and that apparent
differences are harmonised, if we choose, by Transformation.
It is his cure for the common sense of inadequacy and purposelessness in most men. What look like mere futile activities
may be made real if we choose to live in them. For Blake the
universe was a metaphor for some mysterious transcendental
reality, but for Rilke there was ultimately no division. The
world that we see and feel becomes finer and grander, becomes
real, through being seen and felt by us.

This is not, however, all that Rilke says or means. To his
conception of Transformation he added that of Death. The
Tenth Elegy, in all its allegorical complexity and subtlety,
picks up many previous hints and gives a Gospel of Death.
It is a kind of Pilgrim's Progress, a parable of man's state
between the ordinary town with its noisy and aimless activities
and the real life outside. This real life is shown by a Lament
(" Klage ") to one of the youthfully dead, and it contains all
that matters. Rilke develops an idea familiar from *Neue
Gedichte* that the dead have a fuller, more real existence than
the living. He begins with an account of the City of Pain,
with its ready-made church, its booths and shows, its interest
in money and sex. Outside is the other world, with its children, its lovers, its animals, and through this the Lament is
the guide. She shows the great ruins of the past, the trees
of sadness, the strange constellations in the sky, each full of
symbolical meaning, the stream which is the source of earthly
joy. Into this strange landscape Rilke gathers his symbols of
completeness and transformation and unites them into a single
scene of the dead which is full of meaning because it is understood through grief. The subjects of his earlier poetry,
honoured once for their own sake, have become the symbols
of this enhanced existence, of what really matters. These

---

[1] Earth, isn't this what you want : an invisible
Re-arising in us ? Is it not your dream
To be one day invisible ? Earth ! invisible !
(Trs. J. B. Leishman and S. Spender)

once transitory impressions have become permanent in their new setting. They are examples of Transformation. This world of grief and death is the transformed world of which Rilke has already spoken. Death is the final and complete transformer, and he works through grief.

This strange and sombre conception is clear enough in the crepuscular beauty of the Tenth Elegy. In some letters Rilke tended to explain this notion and to claim that it was only part of his whole view of life, a necessary emphasis on one side of a dual reality. Of this the Elegies say nothing. They present a complete vision of death as a liberated and enhanced existence. They are what they are, and not even Rilke's own comments can change them. Later, perhaps, he felt that they fell short of saying all that he believed, and wished to add to his message. But they need no addition and no comment. Formed on a plan, they lead to their majestic and melancholy conclusion, that only in death is Transformation complete. This was the natural end of much that Rilke had thought. In his creative life he felt a struggle to deliver himself from his internal hindrances. By some obscure process he felt that final and complete deliverance comes with death, that only in death is a man really real. It was his version of Mallarmé's superb line on the dead Poe :

Tel qu'en lui-même enfin l'éternité le change.

Rilke saw death not as annihilation but as self-transcendence. He wished to get back to the roots of life, to be like his Eurydice mingled in the earth, to be absorbed in the springs of creation. Like all poets, he imagined a sphere in which he could create in untrammelled ease, and he identified this with the state of the dead. He felt that when he lost himself in intercourse with the Angel, he was to that degree sharing in death. Death was for him a fuller existence not only because his creative moments involved a self-surrender like it but because through death he had known the vivid, stirring power of grief. From an early age he had been deeply touched by grief for the dead, especially for those who died young. It was perhaps the strongest emotion that he knew. Through it he came to believe that the dead had merely changed to a wider sphere of existence. The fascination which death had for him and the inspiration which it brought to his work made him believe that it was somehow enviable, an entry into new and richer experiences. By meditating on it he was able to surmount the wounds which living inflicted on his sensibility. Looking for a real existence and a true source of strength he found it in this other wider, less personal sphere. St. Teresa longed to die that she might know the absolute joy of being with God; Rilke honoured death because he believed that in it he would find what he missed in life and be sustained by powers which hitherto came to him intermittently and uncertainly.

The Elegies stand alone in the poetry of our time. But in Rilke's biography they are closely associated with *Die Sonette an Orpheus* (*The Sonnets to Orpheus*) which were written in an incredible spate of inspiration when he was finishing the latest Elegies. The whole first part, of twenty-six sonnets, was written down in about three days " without one word's being in doubt or requiring to be altered ", and the remainder followed at hardly less speed. In them Rilke's stored impressions burst forth as violently as in the Elegies but in quite a different way. Even the sonnet-form does not prevent these rapturous poems from being songs. In their intricate rhyme-schemes, their variety of melody, their unfailing liveliness and brilliance, they are a complete antithesis to the Elegies. No wonder that afterwards Rilke claimed that the two books must be taken together as giving his dual vision of life. If we are to treat his work as a whole, this is true. But the Sonnets, like the Elegies, are a complete work of art and should first be treated as such. Comparison with the Elegies is useful chiefly for the contrast that it gives. The Elegies deal with grief and death, the Sonnets with joy. If the note of the first is " Klage ", lament, that of the second is " Ruhm ", praise. In the Sonnets Rilke's instinct for song found its last expression. Hampered hitherto by his anxieties and meditative melancholy, it suddenly was liberated and burst forth unsullied. They are songs about song and the spirit of song. While the Elegies moved from the thought of the poet's inspiration to a cult of death, the Sonnets were inspired by a single death to a cult of song. They were written as a memorial for a young girl whom Rilke greatly admired, and from the thought of her death they move to an appreciation of life, of all that she showed when alive and to much else that this suggests. In Orpheus, the singer who tries in vain to call up his beloved from the dead, Rilke found a symbol for himself. But what concerns him is not the attempt to regain Eurydice but the cosmic function of the great poet in whom Nature herself seems to speak. In his kinship with the brute creation, his power to move natural objects by song and so to transform them, in teaching that the body is a tomb from which the soul must escape, Orpheus presents points of resemblance which Rilke could well use. The symbol was good and released many hidden powers in him.

The concept of Orpheus dominates the first part of the Sonnets, and here Rilke implicitly corrects the more rigorous view of death which he put forward in the Elegies. The Spirit of Song, which is in Orpheus and himself, has roots both in life and in death :

> Ist er ein Hiesiger ? Nein, aus beiden
> Reichen erwuchs seine weite Natur.[1]

He still acclaims the importance of " Klage " but recognises that " Jubel ", triumph, and " Sehnsucht ", longing, have their place. But as his inspiration carries him on, he leaves lamentation behind for praise and more and more dwells on the delights of living. His belief is that song is what matters, because song is a permanent force in a world of changing appearances :

> Wandelt sich rasch auch die Welt
> Wie Wolkengestalten,
> Alles Vollendete fällt
> Heim zur Uralten.
>
> Über dem Wandel und Gang,
> Weiter und freier,
> Währt noch dein Vor-Gesang,
> Gott mit der Leier.[2]

He even goes further and says that song is not desire or wooing of something finally won but simply Being :

> Gesang ist Dasein.

[1] Does he belong to this world ? No, from both
The realms does his spacious nature rise.

[2] Change though the world may as fast
As cloud confections,
Home to the changeless at last
Fall all perfections.

Over this transient throng,
Freer and higher,
Sounds on your preluding song,
God with the lyre.

(Trs. J. B. Leishman)

To this conclusion Rilke comes when he sings about his innermost activity. The permanence which art gives, the force with which inspiration comes, the enrichment of personality which it brings, are facets of this essential fact that song is nothing but the Real, the only true existence. It is this that the god gives.

In praising song Rilke is fully conscious of its mystery, and on this he spends some of his most notable imagery. When Valéry says that in poetry " l'oreille parle ", he expresses a paradox which most poets will admit to be true. Rilke sees this and expresses it by a tree growing in the ear :

> Da stieg ein Baum. O reine Übersteigung !
> O Orpheus singt ! O hoher Baum im Ohr ! [1]

There is an audible silence in which every beast falls under the magic of song and the meanest hut becomes a temple in the sense of hearing. Rilke so conveys the miraculous capacity of language for creating. Orpheus sings, and his singing is a tree. This song serves no ulterior end. It is an absolute thing. The young poet must do more than sing about his love : for that source of song will fail. Real singing is something that exists on its own :

> In Wahrheit singen, ist ein andrer Hauch.
> Ein Hauch um nichts. Ein Wehn im Gott. Ein Wind.[2]

The majesty and incalculable power of poetry is like a wind that blows through a god. It cannot be explained ; it is divine.

The spirit of the sonnets is the joy of transformation. It is the poet's own task :

> Wolle die Wandlung. O sei für die Flamme begeistert,
> Drin sich ein Ding dir entzieht, das mit Verwandlungen prunkt.[3]

It has many forms. Things seen and experienced can be transformed in more ways than one. From the complex of his

---

[1] A tree ascending there. O pure transcension !
O Orpheus sings ! O tall tree in the ear.
(Trs. J. B. Leishman)

[2] Far other is the breath of real singing.
An aimless breath. A stirring in the god. A breeze.
(Trs. J. B. Leishman)

[3] Cherish all change. For the flame, for the flame be enraptured,
Wherein there escapes from you something that's bravely transformed.
(Trs. J. B. Leishman)

sensations and memories the poet retains what matters. The unessential is forgotten ; the significant remains. This may in itself be quite trivial by ordinary standards, but the fact that it has stayed in the poet's mind and matured there shows that it is not really so. When Rilke wishes to find an offering for the god of song, he chooses a memory of Russia, a horse on the fields :

> Herüber vom Dorf kam der Schimmel allein,
> An der vorderen Fessel den Pflock,
> Um die Nacht auf den Wiesen allein zu sein ;
> Wie schlug seiner Mähne Gelock
>
> An den Hals im Takte des Übermuts,
> Bei dem grob gehemmten Galopp.
> Wie sprangen die Quellen des Rossebluts ! [1]

The image is complete. Yet it has a secondary meaning, a symbolical importance. The horse who despite his tethering-block gallops into the night is an image of gay confidence and enterprise in the face of obstacles. The poet's memory has enriched his original vision. So more touchingly Rilke recalls another scene from the past, from his childhood, of children playing ball in Prague :

> Wagen umrollten uns fremd, vorübergezogen,
> Häuser umstanden uns stark, aber unwahr,— und keines
> Kannte uns je. Was war wirklich im All ?
>
> Nichts. Nur die Bälle. Ihre herrlichen Bogen.
> Auch nicht die Kinder. . . . Aber manchmal trat eines,
> Ach ein vergehendes, unter den fallenden Ball.[2]

All that remains is the memory of the game, of the actual balls thrown in the air. Even the dead friend, whom the poem commemorates, is in comparison fleeting and transitory. For

[1] White, coming up from the village alone,
On one fetlock a tethering-block,
To spend the night alone, on his own :
How gaily he tossed the shock
Of his mane in time to his mounting mood,
Spite of the dragging clop-clop.
How they leapt the springs of the equine blood !
(Trs. J. B. Leishman)

[2] Unconcerning carriages rolling and swerving,
Houses surrounding us strongly, untruthfully though,— and here
Nothing that knew us. Was anything real at all ?
Nothing. Only the balls. Their glorious curving.
Not even the children. . . . Though sometimes one would appear
Passing, passing, under the falling ball. (Trs. J. B. Leishman)

his sake Rilke recalls the living moment which stays and passes into song.

What the poet transforms takes on a new metaphysical existence. Rilke had in the past written about roses. Two poems of *Neue Gedichte* say what they meant to him. *Die Rosenschale (The Rose-Cup)* is a radiant account of the rose as a type of complete beauty ; *Das Roseninnere (The Inside of a Rose)* conveys the miraculous effect of light in a rose, the sensation that a whole summer fills a room in a dream. In the Sonnets these individual roses, which of old provoked his wonder, have passed into an ideal rose, — almost the flower that Mallarmé honoured :

> Rose, du thronende, denen im Altertume
> Warst du ein Kelch mit einfachem Rand.
> Uns aber bist du die volle zahllose Blume,
> Der unerschöpfliche Gegenstand.[1]

The scent which has charmed men for centuries is like praise in the air. Such a rose has no name. It is something in the mind, richer and more beautiful than any individual flower. And this change is the work of memory. A similar conception fills another sonnet where Rilke calls on his heart to sing of unknown flowers :

> Singe die Gärten, mein Herz, die du nicht kennst ; wie in Glas
> Eingegossene Gärten, klar, unerreichbar.
> Wasser und Rosen von Ispahan oder Schiras,
> Singe sie selig, preise sie, keinem vergleichbar.[2]

From the known flowers the imagination advances to the unknown and is no less at home with them. The poet has made them part of his inmost being. They have their real existence through him, and he through them. The enrichment of the spirit which he finds through the imagination comes from objects which he has himself made real.

So strong is the imagination that it can not only enrich and transform but create out of nothing. Rilke's theory of Trans-

---

[1] For the people of ancient times, rose throned in power,
Your calyx had only a single rim ;
But for us of to-day you're the full, the numberless flower,
The theme whose depths we can only skim.
(Trs. J. B. Leishman)

[2] Sing those gardens, my heart, poured as into a glass,
Those for ever unknown gardens, crystal, unsharable.
Waters and roses of Ispahan or Shiras,
Blissfully sing them, praise them, the un-comparable.
(Trs. J. B. Leishman)

formation might seem to exclude a view of poetry like Shakespeare's :

> And as imagination bodies forth
> The forms of things unknown, the poet's pen
> Turns them to shapes, and gives to airy nothings
> A local habitation and a name.

By pedantic standards this view has nothing to do with transforming things from one order of existence to another. But Rilke was not bound by a mere theory. He knew quite well that some things which moved him and meant much to him were pure inventions. In Italian pictures he had marked and loved the fabulous unicorn, and in *Das Einhorn* (*The Unicorn*) he had portrayed its meeting with a Saint. It is almost purely pictorial, — the surprised Saint, the animal with its ivory horn, its gleaming skin, its rosy lips and white teeth. This impression stayed with Rilke and was transformed in the Sonnets. The Saint has disappeared ; the unicorn remains, an example of what can be done by belief :

> O dieses ist das Tier, das es nicht gibt.
> Sie wusstens nicht und habens jeden Falls
> — Sein Wandeln, seine Haltung, seinen Hals,
> Bis in des stillen Blickes Licht — geliebt.
> Zwar *war* es nicht. Doch weil sie's liebten, ward
> Ein reines Tier. Sie liessen immer Raum.
> Und in dem Raume, klar und ausgespart,
> Erhob es leicht sein Haupt und brauchte kaum
> Zu sein. Sie nährten es mit keinem Korn,
> Nur immer mit der Möglichkeit, es sei.
> Und die gab solche Stärke an das Tier,
> Dass es aus sich ein Stirnhorn trieb. Ein Horn.
> Zu einer Jungfrau kam es weiss herbei —
> Und war im Silber-Spiegel und in ihr.[1]

---

[1] This is the creature that has never been.
They never knew it, and yet, none the less,
They loved the way it moved, its suppleness,
Its neck, its very gaze, mild and serene.

It wasn't, but, because they loved it, got
To be alive. They'd always leave some space,
And it, in that clear space which they'd allot,
Would lightly lift its head, with scarce a trace

Of need to *be*. They fed it, not with corn,
But only with their feeling that it *might*
Exist. And that was able to confer

Such strength, its forehead grew a horn. One horn.
It came up to a virgin once, all white,
And *was* within the mirror and in her. (Trs. J. B. Leishman)

The unicorn is the creation of love and belief. But when it has been created, it becomes a part of the inner life, a symbol of what poetry can do.

In the Sonnets Rilke shows what poetry meant to him, what he got from it and what he hoped for it. The dominating mood is joy. It is a complement to the distress and anxiety of the Elegies, and in Rilke's whole performance the two books must be taken together. While the Elegies reveal his pangs and struggles when he was not creating poetry, the Sonnets tell of his joy when he was. His life passed between extremes of frustrated waiting and rapturous creation, and he assumed that the common human state was like his own, that it knew the misery of aimless emptiness and the concentrated activity of inspiration. His theory of Transformation bridged this division to his own satisfaction. The Sonnets are the songs of his victory. They were composed in a period of extraordinary creativeness when his long-delayed hopes were being unaccountably fulfilled and all his energies were at work. They reflect the confidence and delight that this brought to him. In them his belief in the wider world of death has given place to something wider still, to a scheme which embraces both life and death because all that matters is the spirit of song which belongs to both. Like Valéry, Rilke found in the creative joy of poetry something marvellous and unique. But unlike Valéry, he exalted this to a special and central place, interpreted life through it and thought that it alone gave importance to anything. For him poetry was not one activity among others but a fundamental power. Song was the root of his being, the means of his mystical excitements, the basis of his philosophy. What he found in himself, he applied to others. He stood for an ideal of poetry as a vivifying, preserving force. He was first and always a poet.

The Elegies and the Sonnets, published in 1923, were Rilke's last complete works. The fragments of his posthumous poems suggest that he might have developed the allegorical manner of the Tenth Elegy to new uses and have created a poetry in which abstractions take on a new individuality. But the fragments, interesting and tantalising though they are, are not a complete work. They show no real advance. When at last the Angel spoke to Rilke and answered his prayers, he had responded with his whole being. Into the Elegies and the Sonnets he put all his accumulated impressions and transformed experiences. Then he was empty, almost broken. He wrote that he was caught in a vicious circle like an evil magic ring in one of Brueghel's pictures of Hell, that he did not see how he could continue to live. Physical death came in 1926 in circumstances almost symbolical. Giving some roses to a young girl whom he much admired, he scratched his hand on a thorn. Infection and blood-poisoning of a peculiarly painful kind set in. Rilke lay in agony for weeks and died. He who had always loved girls and roses, who had meditated so tenderly on death, found all three together in the end. His sensibility, which was the chief spring of his poetry, was perhaps a reflection of the physical state which yielded so easily to destruction when it came. In death, as in life, the things which he most admired overwhelmed him.

IV

STEFAN GEORGE

1868–1933

Rilke, who was born on the fringes of the polyglot Austro-Hungarian Empire, owed little in his art to German traditions. He was a cosmopolitan whose most strengthening influences came from France. His verse lacks the usual characteristics of German verse, its emphatic resonance and movement as to a military band. Still less did he care about the fortunes and fate of Germany. He might sometimes be compelled to live in it, but it did little for his work. In strong contrast to him is Stefan George, who was born at Bingen in the Rhineland and displayed in full measures the qualities which Rilke lacked. He became a national poet who not only gave voice to half-hidden ambitions in his countrymen but had an extraordinary influence on their culture. His friends made a considerable contribution to the intellectual life of their time. Their work was inspired and directed by him. He was as much an institution as a poet. But as a poet he counts. The paradox of his career is that he began as an admiring pupil of Mallarmé and ended as a national prophet. His work developed with a logic of its own. His life has a pattern in which personal inclinations, faint at first, were developed into a gospel. His masterful personality grew more and more sure of itself, and with each change he became more German, more at home in a country where learning and speculation had always been more natural than lyric fancy or unpremeditated song, where since the triumph of Prussia the notion of a national mission or " Sendung " has expected a poet more to shape souls than to give pleasure. He could only have existed in Germany. He, not Rilke, is its poet in this tragic age.

George's first original verse owed its birth to contact with France. In the 'nineties Germany had no example and no inspiration for a young man of his gifts. The stale ends of Romanticism had no nourishment in them, and the example which he needed must be found elsewhere. In Paris he felt the enchantment of Mallarmé, and later in *Franken* (*The Franks*) he acknowledged his debt to this city of his youth :

Da schirmten held und sänger das Geheimnis,.
VILLIERS sich hoch genug für einen thron,
VERLAINE in fall und busse fromm und kindlich
Und für sein denkbild blutend MALLARMÉ.[1]

In the poetry of the Symbolists George found the deliverance that he needed. When he returned home, he had discovered his purpose, his style and his theory of art. The verse that he now wrote showed power and maturity. He gathered friends round him, and in *Blätter für die Kunst* his circle, dedicated to the same cause as himself, proclaimed its message and displayed its work. George felt that he belonged to a European movement of which he was the German representative. He saw that if Symbolism was to take root in Germany, it must differ from its French counterpart ; he claimed that it had a national character and was a parallel manifestation of a similar impulse. His friend, Karl August Klein, said that their common aim was " to drag the word from its common daily round and exalt it to a gleaming sphere ". He recalls Valéry's words on Mallarmé : " Il a essayé d'élever enfin une page à la puissance du ciel étoilé ". George's circle felt, as it well might, that poetry in Germany had lost its fire. It needed new aims and a new practice. These they were prepared to supply.

George saw that the problem was largely technical, a matter of defining what poetry was for him. He gave his views in a series of statements which recall some of Mallarmé's *Divagations*. Published in 1894, his apophthegms *About Poetry* may be quoted in part to show his aims :

Every opposing spirit, every reasoning and wrangling with life, points to a still disordered spirit and must be excluded from art.

The worth of poetry is decided not by the meaning (otherwise it would be wisdom, instruction) but by form, *i.e.* nothing external throughout, by stirring every depth in metre and sound, by which at all times the original spirits, the Masters, have distinguished themselves from the followers, the second-class artists.

The essence of poetry is like that of a dream, in that I and

[1] Hero and singer shielded there the secret,
Villiers proud enough to be a king,
Verlaine in sin and penitence saint and childlike,
Bleeding for his ideal Mallarmé.

you, here and there, once and now, stand side by side and are one and the same.

The deepest insight, the strongest impression, are still no guarantee for a good poem. Both must first be transposed into the vocal tune, which demands a certain tranquillity or, even, joy. That explains why every poem is unreal which brings black without a ray of light. Something like this used earlier to be meant by the Ideal.

Beauty is not at the beginning and not at the end ; it is the climax. Art makes its biggest capture when you detect the breath of new, still sleeping spirits.

In this manifesto there is much beside the oracular manner which recalls Mallarmé. The insistence that the mere subject is not enough, the exclusion of political themes, the comparison of poetry to a dream, the emphasis on rhythm, come from the master's gospel. But George was too well versed in poetry to be quite uncritical in his acceptance. The Ideal fades away into a balance of shades in a poem. There is no word about a superior world above the senses, no denunciation of the crowd, no special emphasis on the poet's place in the world. George was too subtle to accept conditions for poetry which did not suit his own gifts. The methods of Mallarmé were well adapted for those who found their wonder in mystical privacy or were eager to explore dusky corners of the soul. It opened new vistas to those who wished to write about half-defined sensations. It required for its proper use a high degree of sensibility and it was ill suited to plain poetry of the emotions. Even in the first days of his enlightenment George was not the man to exploit the possibilities of Symbolism to the full. He relied on other sources than his sensibility ; he had not Mallarmé's mystical trust in the absolute of aesthetic experience. He was highly educated, intellectual and serious. His response to things was not simple or immediate. What came to him did not pass directly into song. It had first to be organised by a cultivated mind and related to a scheme of existence. His sensibility was disciplined at its roots by his intellect. He could never quite abandon himself immediately to excitement. So from the beginning his work is different from the master's, more pondered, more cultivated, more laborious.

The first fruits of George's new activities appeared in three volumes published in quick succession : *Hymnen* (1890),

Pilgerfahrten (1891) and *Algabal* (1892). It is at once clear that George had followed his teachers in taking back to poetry what had been given to music. These poems have their own capacious harmonies. The style recalls Baudelaire's in its slow and loaded movement, its weight and strength and organic structure. The lines stand on their own as if the words in them belonged to each other. This rhythm is not that of ordinary German verse. It is more melodious, more sensitive. The style indeed is more mature than the matter. No poet can find his whole self at twenty-two, and George shows that he was still under the influence of his models. The years were to give him a different scope, but at the moment he followed the new manner with the enthusiasm of a convert. The influence of Mallarmé may be detected in *Hymnen*, where George writes about poetry and poetical inspiration. He tells of visitations of " die Herrin " or Mistress of Vision. In other ages she would be the Muse ; the Symbolists have changed her name and made her more mysterious. George addresses her with deep devotion ; her appearances are like moments of divine epiphany. Her comings are connected with times and seasons, and with skill and care the poet prepares the atmosphere which precedes them. There is a hushed anticipation in *Weihe* (*Consecration*) :

> Nun bist du reif, nun schwebt die Herrin nieder,
> Mondfarbne gazeschleier sie umschlingen,
> Halboffen ihre traumesschweren lider
> Zu dir geneigt die segnung zu vollbringen.[1]

The Mistress is inspiration. Later George was to know more about it. Now he accepts it as a fact and proclaims its mystery. He sees it largely through other eyes than his own.

Another youthful trait is the way in which George loads his verse with sensuous images, especially of hard and glittering things. He has the taste of his time for scented flowers, for jewels and metals. This is particularly clear in *Algabal*, where George dramatises his desire for a gorgeous and uncontrolled existence in the Roman emperor Elagabalus. The young luxurious emperor is presented in the high colours of

---

[1] Now are you ripe. Earthward the Mistress flies,
Moon-coloured veils of gauze around her clinging ;
Half open are her dream-encumbered eyes ;
She bends to you, her benediction bringing.

the 'nineties, as Wilde would have liked to paint him. Hard inanimate objects glitter through verses like

> Für jede zier die freunden farbenstrahlen,
> Aus blitzendem und blinderem metall,
> Aus elfenbein und milchigen opalen,
> Aus demant alabaster und kristall.[1]

These convey the inhuman splendour which George sees in Elagabalus, but their effect is too brilliant to be satisfying. They appeal only to the eye, and even so they are almost blinding. They leave out too much, and make too little appeal to merely human feelings. Against the drab culture of his time George protested by offering something more exciting and more vivid. But the picture is not really imaginative. It emphasises wealth and display but no more. It means something to the poet as a protest and an escape, but his best gifts are not in it. He has learned that poetry appeals through images to the eye, but not that if the sensuous force of an image is too strong it loses much of its significance. This is a defect of youth and inexperience. Of it George seems to have been partly conscious. He suggests that he wished to write strong simple poetry but was as yet unable to do so. Such at least is a natural conclusion from *Die Spange* (*The Clasp*) :

> Ich wollte sie aus kühlem eisen
> Und wie ein glatter fester streif ;
> Doch war im schacht auf allen gleisen
> So kein metall zum gusse reif.
>
> Nun aber soll sie also sein :
> Wie eine grosse fremde dolde
> Geformt aus feuerrotem golde
> Und reichem blitzendem gestein.[2]

---

[1] For every use the friendly colours' gleams.
From metal glittering or dim and dunned,
From ivory or opal's milky beams,
From alabaster, crystal, diamond.

[2] From cold steel I would fashion it,
And like a firm and polished blade ;
But there was no shaft in the pit
With ore so ready to be made.

So now like this it has to be :
A kind of flower I shall mould,
Large, alien, of fire-red gold
And stones that glitter gorgeous!

George already saw that this kind of poetry was a second-best, that his ideal was something different. He foresaw where his true direction lay.

The mystical airs and invocations do not prevent these poems from being concerned with the sensible world. Indeed George was never mystical in the sense that Rilke or Mallarmé was. His place was in this world, but as yet he was not entirely at his ease in it. To express all his feelings he resorted to a kind of self-dramatisation, to writing poetry about a character in whom he saw his own desires satisfied, his own possibilities realised. This helped him to clarify his ideas and to give form to his discontents. It was a useful training for a man whose culture had largely come through books and who approached his creative task with a mind full of history and literature. To shape these disparate elements into a whole he had somehow to unify his personality, and he was helped in this by seeing himself in figures from the past. They showed him what kind of a man he was, what he wanted, what he wished to be. Algabal did for George what Hérodiade did in a not very different way for Mallarmé. It was a focus for his day-dreams. Through it he found something in himself and was able to write a more direct and more personal poetry. In *Vogelschau* (*Augury*), the last poem of *Algabal*, George takes leave of his exotic subjects and comes, as it were, home again. It is a summary of his work and imaginative life up to date. In it George uses nothing but symbols, and his use of them is his own. They form a coherent whole. All the imagery is taken from birds. There is no key, no explanation. All is translucid and brilliant, a real song :

> Weisse schwalben sah ich fliegen,
> Schwalben schnee- und silberweiss,
> Sah sie sich im winde wiegen,
> In dem winde hell und heiss.

> Bunte häher sah ich hüpfen,
> Papagei und kolibri
> Durch die wunder-bäume schlüpfen
> In dem wald der Tusferi.

> Grosse raben sah ich flattern,
> Dohlen schwarz und dunkelgrau
> Nah am grunde über nattern
> Im verzauberten gehau.

Schwalben seh ich wieder fliegen,
Schnee- und silberweisse schar,
Wie sie sich im winde wiegen
In dem winde kalt und klar ! [1]

The poet watches birds as an augur may. He knows that they mean and foretell something if he can interpret it. But these birds are different aspects of George's life : adventures and experiences through which he has passed. After sojourning in exotic and sinister regions he has returned to where he started and has found a change ; a cold wind blows where before the air was sultry. The young poet who felt hampered in his own home and tried strange experiments in the mind, has returned refreshed and clear. In its main character the method is that of Valéry's *Les Pas*. The symbols are all taken from a single sphere and are maintained with complete consistency. But they are presented with circumstances so vivid and so appropriate that the primary and secondary meanings of the poem are transfused. There is no gap between the symbols and what is symbolised. The birds have the variety and qualities of George's adventures ; his adventures are best understood as birds. The Symbolist method is mastered, and the poem gains by this double character which is not in the least ambiguous.

In *Die Bücher der Hirten- und Preisgedichte* (*The Books of Shepherds' and Prize Poems*), 1895, George continued to explore himself and to present the results in subjects drawn from other times and climes. Like other eminent Germans, he felt a strong impulse to master the culture of ages and

---

[1] Silvery swallows I saw flying,
Swallows snow- and silver-white,
In the breezes lullabying,
In the breezes hot and light.

Motley jackdaws I saw skipping,
Paroquets and kolibri,
'Neath the magic branches tripping
In the woods of Tusfery.

Sturdy ravens I saw strutting,
Caddows black and sombre gray,
There in the enchanted cutting
Midst the adders on the way.

Swallows I again see flying,
Swarms of swallows silver-white,
In the breezes lullabying,
In the breezes brisk and bright.

(Trs. Cyril Scott)

countries not his own and believed somehow that he had affinities with them. With characteristic orderliness the book is divided into three sections : Hellenic, mediaeval, oriental. This is partly the poetry of desire and dream. In each of these three worlds George presents much that he likes and would wish to secure for his own life. In the simplicity of the Greeks, in mediaeval song and chivalry, in oriental colour and ease, he sees an imaginary satisfaction for his own inner needs. His poetry differs from Parnassian poetry about the past. Heredia touched on all these worlds and created vivid vignettes of them. But his presentation was entirely objective. George's scenes are projections and extensions of himself. Desires, hampered or impossible in his own existence, are fulfilled in this imagined past. At times the dramatisation fades away, and especially in the mediaeval and oriental sections we forget the setting to which the poems belong. The wandering minstrel may be a mediaeval figure, but he is very like George himself when he sings :

> Sieh mein kind ich gehe.
> Denn du darfst nicht kennen
> Nicht einmal durch nennen
> Menschen müh und wehe.
>
> Mir ist um dich bange.
> Sieh mein kind ich gehe
> Dass auf deiner wange
> Nicht der duft verwehe.
>
> Würde dich belehren,
> Müsste dich versehren
> Und das macht mir wehe.
> Sieh mein kind ich gehe.[1]

Neither in sound nor in sentiment is this very like a song of the Minnesingers. At least we do not think of them when we

[1] See, my child, I'm going,
For it were to pain thee,
Mortal sorrows vainly
Unto thee foreshowing.

For thy sake I'm wary,
See, my child, I'm going,
Lest thy cheeks' so fairy
Roses pale be growing.

Fain would I have taught thee,
But that would have brought me
Grief beyond thy knowing,
See, my child, I'm going.   (Trans. Cyril Scott)

read it, and it needs no reference to them for its understanding. George seems to have found a way through self-dramatisation to a more individual and personal note. The past has not only answered his spiritual needs ; it has helped him to find himself.

In the Hellenic section the antique setting is more emphatically symbolical than in the rest of the book. The poems are true enough to fact and history but they have a secondary meaning which applies to the poet in his own time. George understands these themes through his own life, sees himself in their situations, and through them makes himself more interesting. In *Der Auszug der Erstlinge* (*Departure of the Firstborn*) the theme is that the first-born are sent away from their homes to a new life. They do not know what this is but they believe that they are chosen by the gods for a noble goal. The scene is not familiar in Greek literature and is largely the poet's invention. Later he was to believe that the first-born of a family, the best of the stock, should be severed from parental ties and help to form a new *élite*. Here we may see the first appearance of this idea. The Greek children are the symbol of those who must leave their homes to find a new life ; therefore they go in joy and confidence, and there is no lamentation for their departure. In *Flurgottes Trauer* (*The Field-god's Sorrow*) the natural god embodies the idea that song is born of sorrow and that creation comes through severance of human ties. The god, from whom maidens shrink, must live a lonely life sustained by his trust in a greater god and believe that all will be turned to good. The past appeals to George because it is like himself and still lives in him. He approaches it neither as an historian nor as an aesthete but as one who believes that there are certain permanent things in human life which may for a time be obscured but can be brought to life again. His poems are about the Greeks but they are also about himself, because he feels that he is like the Greeks in the simple stark issues which the creative life forces upon him. By identifying himself with them he relates himself to the past and finds a place in European culture through its unchanging elements. He shows that he is doing what others have done before him. He justifies opinions and feelings which might otherwise seem strange. So this kind of poetry has a double function. As an imaginary representation of the past it has the strength and truth which comes from being written by a man who feels that his problems are its. As a record of the poet's self it gains in depth by showing its affinities to long-established experience.

The triple division of the book corresponds to a real division in George's nature. He wished to make a synthesis of what was most valuable for him in the culture of his time. But his choice of subjects is not a personal whim, or an accident due to his reading. It foreshadows, and no doubt already embodies, a view which later was to be made more explicit by him and his friends, that human character may be divided into " Geist " — spirit,— " Seele " — soul,— and " Leib " — body. The first he finds in the Hellenic world, the second in the Middle Ages, the third in- the imagined East. The full associations of the words are hard to translate into English. " Geist " contains our appreciation of what is noble and tragic in life, the sense of destiny and of sacrifice. " Seele " means much that we mean by " heart " but much also that we mean by " imagination ". It is the force which inspires and warms, which calls men to make great efforts for dimly discerned ends. It is a kind of noble instinctiveness, of zeal and zest for great causes and selfless devotion. It has little to do with the affections. " Leib " is certainly the body, not in its grossness and physical appetites, though these are not forbidden, but in its luxurious and sensuous love of life and pleasure. The trio, " Geist ", " Seele " and " Leib ", were central to George's thought. They were his distinctive contribution to his time. Two of the three had often enough been found in combination before him in German poetry. Hölderlin, for instance, has " Geist " and " Seele ", but not " Leib " ; Goethe, " Seele " and " Leib ", but not " Geist ". George believed in all three and displayed them separately in three worlds of the spirit. He believed both in sacrifice and in pleasure, both in knowledge of one's destiny and in instinctive desires to fulfil it.

For this view of life the three worlds are admirably suited. In each George shows his own background and personal taste. The Greek qualities which he prized were not those which Winckelmann and Goethe found in the antique world, the clarity and godlike ease, the detachment and dignity, the " blitheness and repose ". George saw the Greeks through other eyes, the eyes of Bachofen and Nietzsche. What he valued was the closeness to nature, to the emotions, to the issues of life and death. Just as Hofmannsthal stressed the hatred and revenge in the old story of matricide in his *Elektra*, so George stressed the dangers and anxieties of Greek life. He saw the Greeks not as gods but quite literally as children of nature. His characteristic figures are the first-born sent out of their country to a new life, the hero who kills a monster and goes up into the mountains to die, the women who come with tragic stories to the well, the athletic victor absorbed in his own triumph and oblivious of all onlookers :

> Er geht, mit vollem fusse wie der löwe
> Und ernst : nach vielen unberühmten jahren
> Die zierde ganzen landes und er sieht nicht
> Die zahl der jauchzenden und nicht einmal
> Die eltern stolz aus dem gedränge ragen.[1]

This is not what Pindar would have seen in a young athlete, but the picture, in its restraint and simplicity, is none the less Greek. George seems to have felt that modern life had lost much of its simplicity and directness. These qualities, which he prized, must be restored, and his Greek poems show his attachment to them and their relevance to his own time.

In the Middle Ages George admired the instinctive unity of life, the natural harmony of a society which combined a heroic ideal with a gift for song. His chief figures are the young soldier and the wandering minstrel. The first is what he liked, the second is himself. In the relations between the two he sees what he would like to be the relation between himself and the youth of his time. This is a highly simplified vision of the complex Middle Ages and comes less from history than from the arts. It has none of Dante's omnivorous curiosity and dark emotions. Even its chivalry is seen through romantic eyes ; its poetry is freed from its elaborate airs and graces. It is true that George recognises its religious side and writes with charm a hymn to the Virgin, which has some echoes from songs of the fourteenth century but perhaps owes as much to Mantegna's picture at Frankfurt :

---

[1] He marches, with full footsteps like the lion,
And serious : after many unpraised years
The whole land's ornament, nor does he see
The number of the cheerers, and not even
His parent's pride leap out above the crowd.

Lilie der auen !
Herrin im rosenhag !
Gib dass ich mich freue,
Dass ich mich erneue
An deinem gnadenreichen krönungstag.[1]

George finds in the Middle Ages all that he means by "Seele", the tug at the heart, the devotion to cause whether natural or supernatural, the simple spirit of song.

The third section bears no relation to fact or history. The East which George presents comes from dream. It owes something to Goethe's *West-östliche Diwan* and more to what the West has always imagined to belong to regions of the sun. In it the visions of *Algabal* are given more tenderness and humanity. The notion of " Leib " is widened and made more attractive. The mood is of luxurious musing, of peace and ease in circumstances of great brilliance and brightness. This world never existed except in day-dreams. Its tone is of languorous, delightful rest :

Halte die purpur- und goldnen
gedanken im zaum.
Schliesse die lider
Unter dem flieder
Und wiege dich wieder
Im mittagstraum.[2]

If the Greek and Mediaeval worlds provided George with types and ideals of activity, his imaginary East provided it with a type of dreams, with a contrast to the world in which he lived. It embodies his love for sensuous ease and enjoyment, for the South and the sun. In his composite ideal this was quite as important as the sterner qualities of " Geist " and " Seele ". It was the home of the unfettered imagination, the region in which the spirit can move without responsi-

[1] Lily of the meadows,
 Queen where the roses blow,
 Send thy gladness to me,
 Grant I may renew me ;
 Thou, who art crowned to-day, let thy grace flow.
[2] All thoughts purple and golden
 Hold back in rein.
 Let eyelids close
 'Neath the lilac's boughs
 And the midday drowse
 Lull you again.

bility. It satisfied a deep need in George's nature and it remained a part of his ideal life. He was never one to deride the body or its pleasures, but he needed some symbol to convey what he felt about them. He found it in the East, the traditional home of luxurious ease.

At first sight *Das Jahr der Seele* (*The Year of the Soul*), 1897, is far removed from *Die Bücher*. From the high colours of distance and dream the poet turns to the present, from Greek mountains and Eastern gardens to a great park in a northern landscape, to trees, flowers, streams, fountains, birds. The poems look easy. Their first, literal meaning is perfectly plain. The poet discourses to a friend in moods which respond to the different seasons of autumn, winter and summer. At first sight it looks like an autobiographical record. The title perhaps suggests that it is more, and in a foreword George gives a warning that the " I " and " you " of the poems are often the same person. Neither the scenery nor the persons are what they seem. The poems are a symbolical presentation of a crisis in the poet's life. He passes from the aftermath of the harvest in autumn through the sterility of winter to new life in summer. The " other " whom he addresses is part of himself, that other self which every poet knows in his creative work. The tone of the whole is subdued. The measured accents and quiet colouring fit that time in the poet's life when after a period of enhanced activity he has to rest and wait for his powers to return. In George's life it is perhaps more than this. It is the change to a new self, more conscious of its powers and more eager to put them into poetry. The "other" whom he seeks is his creative soul, which eludes him only to return with renewed and different strength. One task is over ; a new task is about to begin. There is a mood of resignation, of melancholy, which breaks only when summer returns in all its fire.

The two friends in a garden through the changing seasons are the symbols of the poet's divided self. In each poem we must look for the ulterior meaning, for the reference which the symbols have to the poet's complex state. What counts is the mood. In the autumnal landscape, with which the series begins, this is easily caught. Behind lies the exhausted effort of the vintage ; what remains is a kind of weariness both in man and in nature. The quiet poetry of this state belongs to both :

Wir schreiten auf und ab im reichen flitter
Des buchenganges beinah bis zum tore
Und sehen aussen in dem feld vom gitter
Den mandelbaum zum zweitenmal im flore.

Wir suchen nach den schattenfreien bänken
Dort wo uns niemals fremde stimmen scheuchten,
In träumen unsre arme sich verschränken,
Wir laben uns am langen milden leuchten.

Wir fühlen dankbar wie zu leisem brausen
Von wipfeln strahlenspuren auf uns tropfen
Und blicken nur und horchen wenn in pausen
Die reifen früchte an den boden klopfen.[1]

The effect is complete. Nothing breaks the unity of the atmosphere. But of course there is more in the poem than that. The poet and his other self partake of the general weariness. The old life is finished ; only its fruits remain. The symbols are not a code. There is no exact correspondence between the trees and shadows of the poem and any events in the poet's life. The symbolism is of less tangible things ; the movement to and fro, the bright vision even in autumn, the dreaming embrace, the gratitude for something done, are all incidents in the spirit. The poem needs no key. It describes a state of soul and shows its tone and colour, what it means to the poet as an experience.

This method has special advantages for describing conflicts and events in the self. By displaying himself as two characters intimately related, George makes clear the nature of the struggle in himself. It is not dramatic, not sensational. It is like an ordinary human relation. The events in his single life are like those between a pair of friends. For instance, when the poet knows that his old poetry is leaving him, he sees it as a flight of swans :

[1] Midst rich irradiance to and fro we wander
Along the beech-grove, nearly to the bower,
And see across the balustrade out yonder
The almond-tree a second time in flower.

We search for benches free of shade, deserted,
There where never strangers' voices fluster,
Our arms entwined, our eyes in dreams averted,
We steep our souls in gentle lingering lustre.

We're grateful when amidst the soft discourses
Of tree-tops, warming rays towards us travel,
And only look and listen when in pauses
The ripened fruit falls lightly on the gravel.
(Trs. Cyril Scott)

Doch weisst du auch vom tiefen glücke
Und schätzest du die stumme träne ?
Das auge schattend auf der brücke
Verfolgest du den zug der schwäne ? [1]

The scene is so natural, so usual, that its secondary, symbolical meaning emerges with great clarity. The method adds both to the fullness of the poems and to their truth. It helps to present these impalpable experiences at their proper worth. Because the whole tone is so quiet, the slightest variations count, and when autumn changes to winter, or winter to summer, we feel that something very important has happened. In an early poem, *Le Bois Amical*, Valéry seems to have attempted something of the same kind. His companion there is surely his other self, and his conclusion shows the same kind of union or self-fulfilment which George has in mind :

Et puis, nous sommes morts sur la mousse,
Très loin, tout seuls parmi l'ombre douce
De ce bois intime et murmurant ;

Et là-haut, dans la lumière immense,
Nous nous sommes trouvés en pleurant,
Ô mon cher compagnon de silence !

What Valéry makes into a single short poem, George elaborates in a whole series. The theme is rich and submits profitably to his treatment.

It is true that these poems are complete enough even without their symbolical meaning. They are superficially satisfying and consistent. But we can see what is gained by this kind of symbolism if we compare one of George's poems with another which has on the surface a similar theme but has an entirely different character. In the winter section George writes:

Die blume die ich mir am fenster hege,
Verwahrt vorm froste in der grauen scherbe,
Betrübt mich nur trotz meiner guten pflege
Und hängt das haupt als ob sie langsam sterbe.

Um ihrer frühern blühenden geschicke
Erinnerung aus meinem sinn zu merzen,
Erwähl ich scharfe waffen und ich knicke
Die blasse blume mit dem kranken herzen.

[1] But can you probe the silent hollows
Of deeper joys or tearless pain ? —
With shaded brow your vision follows
The graceful swans' receding train.
(Trs. Cyril Scott)

Was soll sie nur zur bitternis mir taugen?
Ich wünschte dass vom fenster sie verschwände. .
Nun heb ich wieder meine leeren augen
Und in die leere nacht die leeren hände.[1]

The dead flowers oppress the poet, and he cuts them. They
are the image of his own lost ideals, of the poetry which no
longer seems to mean anything to him. He wishes to be free
of their memory, but when he has destroyed them, he feels
empty without them. To this a poem of Jean Moréas shows
some resemblance :

La rose du jardin que j'avais méprisée
A cause de son simple et modeste contour,
Sans se baigner d'azur, sans humer la rosée,
Dans la vase, captive, a vécu plus d'un jour.

Puis lasse, abandonnée à ses pâleurs fatales,
Ayant fini d'éclore et de s'épanouir,
Elle laissa tomber lentement ses pétales,
Indifférente au soin de vivre ou de mourir.

Lorsque l'obscur destin passe, sachons nous taire.
Pourquoi ce souvenir que j'emporte aujourd'hui ?
Mon cœur est trop chargé d'ombres et de mystère ;
Le spectre d'une fleur est un fardeau pour lui.

Both poems speak of dead flowers, of the memories that they
evoke, but the difference is enormous. Moréas' poem is, in
the best sense, sentimental. It evokes a state of mind which
we may in certain circumstances find unreal or absurd. It has
the limits of all poetry which describes a situation. It stands
or falls by the importance which that situation has for us.
But George's poem has the additional strength of its symbolism. The flowers, which in themselves might have seemed
insignificant, are important because they are part of the poet's

[1] The flower at my window which I guarded
Safe from the frost in its grey pottery,
Afflicts me for my care all unrewarded
And hangs its head as it would slowly die.

That of its early flowering endeavour
All memory may from my sense depart,
I pick up a sharp instrument and sever
The pallid flower with the sickened heart.

How should it only serve me for derision ?
I wished it from my window out of sight.
But now I lift again my empty vision
And empty hands into the empty night.

life. So when the dramatic end comes, it is entirely in place
and leaves no suspicion of rhetoric.

This poetry of the divided self was not unknown to
Mallarmé, who felt the contrast between what he was and the
ideal poet of his desires. In his *Prose* he dwells on his dual
nature :

> Nous promenions notre visage
> (Nous fûmes deux, je le maintiens)
> Sur maints charmes de paysage,
> Ô sœur, y comparant les tiens.

But George not only wrote more fully about it but was able to
create poetry about the emotions which it aroused in him.
At the end of *Das Jahr der Seele* are some poems which give
its purely lyrical aspects, the feelings that it arouses in him.
These songs are more varied and more melodious than anything he had yet written. In them the poet speaks in the first
person and in the present tense. Their fullness shows how
well he has been repaid by his years of preparation, how his
efforts to express himself indirectly have enabled him to do so
directly. They are intensely personal and have an intimate
appeal. Because they are personal, they are much fuller and
deeper than the half-dramatic songs of *Die Bücher*. Years of
experience are absorbed into these tense, terse poems. The
title of *Traurige Tänze* is perhaps a little misleading. Some
of these songs are indeed melancholy like

> Dies leid und diese last : zu bannen
> Was nah erst war und mein.
> Vergebliches die arme spannen
> Nach dem was nur mehr schein.[1]

But the spirit varies, and some find a kind of joy :

> Es lacht in dem steigenden jahr dir
> Der duft aus dem garten noch leis.
> Flicht in dem flatternden haar dir
> Eppich und ehrenpreis,[2]

[1] This sorrow and this load,— for gaining
What once belonged to me.
In vain for that the arms are straining
That is but mockery.

[2] There smiles in the lengthening year, now,
The balm from the garden, benign.
Weave in thy fluttering hair, now,
Ivy with celandine.   (Trs. Cyril Scott)

or intimacy :

> Keins wie dein feines ohr
> Merkt was tief innen singt,
> Was noch so schüchtern schwingt,
> Was halb sich schon verlor.[1]

Such songs have not the airy sprightliness of Elizabethan songs nor the varied movement of the early Greek lyrics, but they are undeniably songs. They make an instantaneous effect. All that counts is the moment that they convey and the directness with which they convey it. They do this because they present pure emotions in an extremely simple form with a melody that is entirely suited to them. They have no ulterior meaning, no symbolism. With them a new art came to German poetry. Hitherto German songs had been too often composed for the musician. In even the best lyrics of Mörike or Lenau we feel that something is wanting, that they are not self-contained but wait for the musician to complete them. But George's songs sing themselves. They need no help from the composer. In them the springs of George's creativeness unite. Instead of identifying himself with other men, he sings of himself.

With the publication of *Das Jahr der Seele* George really found himself. He might have chosen to continue in this path and to develop its possibilities. But the new kind of poetry which it portended was already forming itself in him. New powers were at work. He had always held the most serious view of his calling and believed that through poetry the soul of Germany might be saved. Now the instrument which he had perfected was to be put to wider and more practical uses. Merely to sing was not enough. The contents and the effect of the song also counted and must be considered. The melancholy of *Das Jahr der Seele* is partly that of a man who feels himself imprisoned in his own personality and needs an outlet, a wider field for his energies. George felt that what he had discovered for himself should be communicated to others. In *Der Teppich des Lebens* (*The Tapestry of Life*), 1900, he showed that his art had taken a new direction. It was the beginning of a great change in his work.

[1] None but thy subtle ear
Marks deep within what sings,
What still so shyly swings,
Half-way to disappear.

The subjective personal poet was to become a seer and a teacher, the voice of deliverance to a barren age. For the moment the instructive tendency was not wholly manifest. George clothes it in poetry which is still poetry for its own sake. But he certainly wished this book to make a mark and to be regarded as something new. For in its forefront he sets a *Vorspiel* (*Prelude*) of twenty-four poems, a kind of *Ars Poetica*, a statement of what poetry is and should be for him. In his time of doubt and idleness he has had a vision of an Angel, and all his life is changed. At first we feel that perhaps George is about to create his own mysticism of poetry. The Angel, both for Mallarmé and for Rilke, is the absolute of inspiration, who works through the poet and even impresses the crowd :

> Eux, comme un vil sursaut d'hydre oyant jadis l'ange
> Donner un sens plus pur aux mots de la tribu.

But George has taken this symbol of the Word and made it the symbol of his own new poetry, in which much is of importance beside the art. His Angel is almost himself, at least his fuller and more responsible self.

The Angel proclaims a message of fuller life through poetry. What counts now in poetry is what it does and what it teaches. George pays service to the Word :

> Das wort von neuer lust und pein ; ein pfeil
> Der in die seele bricht und zuckt und flimmert.[1]

But what really matters is the content of the Word. The Angel's revelation is not mystical, not concerned with aesthetic rapture, but with the best things that George has found in art and history, the fruits of his culture. It is even surprisingly detailed and pays its tributes to Greece, Rome and Italy. The Angel's message to George is that what he has thought valuable is really so, and that the imaginative life as he conceives it is a means to renew himself and the world. This may seem obvious to us, but it is presented with elaborate imagery and detailed description as if the discovery really meant a great deal to George. He seems to have been doubtful about himself and his work, and then to have found an answer to his doubts and a direction for his energies. The

---

[1] The word of new delight and pain, the shaft
That breaks into the soul and jerks and quivers.

Angel not only tells him what to do but fills him with joy and confidence. He suggests that though others may not understand him, he will not falter in his task. It is clear that something had happened to George. In effect his poetry was changed in two ways. In the first place, it became much more objective. What had before been means to express his own moods, became lessons for the world. His old images and symbols became examples of imaginative life which he expected others to share. And in the second place, his old melancholy gave way to a mood of confidence. He had still a place for dark moods, but they were now seen as part of a greater whole. He had found a unity of vision, a comprehensive system which included different parts of himself.

The growing objectivity of these poems after the *Vorspiel* may be seen in George's greater choice of subjects. Past and present, primitive landscape and cultivated fields, religious devotion and bodily pleasure, pass into verse. These poems are descriptive and have their own value as such. Yet we cannot but feel that they are not only chosen with a highly individual choice but that they are somehow built out of the poet's self. They are not really independent vignettes. For instance, in *Die Fremde* (*The Stranger Woman*) a simple ballad tells of a wild woman who comes from afar and, after a stay which causes some trouble, disappears, leaving a child as the only token of herself. It is, on the surface, a primitive subject. There is little trace of an ancient culture in this figure :

> Sie kam allein aus fernen gauen,
> Ihr haus umging das volk mit grauen,
> Sie sott und buk und sagte wahr,
> Sie sang im mond mit offenem haar.[1]

She is interesting for her own sake. But she surely has in her something of the poet who comes from nowhere, wins hatred from his kind, and disappears leaving nothing but the fruit of his labours in a poem. This is a new manifestation of George's old method. The Stranger Woman is an example of something of which the poet also is an example. Behind her and him stands the strange power to create and to amaze, a

---

[1] She came from valleys far away,
Folk passed her dwelling with dismay.
She boiled and baked and prophesied,
Sang in the moon with hair untied.

power which is often not understood and yet is an indispensable element in life. In this figure there is something anti-social and unaccommodating. She does damage to ordinary human relations and breaks up families. She abandons her child when it is born. So too the poet cannot but interfere with established decencies, and when once his poem is written, it no longer belongs to him but to the world ; in a sense it no more interests him. The poem gives a special view of the poet's place and task. He is seen as something primitive and disturbing. The symbols disclose this aspect of his life.

The choice which the Angel, or George, makes from the riches of imaginative experience has the air of personal taste. In some ways it is an extension of the three worlds of *Die Bücher*, but the setting is different. Instead of Greece, the Middle Ages and the East, the division is between life and dream, between action and desire. To the first belong all the different types which make up the pattern of life as George sees it, to the second a variety of dream-laden souls. Together the two make up George's vision of life. He, who is both a man of action and a dreamer, sees other men as examples of one or the other. In his final poem he relates the two together in a single scheme. It is dream which inspires men and in the end strikes them down :

> All dies stürmt reisst und schlägt blizt und brennt
> Eh für uns spät am nacht-firmament
> Sich vereint schimmernd still licht-kleinod
> Glanz und ruhm rausch und qual traum und tod.[1]

The " light-gem " in the starry sky is the reward for the visions and defeats of life. We may recall Valéry's *Ode Secrète*, where the poet's achievements are seen as constellations. George means more than this. His vision is of all tasks in which hope is defeated and yet leaves its undying memorial. This is a heroic view of life in that it stresses glory and risk. What George values is the risk. Dream is an important part of it ; for dream inspires and impels to action. At the end of the book it is clear that George has found a clearer, more emphatic philosophy than anything that he has yet suggested.

[1] All these storm, tear and beat, burn and blast,
   Till for us in the night-sky at last,
   Forms a light-gem that still glisteneth,
   Light and fame, fire and grief, dream and death.

The view of life does not make these poems didactic. As yet George still writes out of his feelings. No doubt he wishes to instruct, and the Angel has a positive message. But the poetry is of things enjoyed and felt ; it contains no abstract imperatives. But because it has a background of conviction, of what is worth seeking and of what should be avoided, it has an austerity and even a moral beauty which are new to George's work. In *Die Bücher* he had written about the Middle Ages ; now what these had to give has been absorbed into his system. He hardly dwells on it. In *Der Jünger* (*The Disciple*) his theme is extremely simple. There is no setting, no local colour. The Disciple is the everlasting type of one who follows a celestial master :

> Ihr sprecht von wonnen die ich nicht begehre,
> In mir die liebe schlägt für meinen Herrn.
> Ihr kennt allein die süsse, ich die hehre,
> Ich lebe meinem hehren Herrn.
>
> Mehr als zu jedem werke eurer gilde
> Bin ich geschickt zum werke meines Herrn,
> Da werd ich gelten, denn mein Herr ist milde,
> Ich diene meinem milden Herrn.
>
> Ich weiss in dunkle lande führt die reise
> Wo viele starben ; doch mit meinem Herrn
> Trotz ich gefahren ; denn mein Herr ist weise.
> Ich traue meinem weisen Herrn.
>
> Und wenn er allen lohnes mich entblösste,
> Mein lohn ist in den blicken meines Herrn.
> Sind andre reicher ; ist mein Herr der grösste.
> Ich folge meinem grössten Herrn.[1]

> [1] Ye speak of joys I crave not, being faulted,
> With me all love pulsates but for my Lord.
> Ye know alone the sweet, I the exalted ;
> I live for my exalted Lord.
>
> More than for any work your guild adjureth,
> Am I sent forth to labour for my Lord,
> Thus, I'll be worthy ; for his grace endureth ;
> I ever serve my gracious Lord.
>
> I know the way leads o'er the barren prairie,
> Where many perished — yet beside my Lord
> I dare all dangers, for my Lord is wary,
> I ever trust my wary Lord.
>
> And should it be his will not to requite me,
> My solace is the vision of my Lord,
> Are others richer, he is the most mighty,
> I follow my most mighty Lord.
>   (Trs. Cyril Scott)

There is a new power in this. The deliberate repetitions, the studied simplicity, convey the Disciple's self-denying, self-effacing spirit.

With this growth in strength goes a more insistently personal note. The poet speaks with confidence for himself. He is not afraid to condemn. In *Der Verworfene* (*The Outcast*) he sketches one who is fundamentally frivolous and treats nothing seriously. He is naturally alien to George's intense earnestness, and is duly judged :

> So kamst du wol geschmückt doch nicht geheiligt
> Und ohne kranz zum grossen lebensfest.[1]

This poem is balanced by poems of personal friendship, like *Juli-Schwermut* (*July Melancholy*), addressed to Ernest Dowson, who was soon to die and in whom George saw a deep world-weariness :

> Nichts was mir je war raubt die vergänglichkeit,
> Schmachtend wie damals lieg ich in schmachtender flur
> Aus mattem munde murmelt es : wie bin ich
> Der blumen müd, der schönen blumen müd ![2]

This intimacy takes a more vivid form in *Winterwende* (*Winter Solstice*), where a friend's vision is praised in words of imaginative admiration :

> Ist von mond — von sonne dieser glanz ?
> Auf verstorbne wege von Byzanz
> Bricht er schaudernd flammt er grell
> Hain und halle macht er hell.[3]

George was now able to approach his friends and his personal problems with authority and to display his feelings directly. The circle in which he lived and which he inspired had

---

[1] So well adorned and yet unsanctified,
Without a crown, you came to life's great feast.

[2] Transience ne'er can rob me of aught that has been,
Languishing just as erewhile on the languishing field,
From languid lips a murmur comes : " How weary
Am I of flowers, of all the radiant flowers".
(Trs. Cyril Scott)

[3] From moon or from sun does this flame come ?
On dead ways of Byzantium
It breaks with menace, burns with light,
Making wood and mansion bright.

become very important to him. He saw in it the gains and the perils of the life for which he stood, and he wrote with power about them.

In *Der Teppich des Lebens* George presents an ideal, not indeed directly, but from different angles, until the parts cohere and we see the heroic goal which he sets before himself and others. This ideal is not completely integrated. It is formed of many disparate factors and does not present a single aspect. Before he published his next book the ideal had taken a living shape and made George's direction much clearer. Like the other inheritors of Symbolism he sought through poetry a great consummation, a change in the world. He wished to revivify Germany. To make his meaning clear even to himself he needed an incarnation of his ideal. The need was satisfied, and the story of it is remarkable. In Munich George met a boy of great gifts and remarkable beauty, known as Maximin. Maximin became the centre of the poet's circle and was deeply admired in it. He was regarded as the perfection of what they most honoured, the type of a new life which henceforth the world must follow and reverence. He wrote poems ; he lavished affection on those around him,— and then, after three years, in 1904 he died. That is the story seen from outside in its bare outlines. But George saw it differently, and it altered his whole life.

This episode had its personal, intensely poignant side. What Maximin's death meant to George only his intimate friends really knew. Some faint echo of his tragic grief may be seen in a letter which he wrote in June 1904 to Sabine Lepsius :

After the gathering winter in Berlin, there has been much anxiety and finality and the annihilating close. I put my trust in an inconceivably early death to guide me in the last abysses.

That was the inner, intimate loss. But George was not one to lament his doom. He was confident that Maximin's death was a call to his courage and to his faith. He transformed the transitory event into something of permanent worth, drew lessons from it, presented it as something that was after all justified in the scheme of things. The change in his feelings about it may first be seen in the foreword which he wrote to a book dedicated to the boy's memory. In this stately and elaborate obituary George has already begun to transform his experience, to see it more as an event in history than as a tragic loss of his own :

The closer we got to know him, the more he reminded us of our ideal, and we honoured the range of his original spirit and the impulses of his heroic soul just as much as their embodiment in form and action and speech. . . . We recognised something strange in him that would never belong to us and we bowed before the unintelligible lot that guided him to a goal unknown to us. . . . He needed no severance from barbarians, as we did in earlier years ; he was too pure for any contact to pollute him, too aloof for any surroundings to touch him. He bore himself with the instinctive pride of one who never recants or serves and with the inimitable dignity of one who has prayed much. His being moved even the insensible crowd of the populace ; they waited for the hour when he passed by, to contemplate him for a moment or to hear his voice.

Maximin embodied the disparate heroic ideals which George had set out in *Der Teppich des Lebens*. In him the poet saw his dreams come true. So both his short life and his sudden death took on a symbolical, apocalyptic significance. He was much more than a transitory, gifted human being. He was the precursor of a new age, the inheritor of all that was best in the past, the type of what the world was to be. He was divine. His death was not a loss but a gain. By it his godlike being was made permanent, his youth preserved in its finest flower. His short span had been enough to reveal what the ideal meant ; his death was a sacrifice which sanctified his every action. Like those whom the gods love, he had died young, and become himself a god.

In his most majestic, most elaborate book, *Der siebente Ring* (*The Seventh Ring*), 1907, George gave to the world the poetry of this remarkable experience and of the gospel which he made from it. The title and the structure of the book show a religious character. It was George's seventh book of verse, and it is composed in seven sections. This formal arrangement is deliberate and suggests connections, hard enough to appreciate, with the alleged magical or mystical character of the number seven. The book contains poems written during Maximin's lifetime and after his death, but its contents are arranged not chronologically but on a more conscious plan by which the poet advances from general themes to themes progressively more intimate, until he closes in private poems to his friends. It suggests that, starting from a general view of the world, he found its particular embodiment in Maximin and applied this to his circle. He transposes his subject to a wider stage and makes it a text on the ills of the world and their cure. But the intimate touch is still there, especially in the central sections. The subject is approached at different levels and from different angles. It has its individual as well as its cosmic significance. George is at pains to stress both. When he announces some important message for the world, his verse moves in solemn majestic rhythms ; when he speaks of his own heart and grief, he commonly expresses himself in song.

If the emotion which George felt for Maximin was love, it was like the Platonic ἔρως which begins with admiration for a beautiful person but finds its completion in activities of the spirit. In George's experience the high interests which he shared with Maximin survived the boy's death and kept their meaning because they had been embodied in him. In the poet's memory they were best and most safely preserved. In trying to make others like him George would fulfil his spiritual duty. If men had Maximin in their minds, they were less likely to falter in their allegiance to what had before his appearance been unrealised dreams. Such is the message of *Der siebente Ring*. It proclaims those powers of the spirit which had been foreshadowed in *Der Teppich des Lebens*, but with a greater confidence and pride. For now George knew what they meant in fact. He felt that his old beliefs were justified, that the hopes he had of a new Germany were not false. In Maximin he saw the fulfilment of aims in which others had failed. The great German heroes of the past had striven to break through their surroundings to dimly discerned goals, but without success. Their country remained with its haunting sense of incompleteness. But Maximin was an example of success and completeness. The spiritual life for which the poet lives seemed at last to be spreading abroad to other spheres and to have created a young man who had no sense of lack and was not touched by the drabness of his time. If such things could happen, the world must know about them and learn through them to deliver itself.

The experience, and the conclusions which George drew from it, are certainly remarkable. It is not sufficient to quote parallels from the cult of boyhood in ancient Greece. This cult, in so far as it was a cult, usually lacked the cultural content and the spiritual ambitions which George gave to his. Theognis' poems to Cyrnus hold out no hope of a reformed world ; they are concerned with a purely personal relation, its hopes and its despairs. Plato is nearer to George, but between their circumstances there is an important difference. Plato saw that the emotion of love could be transmuted and transposed to another sphere, but the basis of his thought was the cult of boyhood which was common in his time and took the place that was later held by the cult of woman. At least he conformed to contemporary habits, and his conclusions, surprising though they sometimes were, were deduced from habitual ways of thought. In George's Germany there was nothing really like this. Such cult of boyhood as existed was in the nature of things confined to a few people, and was in many cases purely esoteric. George's taste for it remains an idiosyncrasy which most of his contemporaries did not share. So when he erected his taste into a gospel, he emphasised his severance from his age. He proclaimed a salvation which must necessarily appeal only to a few. Of this he was conscious, and he had his answer. He felt that the boyhood of Germany, handsome, serious, spiritual, was the greatest and surest hope. The grown men, brought up in a materialistic age, had little to give to the future. The women were too absorbed in domestic tasks to take up the hard labours of the spirit. George could support his preference with arguments and in the person of Maximin point to an accomplished fact. Here in a living figure were realised all his ideals.

From an impartial distance George's cult of Maximin might be regarded as the peculiar illusion of a man who is so deeply imbued with the past that he sees the present in its light. Nor is this entirely untrue. George certainly owed much to the Greeks in his conception of Maximin. Like them he lived in an intimate male circle, and in this he prized with all the enthusiasm of a scholar and an aesthete qualities which are obliterated by a more ordinary life. He prized too the peculiar sense of unity which comes from the pursuit of common aims. In Maximin he found someone who understood and embodied those aims so finely that he must be of divine quality. George's circle would see nothing strange in such an admiration, and George could pursue it naturally and

with ease. His circumstances favoured his adaptation of
Greek ideas to his own life and prevented him from minding
that the experience was fundamentally esoteric. He felt that
if others could see things as he did, they would be the better
for it. Nor did he think this impossible. Just as in the Middle
Ages Germany had presented its ideal in such a masterpiece
as the Rider of Bamberg, so George seems to have felt that it
might again recognise such an ideal, and that if it did, the
gain would be great. The strength of his confidence and conviction shows how much George owed to his culture, how
strongly it shaped his life. He had found his values in a study
of the great civilisations of the past. It was only natural that
he should interpret the present through what he had learned
from them.

In *Der siebente Ring* George's poetry falls roughly into two
classes : the first meditative if not instructional, the second
lyrical. The division corresponds to a difference of subjects.
The first, seen especially in the opening section of " Zeitgedichte ", songs of the time, fourteen poems in the same
metre and of the same length and structure, describe or praise
a series of men and peoples who mean much to the poet. They
are examples of the heroic spirit at work in different times
and in different manners. They include figures so diverse
as Dante and the Hohenstaufen Emperors, Goethe, Nietzsche
and Leo XIII. Diverse as they are, they have this in common,
that they all saw beyond their times and came into conflict
with them. They are heroic because of the grandeur of their
aims and the courage with which they pursued them. And
though they come from different climes, they are all in their
ways connected with the German spirit. George was no
limited admirer of his country. He knew that in the past it
owed much to foreign lands and had a great gift for learning
from them. Therefore he praises the Romans who have left
their visible mark on Trier, the Franks who made French
civilisation and were ultimately responsible for all that it
brought to Germany, Dante who had his vision of a Christian
and Imperial Europe. He believed that the German spirit
reaches its full dimensions only when it gets life from abroad
and that this is its special gift and mission. When facts
forbade this, George felt that something was missing and
wrong. The tragic failure of Nietzsche shows how deadly
Germany may be to its most gifted sons. In the past Germany

had gained much from contact with other lands, and in return it had given them understanding and devotion. It was this side of German life which George praised and wished to vivify. With all his German qualities he was a good European. The poetry of this section is richly, even heavily laden. Unlike much contemplative verse, it is not abstract. It moves through vivid imagery and strong personal impressions. It is informed by the personality of a man who enjoyed many things in life and in art, who accumulated impressions and memories and pondered them until they became part of himself. The intellectual effort that has gone to their shaping gives them a special dignity and strength. The words are chosen with judicious care ; the slow rhythms suit the brooding mood, the charged atmosphere of sombre meditation. When George writes of Nietzsche,

> Hier sandte er auf flaches mittelland
> Und tote stadt die lezten stumpfen blitze
> Und ging aus langer nacht zur längsten nacht.[1]

not only is the judgment truly and nobly made, but every word tells. The majestic march of the verses contributes to the vision of the angry seer thundering in vain against his times and passing through madness to death. This associative power wakes more than emotions. George, like Milton, appeals to memories of the past and hints at great backgrounds. When he writes of Frederick II

> im blick
> Des Morgenlandes ungeheuren traum,
> Weisheit der Kabbala und Römerwürde
> Feste von Agrigent und Selinunt,[2]

the proper names conjure up the strange mixture of East and West at the court of " Stupor Mundi ", and the associations are carried further in the names of Agrigentum and Selinus, old Greek cities, which hint that Frederick, true pagan that he was, had amongst other affinities something essentially Hellenic. The resounding names recall the youth of the world and bring the Hohenstaufen emperor nearer to it.

---

[1] Here sent he over the flat middle-land
And dying town the last worn thunderbolts
And went from long night to the longest night.

[2] In vision of the East's enormous dream,
Cabala's wisdom, Roman dignity,
Feasts of Selinus and of Acragas.

STEFAN GEORGE

At the start of his " Zeitgedichte " the poet promises

> dass morgen
> Leicht alle schönheit kraft und grösse steigt
> Aus eines knaben stillem flötenlied.[1]

The promised song is metaphysical, a renewal of strength through the example of Maximin. It too passes into poetry, and the songs of *Der siebente Ring* show what George could do with it. At the centre of the book, in the section "Lieder", or " Songs ", he found the highest level of his lyrical gifts. In it his personal tragedy purified and strengthened his style. Before Maximin's death he often wrote in the elaborate manner favoured by the 'nineties. There is an undeniable charm in much of this, an intricate artistry which catches some of the complexities of melancholy in

> Leichte seele — so sagt ich dir — was ist dir lieben !
> Ein schatten kaum von dem was ich dir bot. .
> Dunkle seele — so sagtest du — ich muss dich lieben
> Ist auch durch dich mein schöner traum nun tot.[2]

But the very sway of the rhythm, the ingenious balance of the phrases and the artful repetitions, dull the outline. The mood reaches no clear climax and is not intended to. But in the short concentrated poems of " Lieder " there is no such indecisiveness. In the short lines and short sentences, the almost total lack of decoration and of images except of the most necessary kind, the pathetic defeated close, George truly expressed his grief. No other poems of his are so intensely personal. Two examples will show the level of his art :

> Kreuz der strasse. .
> Wir sind am end.
> Abend sank schon. .
> Dies ist das end.
> Kurzes wallen
> Wen macht es müd ?

[1]   To-morrow
All beauty, strength and greatness easily
Come from the quiet flute-song of a boy.

[2] Flighty soul — I said to thee — what means thy loving ?
Hardly of all I offered thee a shade.
Sombre soul — thus didst thou say — I needs must love thee,
Although through thee my fairest dream be dead.
                             (Trs. Cyril Scott)

Mir zu lang schon. .
Der schmerz macht müd.
Hände lockten :
Was nahmst du nicht ?
Seufzer stockten :
Vernahmst du nicht ?
Meine strasse
Du ziehst sie nicht.
Tränen fallen
Du siehst sie nicht.[1]

The misery of knowing that there is no hope of return for what has gone is wonderfully caught in these verses, where the repeated " nicht " and the economy of rhymes give an appalling sense of defeat and despair. No less striking and perhaps more moving are some other lines :

Im windes-weben
War meine frage
Nur träumerei.
Nur lächeln war
Was du gegeben.
Aus nasser nacht
Ein glanz entfacht —
Nun drängt der mai.
Nun muss ich gar
Um dein aug und haar
Alle tage
In sehnen leben.[2]

[1] Lo, the crossways. . . .
We're at the end.
Night hath fallen. . . .
This is the end.
A moment's wand'ring
Whom maketh tired ?
Too long for me though. . . .
Pain maketh tired.

Hands entreated ;
Yours neared them not ?
Sighs oppressed me ;
You heard them not ?
Here my home-way,
You go it not.
Tear-drops trickle,
You know it not.
(Trs. Cyril Scott)

[2] In the wind's weaving
All I could say
Was a dream-show.
Nought but a smile
Came from your giving.
In the wet night
A flame alight.
— May drives on now,
And now must I
For your hair and eye
Every day
Live on in grieving.

The tragic compression of the last four lines could not be bettered. In them George tears off his trappings and lets his poetry come out in naked grief.

This central experience is enclosed with poems of a different character, and when we try to judge the book as a whole, we are forced to treat it, as its author intended, as a revelation. It has an apocalyptic character, and to this many poems contribute. For such a revelation symbols are indispensable. George's subject is in its way religious and demands the usual appurtenances of religious verse. No other means are adequate to it. The uncommon nature of his subject prevented George from using any traditional body of symbols. With sound judgment, he presented the life and death of Maximin in a religious scheme whose elements, familiar from Christianity, are hardly less familiar from other revealed religions. His god is incarnate and has an earthly life, with the accepted progress of advent, miracles, presentation, suffering, ascension. He invites and gets prayers. Even when he has gone, he can make his presence felt. The poems are hardly even symbolical. We may well accept them for what they claim to be, the chapters of a divine life, the record of a revelation. Such George believed them to be, and though at times he may have idealised the reality, he still expects his version to be treated as truth. The remarkable thing is that this highly unusual gospel is undeniably impressive. George makes us feel that there is a mystery in it. In *Besuch* (*Visitation*) there is real imagination in the idea that the god may come back in twilight to some closely described familiar scene ; in *Die Verkennung* (*The Mistake*) there is truth and insight in the disciple who prays for his Lord and does not recognise him when he comes:

> Der fremde schwand . . . der jünger sank ins knie
> Mit lautem schrei . . . denn an dem himmelsglanz
> Der an der stelle blieb ward er gewahr
> Dass er von blindem schmerz und krankem hoffen
> Nicht sah : es war der Herr der kam und ging.[1]

In *Entrueckung* (*Withdrawal*) the struggles and consolations of faith are portrayed in the believer who tries to regain his lost

---

[1] The stranger vanished . . . the disciple knelt
With anguished cry. . . . For in the holy glow
That bathed the spot, he saw, what in his blind
Despair and sickly hope he had not seen
Before : it was the Lord who came and went.
(Trs. Cyril Scott)

Lord and suddenly finds himself sustained and comforted. The strength of this poetry is that for George Maximin really was a revelation, a god. His all too short stay on earth and his sudden death moved the poet to the depths of his being. He felt that he had seen something of vast significance, and this feeling passes into his verse.

Maximin embodies the triad of Spirit, Soul and Body. Each of these was manifested in him and is recorded in different poems of *Der siebente Ring*. The first inspires those poems in which his spirit is seen as revivifying the world no less than in his own sacrifice for it. The second is portrayed in types dear to George's heart like the young Templar and the heroic soldier. The third appears in many moments of physical joy and in the language of love which is often used. In Maximin George's ideals were made flesh. The experience shaped the rest of his life. Once he knew what he believed and saw it realised, he never looked back or turned to other aims. Thenceforward his imaginative and creative existence seems to have been passed in a kind of communion with the dead Maximin, a meditation of what he had been and represented. The personal results had passed into poetry. Wider aspects had been duly considered and celebrated. There remained the sterner, less poetical task of translating the ideal into fact, of driving home the lesson and the revelation. George, with complete consistency, did not shrink from this. As years passed, he saw himself more and more as a leader of thought, an inspirer and promoter of ideas and ideals. He sought to create a circle of men who should refashion Germany in fact as well as in spirit. He himself was still the poet, the Master, the man whose power over others was won and maintained through the word. But even in him there was a perceptible change. The springs of song were drying up. He wrote less, and between 1907 and his death in 1933 he published only two volumes of poetry. Nor was it only in quantity that his work suffered. Something else was passing from it : the gift for song which he had raised to such powers. The teacher was in conflict with the singer and had the better of the struggle. Even in *Der siebente Ring* the part called " Tafeln " (" Tablets ") is often curiously didactic. George deals vehement blows against matters of the day, the Russian Revolution of 1906, political parties, Berlin, the German public. In *Der Stern des Bundes* (*The Star of the Company*)

(1914) George is for the first time directly and unaffectedly didactic. The book gives rules for those who would follow his gospel. It was intended in the first place for his own inner circle, who were to be the "inner state", "der innere Staat", an example for an ideal state, and were to display in their lives and work the ideals of Maximin. For them he wrote a kind of secret book, which gave the manifestation of "Geist-Seele-Leib" in a new religion, a new state and new laws. He saw himself not indeed as a philosopher-king, for philosophy never meant anything to him, but as a poet-king who should rule over a Platonic state of wise poets. *Der Stern des Bundes* is the book for this state. It is more concise, more dogmatic, far less lyrical than anything he had yet written. The predominant form is of short unrhymed poems, and rhyme is only occasionally admitted to mark the final poem of a section. The whole has an instructional plan. The first part proclaims the need of the world for a great rejuvenation in its "Geist"; the second is concerned with its "Seele" and gives the inner emotions and relations of this perfected society; the third deals largely with its "Leib" and lays down rules of behaviour. From the great proclamations of the Introduction we are brought to rules and regulations. The whole air, the language and the structure, are poetical. But it is a kind of poetry which invites questions and is accepted with reservations and even with misgivings. George had moved far from those early days when he said that poetry must be rid of "every reasoning and wrangling with life". The poet had become in real earnest a teacher. He had forsaken his French doctrine, and in true German style come to believe that the poet is more than a master of words, that what counts is his message, his vision of a new world, his power to transform humanity.

Der Stern des Bundes raises questions about the nature of poetry, and since George must have known what he was doing, these can hardly be shirked in any discussion of the book. In the first place it is written for a select society of friends. Hitherto George had addressed the world. Like the Symbolists, he may have despised it and condemned it, but he wished to influence it and to be read by it. His occasional obscurities, his scanty punctuation and curious treatment of capital letters, perhaps indicated a contempt for the average man, but none the less he would have liked a public which could appreciate him. His work had not so far required any inside information for its understanding. It was intelligible to anyone who knew what poetry was. But in *Der Stern des Bundes* he changes his position and writes for a chosen few, for a circle of friends and disciples to whom he entrusts his mission. He is now concerned only with a choice band of initiates. This affects the character of his poetry. In many of these poems we feel that if we only knew the background better, we should appreciate the poetry more. The texts are not obscure or ambiguous, but the atmosphere in which they were born and to which they refer is hard to recapture. Without a knowledge of it we grasp only half the poet's meaning. It is of course true that much here must be seen in the light of George's earlier work, especially *Der siebente Ring*, and that there is much in Proust's saying that " les grands littérateurs n'ont jamais fait qu'une seule œuvre ". *Der Stern des Bundes* is practically unintelligible without some knowledge of Maximin and what he meant to George. But that is not the trouble. This knowledge is easily acquired, and the poet is within his rights when he demands it. A real difficulty is that even when we have this knowledge we still miss the poetry. The situations implied are often of too little significance as they are presented. There may be great backgrounds to them, but we do not know them and cannot reconstruct them. To write for a small circle is no new thing. Sappho and Pindar wrote not only for a few friends but for special occasions. Yet in them we feel no lack, no esoteric mystery. Their words hold their full value for posterity. The difference between them and George is great. We understand them because they lived in a simple age when ideas were held in common and the poet was like other men. George, unlike them, is not only intimate but esoteric. Few outside his own friends can know all that he meant or grasp the full importance of this or that situation in his poems. Commentaries hardly help, because they can only explain, while what is needed is the creation of an atmosphere, of the air in which the poetry was born and moves. Of all this George was no doubt perfectly aware. These poems were meant for a select few. Their appeal is meant only for a circle of initiates. For others there is an intervening veil which no imagination and no insight can quite pierce. George presents results, not the process by which they are reached. But for the average lover of poetry it is the process, with all its dependence on emotions and excitements, that counts. We value poetry less for its conclusions than for the experience which creates and colours them. *Der Stern des Bundes* is a book of conclusions.

Another, more familiar, question raised by *Der Stern des Bundes* concerns the didactic element in poetry. The Symbolists had turned with horror from all attempts to instruct. Nothing, in their view, was more hostile to the spirit of song. George himself had once agreed with them. But now his views had changed. He felt that he must teach. No longer was he content to leave instruction to be done indirectly through song ; he must announce truths and give orders. When he writes

Glaube

Ist kraft von blut ist kraft des schönen lebens,[1]

he does not even adorn his bare dogmatic statement. We are forced to consider it as a statement of fact, to accept or reject it. George might have defended such apophthegms by Greek precedent. All Greek poets, even Homer, have their share of gnomic sayings, and no one has thought the worse of them for it. Yet the modern dislike for such sayings is more than a fad of Edgar Allan Poe. When the French Symbolists rejected them, it was no doubt because they felt that many of Hugo's resounding judgments were neither poetry nor truth. They might point to De Musset's couplet

Les plus désespérés sont les chants les plus beaux,
Et j'en sais d'immortels qui sont de purs sanglots

and say that it is both sentimental and untrue. The poets of the nineteenth century were too fond of making statements with an air of great profundity but without any real insight. Yet there is a gnomic poetry which is still poetry. Polonius' advice to Laertes may come oddly from the cynical old courtier but it has moved many hearts. The question with George is really whether his advice succeeds as poetry. At times it does. He shows real power when he denounces the hollow pretensions of the age. But at other times he seems almost trivial in his insistence on this or that opinion or behaviour. When a poem begins

[1]

Belief

Is strength of blood, is strength of lovely life.

Die weltzeit die wir kennen schuf der geist
Der immer mann ist, ehrt das weib im stoffe . . .[1]

the tone is so unashamedly dogmatic that all poetry seems to be lacking. Or when a poem, without further ado, begins

Ein wissen gleich für alle heisst betrug.
Drei sind des wissens grade,[2]

it presents a formidable front to those who look to find delight in it.

The fact is that it is wrong to judge this poetry by aesthetic standards. It is written for a different end. George seems to have thought that for his new world he could legislate in verse because verse was the only instrument sufficiently concise and cogent for his needs. Just as the Greeks used verse for matters so different as philosophy, astronomy and zoology, so George uses it for instruction. Nor can we complain that this poetry is dry and esoteric. It is written, as he himself says, " for friends in a narrow circle ". The outer world has no claim to criticise it or even to understand it. For such a function verse may well have its uses, but it abandons its claim to be considered as poetry. What matters is the instructive result. It seems that *Der Stern des Bundes* was read by many outside the few for whom it was written, and that in the Four Years' War it had, according to the author, a special success on the battlefield. It certainly contained a message which appealed to the then youth of Germany. The author succeeded better than he had foreseen in influencing opinion. His views carried weight. In so far as he proclaimed a new order, this is intelligible enough. Soldiers must comfort themselves with the belief that they are making a better world. In George's case the gospel was in many respects presented with a strong appeal. It denied differences of birth, even of race. Its emphatic optimism could not fail to win converts. Its appeal to a natural elect, to a chosen few, was flattering to those who felt that they were of this number. Yet, when all is said, its actual message is itself esoteric. George demands that his own highly individual ideas should be accepted uncritically by a band of devoted disciples. For him they

[1] The world's time that we know was made by spirit
For ever male, honours the female substance. . . .

[2] One knowledge like for all men is called fraud.
Three are the grades of knowledge.

must give up their independence, their private tastes, their traditional beliefs. What counts is the unity of the company in its single common aim, the re-creation in the world of the ideal embodied by Maximin. What exactly this means can be known only to those who really knew Maximin or are willing to accept the poet's account of him. It is a considerable demand, yet it won adherents. The book was undeniably influential. It stood in a way for a kind of aristocratic ideal, for a well-founded culture and for certain noble qualities of heart. The mere fact that it made an appeal shows how disintegrated German life had been by the political and economic developments of the preceding fifty years. George was at least right in thinking that he would find men to listen to his message.

As George framed his ideal for practical purposes and came to see more clearly what it implied, he came also to feel the gap between it and reality, the sickness of his age and its need for a cure. In the halcyon days before 1914 he saw only a society so dead to the spirit that it needed a violent awaking. He depicted his god as denouncing the nullity of the world and turning in wrath away from it ; when everything was to be had, the soul was starved :

> Alles habend alles wissend seufzen sie :
> " Karges leben ! drang und hunger überall !
> Fülle fehlt ! " [1]

For this George had his solution. It was war. It was too late for any other cure. The sacrifice must be of blood :

> Zehntausend muss der heilige wahnsinn schlagen,
> Zehntausend muss die heilige seuche raffen,
> Zehntausende der heilige krieg.[2]

With prophetic ardour he foresaw war. He even desired it, feeling that it alone could bring the necessary change of heart and soul. This strange and sinister desire was by no means unique at the time. Before 1914 there were many who thought that war would bring a kind of redemption and restore man-

---

[1] Having all things, knowing all things, they bemoan :
" Paltry life ! distress and hunger everywhere !
Plenty fails ! "

[2] Ten thousand must the holy madness strike,
Ten thousand must the holy sickness seize,
Tens of thousands the holy war.

kind to some pristine purity and manliness. The young poets of 1914 went gaily to battle in this belief. No doubt they were impelled partly by a desire to break the bonds of a too organised life, partly too by a more primitive appetite for excitement which easily disguised itself as something nobler. Yet it is odd that George should have shared these illusions, and failed to see that the European culture which he prized so highly could only suffer irreparable damage from such a catastrophe as war. The truth seems to be that as he grew older his contempt for existing society increased and he viewed the prospect of its destruction with some complacency. His ideal had taken so strong a hold on him that it was beginning to weaken his grip on reality.

The war came, but George did not find in it what he desired. It did not even purify the German people. In *Das neue Reich* (*The New Realm*) (1928) he published some war poems which show a singular detachment except when his own friends are concerned. He saw that modern war has few heroic qualities, that in it machines are more important than men, that it fails to fulfil the high hopes placed in it. He saw the hollowness of

> Spotthafte könige mit bühnenkronen.[1]

He knew that

> Ein volk ist tot wenn seine götter tot sind.[2]

He realised that the end of the war would not be the end of its miseries, and that the worst years were still to come. Above all, he now saw that war brought destruction to his ideals, or at least postponed the possibility of their fulfilment. He had wished for war, but not for this war. His ideal hero was something more than a soldier; his fight belonged to the spirit more than to politics. But he had desired a change in the world through blood and could not rightly complain when blood was shed. What mattered most to him was his own circle. When members of this were killed, he honoured their memory with noble and touching verses. For here his heart was; here his touch was sure. His efforts to be a prophet had been answered by the grim denials and humiliations of brutal fact. In his intimate world he was safe. He seems to have felt

[1] Ridiculous monarchs with their pasteboard crowns.

[2] Dead is a people when its gods are dead.

this consciously or unconsciously. For in his last years the gap widened between the ideals which he revered and the reality which he despised. Of old he saw the world as passing between dream and death. Now his own life was to follow a similar pattern, to pursue familiar dreams and to desire something like death for what lay outside them.

The fierce satisfaction which George took in the thought of the wrath to come was revealed in his short poetical play *Der Brand des Tempels* (*The Burning of the Temple*). In this an old civilisation has fallen to a barbarian conqueror, and we might expect a lament over lost, irrecoverable beauties. But to the conqueror, who brings destruction, George gives a strange power and appeal. He is a type of something new and startling, who hates all things that have a hold on human hearts and is as hard on himself as he is on others. The temple is the last, most valued possession of the captured town, and just because it is this, the conqueror gives orders for it to be burned. The play ends with the words :

> Der tempel brennt. Ein halbes tausend-jahr
> Muss weiterrollen bis er neu crstehe.[1]

But this conqueror, this second Genghiz, is not portrayed with hostility or horror. Even his victims feel a kind of admiration for him ; his subjects serve him with unstinted and uncritical devotion. He is an embodiment of power, and he pursues power not for its own sake but for some abstract ideal which it represents. He is the absolute Puritan, the destroyer of all idols in the market-place or in the heart, the rigid judge who is moved by no mercy and no sentiment, whose only god is an unhewn stone, who looks young but is ageless in word and thought. He is a vision of the none too distant future, a prophetic forecast of the shape of men to come. Into this vision George has surely put some of his own distaste for the age in which he lived. There is a hidden pleasure in the prospect of this annihilating force at work in an ancient world.

In contrast to this sinister reality are poems of dream. Behind these lies the experience of George's life with Maximin, of the visions which once irradiated his being and to which he still held, though he knew that their realisation

[1] The temple's burning. Half a thousand years
Must roll away before it stands up new.

K

was far indeed, if not impossible. *Das Lied* (*The Song*) is a ballad of a man who has been in fairyland and comes home to be treated like an idiot. There is a painful contrast between his memories of what he has seen and the contemptuous pity which he finds on his return, when only children listen to his songs. The man is the poet who has had his visions and told them to others, only to be mocked and pitied. The poem is George's cry of failure, of sorrow that he has not been able to make others see what he himself has seen. It gives the discord between his imaginative existence and the real world about him. Yet though he knew that his dreams were perhaps only dreams, he clung to them. In *Seelied* (*Sea Song*) he tells of a beautiful child who from time to time appears to a lonely figure on the sea-shore until it is all that matters to him. It is the record of old age longing for the companionship of youth and fearing that it may be deprived of it. Over its charming scenes hangs the menace of coming loss. The child is not sure to come and the watcher waits anxiously for him. The child is hardly of this world. He has much of the brightness of a vision :

> Mit gliedern blank mit augen klar
> Kommt nun ein kind mit goldnem haar.
> Es tanzt und singt auf seiner bahn
> Und schwindet hinterm grossen kahn.[1]

Before this vision nothing else counts, least of all the comfort and securities of home. The watcher shapes his life for these moments, and without them he is empty :

> So sitz ich, wart ich auf dem strand
> Die schläfe pocht in meiner hand ;
> Was hat mein ganzer tag gefrommt
> Wenn heut das blonde kind nicht kommt.[2]

The superficially simple ballad is a record of George's life. He is the old man, Maximin the child, seen in retrospect as a type of all that the poet most admires and loves.

[1] With glowing limbs, with candid stare,
There comes a child with golden hair.
He goes his course with song and trip
And fades behind the bulky ship.

[2] So sit I, wait I, on the strand,
My temples throbbing in my hand ;
For what have passed my hours away
If the gold child comes not to-day ?

This life of memory and dream has its pathetic side when it is brought into conflict with harsh facts. But in itself it has its compensations. It is significant that the last poem of *Das neue Reich* proclaims the permanent joy which he found in the companionship of his ideal. No doubt, as certain poems suggest, he found other examples of this ideal embodied in living persons, but what counted was the ideal itself, which transcended its examples. The memory of Maximin, and devotion to the qualities which this memory sustained and unified, have in this final poem found their right expression in an ideal region of the mind. The poem honours not a personality but a perfection, and seems to be concerned as much with the whole life of the imagination as with any individual characteristics. It is the fitting conclusion to George's work :

> Du schlank und rein wie eine flamme,
> Du wie der morgen zart und licht,
> Du blühend reis vom edlen stamme,
> Du wie ein quell geheim und schlicht,
>
> Begleitest mich auf sonnigen matten,
> Umschauerst mich im abendrauch,
> Erleuchtest meinen weg im schatten,
> Du kühler wind du heisser hauch.
>
> Du bist mein wunsch und mein gedanke,
> Ich atme dich mit jeder luft,
> Ich schlürfe dich mit jedem tranke,
> Ich küsse dich mit jedem duft.
>
> Du blühend reis vom edlen stamme,
> Du wie ein quell geheim und schlicht,
> Du schlank und rein wie eine flamme,
> Du wie der morgen zart und licht.[1]

[1] You who are pure as flame and slender,
You shoot from fine strain flowering,
You like the dawn serene and tender,
You like a simple, secret spring,

My fellow through the sunlit meadows,
Thrill round me when eve darkeneth,
Lighting my path among the shadows,
You cooling wind, you fiery breath.

You are my longing and my thinking,
I breathe you in all air that is,
I sip you when my lips are drinking,
In every fragrance find your kiss.

You like the dawn serene and tender,
You like a simple, secret spring,
You who are pure as flame and slender,
You shoot from fine strain flowering.

The poem is addressed to an ideal person, yet it might almost be addressed to the poet's inspiration, to the power which informs his poetry. The living boy who was Maximin, the others who have in one way or another recalled him, are themselves but examples of a universal power, of the spirit which increases life and sustains it.

It might be wise to close consideration of George with this characteristic poem. It shows how he who began with the ideals of Symbolism and then made great efforts to translate them into life was in the end content that they should be ideals. He now saw that the changes which he had wished for the world were all but impossible and that he must content himself with creating a small select society which understood his aims and followed his example. His fate was no worse than has befallen other poets. He had his renown, his influence. He wrote up to his own high standards. Yet since he shows the great difficulties which beset any poet who wishes to extend the sphere of his authority and to impose his ideals on the multitude, we can hardly pass by the malign and ironical fate which gave to George's most sacred notions a publicity quite beyond his wishes. The National Socialists, with their peculiar gift for adopting and defiling ideas that have in their time been of real value, did not spare George. In some ways he might even be thought to have promoted and helped this perversion of a gospel. The swastika had long appeared on his books. He had introduced such phrases as " der Führer " and " Heil ". He had proclaimed the superiority of instincts to brains, of deep inherited qualities to anything imposed from without. He had preached the beauties of " Gemeinschaft " and corporate life, the heroic ideal and the right of the German to lands not his own, the inferior position of women as wives and mothers, the government of mankind by a select class. Nor were the National Socialists slow to see a possible ally in George. They offered him high honours and a position suited to Germany's chief poet. For a time he seems even to have played with the idea of compromising with them. He was old. He did not wish to be neglected, to lose his position, his influence. No doubt, like many others, he was blind to the real truth and deluded by his own phrases when they were repeated to him. But he made his decision. He rejected all the offers with contemptuous silence and left for Switzerland. He was a sick man, but a simple operation might have saved him. He refused to have it and died in December 1933 at Locarno, without having made any gesture of friendliness to these self-appointed friends. Perhaps his human record in this last year is not impeccable. But what matters is the more serious question of his poetry. We may well ask whether it really was all that the Nazis claimed it to be when they wished to win him to their side, and whether he was really a prophet of one of the most destructive movements that the world has seen.

In a chapel of the great church at Orvieto, Luca Signorelli has painted the coming of Antichrist. A figure comes down from the sky who looks like Christ and does miracles like his. The children gather to him ; the sick are healed ; the dead are raised. But he is an impostor and his miraculous works lead to angry quarrels and violent deaths. George knew the picture, and in *Der siebente Ring* he wrote a poem on " Der Widerchrist ", the Antichrist who turns water into wine and holds converse with the dead. The figure is no doubt a symbol for all impostors and imitations and shows what disaster they cause. George's own feelings about the type are emphatic. He shows the unholy power that it has over men and denounces their devilish joy :

> Ihr jauchzet, entzückt von dem teuflischen schein,
> Verprasset was blieb von dem früherem seim
> Und fühlt erst die not vor dem ende.

> Dann hängt ihr die zunge am trocknenden trog,
> Irrt ratlos wie vieh durch den brennenden hof. .
> Und schrecklich erschallt die posaune.[1]

George's vision of Antichrist may be applied to his own experience in 1933. The high and holy things which had meant so much to him were flung about in propaganda by men who had no care for their real meaning. They stole his vocabulary and his ideas for ends which were not his. He had dreamed of a new chivalry of the spirit ; they created a nation of cut-throats. He believed in the leadership of a few select

[1] You clamour, enticed by the devilish show,
Lay waste what remains of the sap from the spring
And feel your need first when the end comes.

Then you hang out your tongues on the emptying trough,
Stray like herds without aim thro' the courtyard in flames;
And fearfully rings out the trumpet.

souls ; they demanded servile obedience to a gross image of themselves. He wished Germany to hold an honoured place in a Europe which it loved and understood ; they saw nothing but opportunities for loot and bloodshed. Even his less attractive ideas, his exclusiveness and intolerance, had their positive side ; they were part of his desire to create a male society conscious of its responsibilities. The reality was far from George's ideal. All good things can be made to serve base ends ; all fine phrases can be twisted to cover what does not belong to them. False gods may win because they are like the true ; Antichrist has many of the marks of Christ. But the end is disaster. The destruction which George, not altogether unwillingly, foretold, came, but not in his form or in the way that he wished. It was his temple that the conqueror destroyed.

And yet, though he would have hated the idea and would never have admitted it, it is surely true that when George tried to remake the world through poetry, the undertaking was full of menace even for the things that he most valued. By imposing his imperious will and forcing his special notions on others, he denied the independence which is the lifeblood of all true art. Not one of his followers was comparable to him as a poet. His poetical achievement was his own ; it could not be adopted by others. What was dangerous for art, was still more dangerous for life. The European tradition which he honoured and made the centre of his system has survived through the variety of the forces at work in it. To reduce these to a single scheme and to exclude anything that seems alien is to strike at the life of this tradition, to frustrate possibilities of growth, to turn a creative force into a dead dogma. The joy of living which creates the arts is infinitely removed from the desire to make everyone conform to a pattern. George believed that he was giving life to the sick. In his own circle this was no doubt true. But in the wider public reached by his books his extremely special view of life was bound to restrict and discourage many excellent activities. He asked for obedience and devotion from a people all too ready to give them. The result was that he aggravated a deep disease in the German people. He is hardly to be blamed. His motives were excellent. But he was a poet who lived among visions, and when he gave these to men, they took on strange and dangerous forms. George's destiny illustrates

with peculiar poignancy the place of the poet in the modern
world. He wished to take his place in life, to have a great
influence over it, to bridge the gulf between art and reality.
But the art which was in its own place and within its own
limits so noble and distinguished was not the medicine to heal
his age.

V

ALEXANDER BLOK

1880–1921

In the hundred and fifty years of its existence Russian literature has responded with extraordinary effect to impulses from abroad. Some of its most inspired works owed their first beginnings to foreign models. Just as Tolstoy was fired to write *War and Peace* by Stendhal's *La Chartreuse de Parme* and, even more paradoxically, Dostoyevsky found the form of his novels in Dickens, so Russian poets have often begun by imitating French and English models. Krylov's Fables, which have some claim to be the first work of modern Russian poetry, started by being a translation of La Fontaine ; the flawless craftsmanship of Pushkin and Lermontov derived its romantic air and some of its verse-forms from the slap-dash poetry of Byron. In most cases the Russian imitators have surpassed their originals in power and quality. In almost every case they have created something quite new. So strong is the taste for the arts in Russia that any writer who is worth the name has often a higher standard of craftsmanship and a greater emotional range than his Western models. He improves his borrowed form and gives to it an intensity of emotion which transforms its character. If he adopts a new theory of art, he is not afraid to pursue it to its limits. But because foreign models have meant so much to Russian writers, the progress of their poetry has been spasmodic and intermittent. There have been periods when prose has been in the ascendant and poetry has fallen almost into disuse. This was certainly the case in the middle years of the nineteenth century, when the literary stage was dominated by the great novelists. It was again the case at the end of the century, when a slackening of official control produced a great activity in the short story and the drama, forms in which ideas could be presented to a wide public. This prose was realistic and critical, the counterpart of the realistic novel in Western Europe. It answered some needs in the Russian soul, but not all. The desire for poetry was unsatisfied. In the ordinary process of reaction poetry came again to the front. This time its first impulse came from France and from the Symbolists.

The new poets proclaimed that they were Symbolists and, true to their country's character, gave a whole-hearted devotion to what they believed to be a new kind of poetry. The French doctrine appealed to them for several reasons. It proclaimed high artistic ideals at a time when Russian poetry had sunk to a low level, and those who had hopes for it welcomed the positive message. It disclaimed any connection with politics, and these poets were at first eminently un-political. Its mystical character appealed to a people which had always used the language and symbols of the religious life and saw nothing very unusual in prophets and holy men. In its first years Russian Symbolism was connected with the names of Constantin Balmont and Valery Bryusov. They fought the first battles, earned the first abuse and the first praise. They conformed to good European models, quoted the right texts from Baudelaire and Verlaine and were well acquainted with Poe. They made much of Goethe's lines :

> Alles Vergängliche
> Ist nur ein Gleichnis.[1]

Their verse had a new richness and a new music. They were fully conscious of what was owed to the Word. Balmont expressed his mysterious hopes for the Russian language as he wrote it :

> I,— a rending asunder,
> I, a sporting of thunder,
> I, a stream finely-spun,
> I, for all and for none.[2]

Bryusov saw that Symbolism was a subjective view of art and said, " Every secret is in us, every darkness and dawn ". His friend Fedor Sologub went even further, " I am the god of a secret world. The whole world is in my visions alone." It is clear that with such beginnings Russian Symbolism made no reservations. It was prepared from the start to make great claims for itself. It undoubtedly did good work. It rid Russian poetry of much sentimental matter. It turned atten-

---

[1] Everything transitory
    Is but a likeness.

[2] Trs. P. Selver.

tion to technique, to expressiveness, to the music of words. But its final performance would have been only of secondary value if it had not inspired a man of far greater genius than Balmont or Bryusov. Its chief claim is that it gave a doctrine and a direction to Alexander Blok.

Blok served hardly any apprenticeship in poetry. His early verses are astonishingly mature, and an onlooker might have thought that here was an exquisite and gifted poet who had done at twenty-three what he would probably spend his life in repeating. Born in 1880, by 1904 Blok had given Symbolism a new character. He was the centre of a circle which was interested in much more than mere poetry. In 1901 and 1902 Blok was the subject of a remarkable experience. He lived in spiritual association with a Beautiful Lady. He had learned of her from the mystical philosopher Vladimir Solovyev (1853–1900), who in the intervals of writing comic verse had moments of mystical ecstasy, of intimate communion with the Divine Wisdom. After studying her in the reading-room of the British Museum he had a vision of her in the desert near Cairo. He was a strict Orthodox Christian and believed that she was a manifestation of God, though his irrepressible humour could not be prevented from bursting into his accounts of her. This Sophia or Divine Wisdom was the object of Blok's devotion. Beginning as an undefined " She ", she becomes " the Queen of Purity ", " the Beautiful Lady ", " the Mysterious Virgin ". But Blok's feelings towards her are of a curiously personal kind. When he married the daughter of the chemist Mendeleyev, it happened that her name was Lyubov, the Russian for " Love ", and the event was regarded as a kind of mystical union in which the poet was united to an incarnation of his vision. · His friend Andrey Bely treated the whole thing as of the greatest importance. Blok's poetry, in his eyes, was the record of something vastly more exciting, a religious experience full of portentous promise.

Blok's poetry of these years, his *Verses about the Beautiful Lady*, must be seen against this background. They are undeniably mystical and have even an Orthodox Christian air. They are poems of prayer, of meditation, of religious joy. The object of his devotions is, it is true, addressed in the language of love but of love so deeply respectful and devoted that it can hardly be intended for a human being. It has some parallel in Dante's cult of Beatrice, but is more formless, more instinctive, more emotional. Beatrice symbolises much that Dante honoured ; the Beautiful Lady exists almost on the edge of consciousness, and is hardly even a vision. For the poet she absorbed his being and filled his verse. In it there are no clear outlines. All is mist and solitude, but in this vague world the poet waits anxiously for her, hears at dawn or sunset her footsteps in the infinite sky, feels her withdrawal into vast orbits of space, shuts his eyes or cries to her, hoping that she will answer him. There is no direct revelation, no contact. The poet hovers in rapt expectation on the brink of some unimaginable event. This is the poetry of a young man who concentrates all his thoughts and feelings on a single experience, a single hope.

For an experience of this kind the method of the Symbolists was admirably suited. Everything that happens must be stated in metaphor and symbol ; all that matters is the subtle recreation of a mood, an atmosphere. Put into prose the poems mean little, and they resist attempts at translation. Their effect is almost purely magical. They create a feeling of an intimate and mysterious relation which cannot fully be understood. Even natural facts like the coming of spring become in them part of a ritual, and the language of devout love, at times remarkably personal, is never addressed to a living person. Nothing can be " plus vague et plus soluble dans l'air " than this poetry. It satisfies all Verlaine's desires for pure art. It is naturally praised for this aesthetic beauty, for being almost as free of meaning as music. By the mysterious quality of his verse, by his symbols adapted to this middle state between dream and waking, by his cadences and choice of words for their expressive subtlety, Blok re-creates in his readers the indefinite emotions which he had for the Beautiful Lady. Valéry has said that a poet's task is simply to transfer to another his own state. That is what Blok does. Through his rhythms and the power of his words he conveys his own unique, extremely private state.

For Blok and his friends the Beautiful Lady was not a poetic fancy but a real fact. She became almost a cult and aroused incalculable expectations. For Bely and for others she was a manifestation of divine Wisdom and Love, the Eternal Feminine that exists in God. The earlier Symbolists had quoted Goethe as saying that everything transitory is but a simile ; Blok's disciples went on to quote

Das Ewig-Weibliche
Zieht uns hinan.[1]

They felt that an experience of this kind could not be complete in itself, that it pointed forward to something of cosmic significance. Bely records how the circle trusted in the vision as a direct manifestation of God and waited for some overpowering revelation to come. It never came. While they were still waiting, the experience ceased. Blok had already begun to write poems about his fear that the Beautiful Lady would desert him, and before his volume of poems about her was published, in 1905, he found himself emptied of his ecstasies and confronted by disciples who complained that they had been betrayed. The end of this extraordinary marvel was a turning-point in Blok's life and poetry. He had to make a fresh start, haunted by the gnawing conviction that he had been tricked, that he had failed in a task which had absorbed his whole being. The disillusionment was deeply embittering and made him a far less happy man. But out of the conflict with himself he began to make a new kind of poetry. He was too deeply accustomed to his other world to bring all his thoughts at once to earth. Indeed he never lost his old transcendentalism. But because his attention was now turned to reality, because he knew the bitterness of defeat, the gain for his poetry was inestimable. He had been subtle and delicate ; he became powerful and profound.

The contrast between vision and reality determined much of Blok's later poetry. By nature and circumstance he had been accustomed to looking for something real behind what he saw, for hidden mysteries and inner meanings. He had believed in ideal love and purity, in heroic devotion and self-sacrifice. He found himself confronted by facts which did not conform to his dreams, by ugliness and discord which he had to accept, by a disorder which was the antithesis of the old divine order which had meant so much to him. He turned from vision to ironical realism. His second volume began with the words

Gone to the meadows, you will not return

and was his farewell to the Beautiful Lady. He felt humili-

[1] Eternal womanhood
Draws us on high.

ated. He, who had assumed heroic airs, was now a " poor knight " with a cardboard helmet and a wooden sword. He found substitutes for her, but they were not entirely satisfactory. In one of his most famous poems, *The Stranger* (1906), he paints a realistic scene of a pleasure resort near Petersburg. Here he sees a woman, entirely modern and fashionable in her clothing. He does not know if she is real, is fascinated by her, seems to look through a dark veil and see an enchanted horizon. He feels that he has a unique treasure, and that he alone holds the key. The vision certainly means much to the poet, despite the worldly setting and despite his own final admission that " Truth is in wine ". The poem gives the contrast between his dream and the reality which he was beginning to know. But it is noteworthy that the dream is what really counts.

Blok's first reactions to his loss of the Beautiful Lady may be seen in his first lyrical plays. His natural gift for the drama was extraordinary. With no apparent preparation he created his own kind of play, intensely poetical and yet full of wit and irony. His dramatic world makes no claim to be realistic. Its characters are not tied down by the ordinary rules of behaviour or even of the physical universe. But the effect is brilliant, so brilliant indeed that we may not at first see the cruel spirit which informs the plays. In *The Puppet Show* (1907) Blok produced a comedy of the old pantomimic kind with Pierrot, Harlequin and Columbine. Under its gay appearance it is a satire on Blok's mystical experiences and the mystical hopes of his friends. His Harlequin and his Pierrot, the one gay and the other sad, are both equally absurd. They, and the inarticulate Mystics with them, await the arrival of a Well Beloved. She comes and is Death. She becomes a young girl, and Harlequin takes her off, only to find that she is a cardboard doll. The whole great expectation is thus satirised and made absurd. Even the sky into which Harlequin throws himself in a splendid moment is only a piece of painted paper that the clown takes out of his head. At intervals the author appears on the stage and makes disparaging remarks. Despite its absurdity *The Puppet Show* is the reflection of Blok's disillusion. What once meant so much to him, now means nothing. He can make fun of it and show how absurd it is. But it is full of hidden bitterness, and it is not surprising that Blok's friends were horrified at it and regarded it as a betrayal of their ideals.

The Stranger (1906) is a kind of expansion of the poem with the same name. It too is double-edged. Under its dreamy and romantic air it hides a sharp satire and irony. The Stranger Woman is the object of the poet's ideal love, a star fallen from heaven. The laugh is not against her but against the poet, who begins by being thrown out of a bar for being drunk, then, as he is being dragged along by two policemen, sees the Stranger and does not recognise her, though he is in love with her. Later, he sees her again in a drawing-room, seems to recognise her and yet cannot. Unrecognised, she disappears, and the star, whose fall has caused much anxiety to an Astronomer, again shines in the sky. The Stranger remains remote and beautiful, but the human society which she meets is indeed pitiful. Blok makes his characters show the futility of their lives by the banality of their conversation, their stupid views about progress, peace, happiness, comfort. The conversation in the drawing-room has a sinister resemblance to that in the bar. The sodden poet is a pathetic and even revolting figure ; the young man who goes off with the Stranger and promises to teach her of earthly love is simply vulgar ; even the Astronomer, who cannot understand why a star is missing from the sky, is absurd. The whole play looks like farce and can be enjoyed as such. In it Blok was able to surmount some of his feeling of emptiness, to find his distance from something which had meant a great deal to him. Unable to forget his loss, he turned it to mockery.

The irony of his plays had helped to assuage Blok's particular grievance about being tricked. In his lyrical poetry he still kept much of his old visionary self and Symbolist methods. Moving between contrasts of dream and reality he saw that he must still use symbols for what was still visionary, if not mystical, verse. But now he used them not for a single metaphysical scheme but because they conveyed his complex, often irrational states of mind. He still saw reality through a haze of imagination. He wrote charming poems about the Neva Delta, a land of mist and fog, of endless marshy plains where everything fades from sight and the division is imperceptible between life and mirage. This was his home, his own place. He felt at ease in its ambiguous air, its half-tones and half-lights, its strangeness and its mystery. This atmosphere and this mood affected much of his verse. He wrote about his feelings through imagery and transposed them into imaginary scenes. When, for instance, he felt that his life had taken a new direction, he wrote :

> Life, our bark, has stranded
>   On a shoal profound.
> High the shouts of labourers
>   Far away resound.
> Over the blank river
>   Drift alarms and song.
> See, and Someone enters,
>   Grey of coat, and strong,
> Shifts the timbered rudder,
>   Lets the sail go free ;
> Breasting at the boat-hook,
>   Pushes off to sea ?
> — Quietly the crimson
>   Poop wears round at last ;
> Look, the motley houses
>   Now have flitted past !
> Far away, they're floating
>   Gaily ; yet, think I,
> Us they ne'er shall carry
>   With them as they fly.[1]

This is not an allegory, though it looks like one. The essential facts are in the poet's mind ; the important figure who intervenes to save him is not a person nor an abstraction but a power in himself. The houses that seem to float past are his old life, and what counts is his sense of deliverance. The method is quite simple. It relies for its main effect on its verbal harmonies and its sense of mystery. In it Blok has not attained to his full powers. But he shows in what direction he is moving.

With his mystical temperament Blok came more and more to find symbolical importance in things and to interpret ordinary happenings as instances of mysterious divine laws, and developed his Symbolism in new ways. He sees, for instance, a woman growing old in her hut after her daughter has died, sitting and sewing with needle and thread. The scene is perfectly simple, but in it Blok finds an ulterior meaning. The thread is associated with the thread of life, and through this the old woman is a symbol of the cosmic process which eternally fashions new shapes. This method could be

[1] Trs. Oliver Elton.

extended, and in *Son and Mother* Blok uses it to great effect. The Son leaves his Mother for a glorious life, is persecuted and wounded and comes home to die. The myth stands for the poet who leaves his home for great adventures, suffers and fails and finds that in the end his only peace is at home. The poem is symbolical in intention and detail. There is confidence and glory in the Son's departure :

> Songs may his lonely mother sing ;
> Golden happiness she knows.
> There is joy in suffering,
> If to high renown he goes.
>
> In panoply that blinds the eyes,
> Through mist, they say, the Son will go ;
> His soul with dwellers in the skies,
> With Mother Earth his heart below.
>
> To-morrow morn the cocks will call
> And night flee frightened in her track :
> The hunting-horn, when dawn-mists fall,
> Sounds raucously behind his back.

Then his enemies attack the Son, and his Mother sees them hit him with their arrows. To him this is a deliverance :

> There blows a purifying breath
> Of wind from heaven's azure air.
> The Son throws down his sword of death
> And takes the helmet off his hair.
>
> Outstreaming from his stricken breast
> Flow blood and fiery songs of praise :
> Hail, distance, who deliverest,
> From the night's dark and misty ways !

The Son returns to die, and in his death the Mother knows nothing but joy. This is the poet's destiny, and he welcomes it. The symbolical story is his own. It tells of his romantic dreams, his sufferings and his final peace.

By 1909 Blok's new manner was complete. His whole style had changed. Diffuseness and vagueness have given place to a hard outline, an economy of effects and a boldness of imagery unique in Russian verse. The varied rhythms of his earlier verse are succeeded by more regular and more resonant forms. Blok now says in four lines what before took eight, and the concentration is a great gain. There is now little place for rhetoric or the lesser emotions. All is clear, grand, direct and powerful. Blok's mastery of his material may be seen in his *Ravenna* (1909), which has no profound personal note and is indeed a by-product of travel :

> Interred in ages past thou keepest
> All frail and momentary things,
> And like a child, Ravenna, sleepest
> Beneath Eternity's drowsed wings.
>
> No slaves, with their mosaics loaded,
> Now pass the Roman gate ; and all
> The gilding burns away, corroded,
> On the basilica's cold wall.
>
> The rude sepulchral arches weather
> Beneath the ooze's lingering kiss ;
> O'er coffined queen and monk together
> For ever creeps the verdigris.
>
> Dumb are the burial-halls, and shady
> And chill their doors, lest Galla rise.
> The very stones, that sainted Lady
> Would calcine with her sombre eyes.
>
> Forgot are wars, wiped out for ever
> Their trail of blood, their harms, their rage.
> Placidia, wake not ! chant thou never
> The passions of a vanished age !
>
> Far out the sea has ebbed ; a riot
> Of roses clasps the wall, in bloom ;
> The storms of life must not disquiet
> Theodoric, dreaming in his tomb.
>
> The people, and the homes they sat in,
> The vine-hung wastes are graves. Alone
> The lettered bronze, the sovereign Latin,
> Rings like a trumpet on the stone ;
>
> And only the Ravenna lasses
> With mute fixed looks, forbear to hide
> A rare, a shy regret that passes
> For that still unreturning tide.
>
> Sole, nightly o'er those valleys bending,
> The wraith of Dante aquiline
> Counts on the future, to me sending
> His song of the New Life divine.[1]

Ravenna, secluded in its remote marshes with its memories of ancient splendours, its tombs of Galla Placidia, Theodoric

---

[1] Trs. Oliver Elton.

and Dante, lives in this poem. The atmosphere of peace and decay, of retiring sea and rising ooze, proclaims to Blok its death. But at the same time in the tomb of Dante with its proud epitaph he sees a message of hope in the endurance of poetry and of a new life for himself.

Blok had found himself as a poet. His growth in power went with an improvement in technique. He spoke more directly and more effectively than before. He who had known the high serenity of vision was now the prey of conflicting and violent emotions over which he had little control. Like many Russians of his time and class, he followed his emotions without plan or purpose, and since he did not see where he was going and still lacked any ideal to unify his life, he often felt that he was wasting himself in fruitless effort. From this his only refuge was poetry. To it, with an extraordinary vitality, he devoted himself. He wrote straight out of his emotions, and, being more emotional than most men of his own or most other times, he covered a remarkable range. What he felt, he transposed into song so powerful and so direct that it is unique in this century. This poetry is entirely personal. Blok was not prevented by shyness or irony from writing in the first person about himself. In many of his poems there is a deep gloom, the result of his disillusionment. He tries by various means to get away from it, only to find himself back where he started. In his *Dance of Death* he sees himself as a corpse come back from the grave to mix among the living. He goes through the common round of busy life and pleasure. The clamour hides the rattling of his bones, until when he addresses a beautiful woman, she hears the uncanny noise in her ears. This is his symbol for his sense of incompleteness, of acting a macabre part in life, of not being really alive. In the second part of this poem his despair is stated with extreme simplicity and shows the concentration of his art:

> Night, a street, a lamp, a chemist-shop,
> A meaningless and dull world.
> Live another quarter of a century —
> All will be the same. There is no way out.
>
> Die — you will begin afresh,
> And all will be repeated as of old.
> Night, the canal's frozen ripple,
> The chemist-shop, the street, the lamp.[1]

[1] The original is rhymed.

What strike here are not only the thought and the repetition which drives it home but the remarkable aptness of the imagery. The Symbolist, cut off from his ideal world, still knows that poetry lives by individual things and that despair becomes more forceful when it is presented in this extremely concrete way. The scene is an ordinary scene on a dark night in a northern winter, but it has the very drabness and squalor of the mood which Blok wishes to present. His despair may be that of the poet whose task is so exacting that he feels empty and hopeless. But nothing is said of the causes. What matter are the mood and its moment. They make everything else irrelevant.

Blok found various ways of escape from this numbing gloom. His powerful temperament swept him into most of the excitements known to the human soul, and much of this passed directly into poetry. He had a gift of seeing only one thing at a time and concentrating his powers on it. He is usually economical of imagery, but when his images come, nothing can withstand them. The brilliant pictures which he introduces lift the passions into the realm of pure art since they give exactly the right emotional note. Through them the poem finds its individuality, takes it readers by storm and makes them catch the poet's intonation. He places some compelling, concrete image as the keystone of a poem and makes it co-ordinate the lines and carry their weight. It contains what is most important and subdues the details to the unity of the main design. In one splendid poem Blok proclaims his joy at being free of his passions and can hardly remember the names of his old loves. Then he ends with a vision of himself on some snowy cliff from which he sends down an avalanche into the valleys where once he loved and kissed. In another poem when he wishes to show the impenetrable barrier between himself and a southern girl who loves him, he says that she is like a dream piercing the snowstorm of his life. Such images make the poems which contain them. They are usually preceded by a powerful and direct statement of his feelings, and they show by contrast how vivid and exciting his experience is.

No less remarkable than the power of presentation is the great range of subject, the endless variety of these poems. In his poems of love Blok has struck more chords than any writer of our time. What Yeats has done in depth and intensity, Blok has done in variety and range. No doubt he was helped by his lack of false shame and of other civilising qualities inimical to genius. If we allow him every advantage in his circumstances, remembering that he lived in a society singularly free and candid, his performance is still astonishing, because men seldom taste so many possibilities of passion without losing much of their personality in the process. In some ways Blok recalls Verlaine who equally had no reticence, but the resemblance is superficial. Whatever Blok touches, he treats with intensity and power. He has none of Verlaine's air of indiscretion or love of being naughty. At one extreme his love-poems move in a region of pure spirit. His old idealism asserts itself and he sees his love coming as an angel-shape when the scent of mint is in the air. At the other extreme are his poems of guilt, when he explores the dark places of lust, discord and degradation. In *Humiliation* he describes a scene in a brothel. The details are extremely realistic, — the shoddy, pretentious furniture, the mixed company of merchant, cardsharper, student and officer, the girl whom he knows that he does not love. The poem is entirely true to life and contains no word of condemnation or complaint, but it is deeply moving. The poet's discovery that the whole thing is false is portrayed so naturally and directly that any kind of comment from him would strike a wrong note.

Like most Russians, Blok knew well the meaning of shame and guilt. No doubt it did not prevent him from doing certain things, but if he did them, he was powerfully aware that they were wrong and that he would regret them. In *The Steps of the Commander* (1912) he gives his own version of a famous story. The Commander is the Commendatore of Mozart's *Don Giovanni* and of Pushkin's *The Stone Guest*. The setting is that of Don Juan's last night with Donna Anna, the night of his death. But the whole poem turns on the subject of retaliation. Every action seems to be caught in a fatal series which leads to only one end. The verse stresses this by its emphatic repetitions. The end comes when the Commander enters and asks Don Juan if he is ready for him :

> To the cruel question comes no answer,
>   Comes no answer. Voices fail.
> Dread is the rich bedroom at the dawn-hour ;
>   Servants slumber, night is pale.

At the dawn-hour it is strange and chilly,
At the dawn-hour night's thick veil.
Queen of Light ! where are you, Donna Anna,
Anna, Anna ? Voices fail.
Only in the cruel mist of morning
Hours resound with their last breath.
" Donna Anna rises at your death-hour,
Anna rises at your hour of death."

This is Blok's version of the story as he knows it from his own experience. The sense of doom which it presents is the reflection of guilt well known and sharply felt. The mysterious Commander who comes in from the night " like an owl " is the emblem of doom. The scene which he finds is of lust and cruelty, and the end comes with an inevitable, relentless march.

In this poetry there is often a variety of content, a movement from one mood to another, especially when Blok indulges the pleasures of memory and surveys in retrospect what has happened. His strong undeceived intellect did not shrink from contrasting the promise of a great occasion with its actual end. He can convey both the illusion which was once his, and his later knowledge of its falsity. Such a contrast need not imply any great hope or disaster. It can make a simple poem of sentiment :

Here in the dusk, as winter fled,
Were she and I, — no soul beside.
" Stay, let us watch the moon," she said,
" Into the rushes plunge and hide."
But, as a light air floated past,
Rustled the whispering reeds, and went,
Some blue transparent film it sent
Of ice ; her spirit was overcast. . . .
She's gone ; no soul is here beside.
" Tra-la ! " so hum I, pacing fast.
Only the moon and reeds at last,
And bitter almond-scent, abide.[1]

This is an unembellished record of fact. The tone is kept quiet, as suits a not very important occasion. But it is undeniably true to life. The occasion had its interest, and the poet preserves it. Deeper and more characteristic is another poem in which memory plays another, more poignant part :

[1] Trs. Oliver Elton.

What long-forgotten gleam is this ?
    An instant through the violinning
    I catch a different strain beginning !
That low deep voice of hers it is,

— Of her, my friend of old, replying
    To my first love, and I recall
    It always on the days when fall
The snowstorms, blusterously flying ;

When traceless melts the past, and when
    'Tis only alien passions tell me,
    Tell me a little, now and then,
Of happiness that once befell me.[1]

At such times he could recollect emotion almost in tranquillity, but not quite. The snowstorms outside are the image of the torment that once was his and is still liable to return.

The same extremes of happy vision and dark gloom are to be seen in Blok's other poetry. He was capable both of losing himself in a rapturous vision and of being crushed by cosmic despair. For each kind he found an appropriate style. The first called for his decorative gift, his use of the senses, the second for grand imagery of prophetic import. He knew what happiness was, especially in his imaginative life, and at such times he doubted the reality of the world about him. He could write in a mood of pure fancy :

Pipes on the bridge struck up to play ;
Flowers tipt the apple-spray ;
And one green star, aloft, away,
Uplifted by an angel, lay.
Miraculous, on the bridge to-day
To look into the deeps that stay
Aloft, so far away !

The pipe sings loud, the star climbs high,
(Now, shepherd, homeward ply !)
Beneath the bridge the wave sings by :—
" Ah, look, how fast the waters go !
(Forget for ever all thy care)
Thou never saw'st so deep a flow,
So lucid, anywhere. . . .
Or listened'st to such deeps below
Of silence, anywhere. . . .

Ah, look how fast the waters go ;
When didst thou dream it ? Dost thou know ? "[2]

[1] Trs. Oliver Elton.   [2] Trs. Oliver Elton.

The poem looks almost slight, so well sustained is its mood. But it has its own grandeur. The poet sees himself between the deep skies and the deep waters and enjoys a moment of almost unreal happiness. The mystery somehow comforts him. He is in harmony with nature and does not know nor very much care whether this is an illusion or the truth. It is enough that he feels it.

At other times Blok looked out from his own depths onto the world and foresaw some fearful disaster ahead, far worse than anything he had suffered himself. At such moments he took on the full stature of a prophet who neither warns nor denounces but pities the victims of a cosmic disorder. In *A Voice from the Chorus* he warns his friends of the dark future that lies before them :

> We weep, how often, I and you
> Over our lives' poor pitiful ways,
> But if, my friends, we only knew
> The cold and gloom of coming days !

> To-day a dear one's hand you press,
> You played with her and smiled ;
> You weep to find untruthfulness
> Or in your hand a knife caress,
>   Poor child, poor child !

> There is no end of craft or lies :
> No sign of death appears.
> A blacker light will blind the eyes,
> And madder planets sweep the skies
>   For years, for years !

> The last age shall be worst of all,
>   And you and I shall see
> The sky wrapped in a guilty pall ;
> Laughter on lips shall freeze and fall, —
>   Anguish of Not-to-be . . .

> You wait for spring, my child, but none
> Shall greet your eyes.
> To heaven you call out for the sun —
> No sun shall rise.
> You cry, but crying, like a stone,
> Falls down and dies.

> Be happy with your lives and ways, —
> Stiller than water, low as grass.
> Oh if we knew what comes to pass,
> The cold and gloom of coming days !

When he wrote these lines Blok was not turning his own defeats into a vision of universal disaster. This was his authentic insight into the future, his interpretation of the limited life, with its dramatised emotions and petty pretences, which he saw around him. Nothing could be farther from George's stern demand for a purification of the world through blood. The fearful chaos which Blok sees in the universe is made clearer by his tragic vision of life.

Pity and tenderness, pity for a generation doomed to disaster, tenderness for those who cannot defend themselves against the blows of chance, these are outstanding qualities of Blok's poetry when he wrote in a prophetic vein. Abandoned by his dreams, he wrote from the excitements of his varied life and forgot his own disappointments in the sorrows of others. He looked on himself with dispassionate eyes. His poetry records his tempests and torments, but it is controlled by an intelligence singularly candid and free from prepossession. We feel no suspicion that he is ever dramatising himself in the cause of literature or adding anything for effect to the pure originating emotion. In his high creative moments he possessed a vision so vivid that he can call up almost any scene and present it to the inner eye. He often makes his point by some specially appropriate picture and sums up in it exactly what he feels. His imagination moved naturally in such scenes. Other poets, for instance, have wondered how death will come to them ; Blok too considers it in a series of short sketches :

> Some night of Easter by the Neva,
> In wind and ice and snowstorm, shall
> Some beggar-woman with her crutches
> Move my still body where I fall ?
>
> Or in the countryside I love so,
> When the gray autumn rustles round,
> In rain and mist shall the young vultures
> Devour my body on the ground ?
>
> Or in an hour of starless anguish,
> Inside some room's four walls, shall I
> Submit to iron fate's compulsion
> And lie down on white sheets to die ?

Then, after he has considered the possibilities and wondered

how much memory will be left to him after death, Blok
suddenly announces his faith that something will survive :

> But I believe — not past pursuing
> Goes all I loved with such desire,
> All our beggared life's poor trembling,
> Our unintelligible fire !

The careful examination of the future, and the different forms
that it may take, are brought together and fused in this final
declaration of trust. When it begins, the poem does not seem
likely to take any firm shape ; then suddenly at the end it is
seen to be completely dominated and held by the central
formative idea.

In these strong, straightforward poems Blok's qualities
have passed outside his own time and he writes, as great poets
have written, of fundamental things in masterful words. If
he had always written like this, we might doubt if he had ever
learned more from Symbolism than a high standard of craftsmanship and a belief in the importance of his own feelings.
He could have learned as much from his own countrymen
Pushkin and Lermontov. But though he had been brought
to earth and though he had made his style more direct and
more forcible every year, yet fundamentally, despite his early
crisis and the despair which it induced in him, Blok always
kept something of his old visionary self. He was not one of
the poets in whom the capacity for immediate expression fails
and must be replaced by laborious effort. He remained
indubitably inspired. His experience of poetical creation was
always remarkable and in a sense outside himself, certainly
outside his full control. He was conscious of this and greatly
excited by it. The process by which he came to write became
a subject for his poetry. In *To the Muse* he describes what a
pain and cost it is to him. The Muse may be marvellous, but
she is also infernal. It is she who drives him to find song
in dark places and forbidden delights, who seems to bring
a message of ruin and to enjoy humiliating him, who gives a
fatal consolation in treading down holy places and plants an
insane pleasure in the heart. The suffering that she brings is
wormwood. This is one side of the picture. Blok's temperament drove him through many humiliations and sufferings.
In these he found subjects for his poetry. Therefore he saw
his lot as accursed. But for this he received an incalculable

reward. In *Demon* he shows what this is. His demon carries him over high mountains and bottomless abysses, through showers of ethereal flame to heights where earth seems a star and a star seems the earth. Then at the end of this rapturous journey he is dropped like a cold stone in the glittering void. In these flaming images Blok gives the contrast between his creative and his ordinary life, between the sense of celestial power which he has when his full faculties are at work and of absolute collapse which follows. The gap between his poetry and his life was enormous. But what finally counted was the vision, the ecstasy of creation, the flight of his untrammelled spirit through the void.

The clearest expression of this contrast and conflict is in *Artist* (1913). Blok begins by telling of his usual life ; while other men marry, make merry and die, he waits in deadly boredom for those bells in the sky which are a sign that the moment is near. When it comes the whole world changes. He asks if it is a whirlwind on the sea, are paradisal birds singing among the leaves, does Time stand still, are the apple-trees of May letting their snowy blossoms fall, does an Angel fly past. He feels the moments grow long in an unreal peace and the past unite itself with the future. It is a state of blissful unreality :

Nothing is present or pitiful here.

His soul is filled with a new strength. But then comes the crisis and the end. The soul gives place to the reason ; the reason conquers the soul and kills it. The bird, who was before free and gay, who meant so much to the poet, is imprisoned in a cage, where with clipped wings it swings on a hoop and sings the songs that it has learned by heart. Others may listen to them and like them, but for the poet the deadly time of waiting begins again. In the contrast between the boredom of waiting for inspiration to come and the sense of rapturous, unreal, timeless joy which he has when it comes, between the new soul which is then his and the ordinary reason which destroys it, between the portentous promise of his ecstasy and the captive bird which is all that remains from it, Blok marks the extremes between which his life passes. The fine frenzy is what matters, more than its results, much more than his ordinary life. The actual poem is but a small emblem of this supreme joy and this sudden, unreckonable, contentment. The essential fact in Blok's life was this power which filled him with strength and made him a poet in a far more vivid sense than a mere writer of poems.

As the creative vision remained sublime and uncontrollable for Blok, he attached a great metaphysical importance to it and never acquiesced in any sceptical philosophy. He based his view of life on his inspired moments and made a system which put the creative process at the centre of the universe. For him the important, the only reality was what he called the " Spirit of Music ", and on this he built his metaphysical system. The Spirit of Music is that exaltation of vitality which the artist finds in his inspiration and the ordinary man in his moments of absorbed energy and all-sufficing activity. It is transcendental and it takes the artist outside the ordinary world. Blok says of it :

There are, as it were, two spaces : one is historical and exists in the calendar, the other is musical and cannot be reckoned. It is only time and space of the first order that are invariably present in the civilised consciousness. We live in the second only in those moments in which we feel that we are close to Nature, when we surrender ourselves to the musical wave which rises out of the universal orchestra.[1]

The experience described poetically in *Artist* is here exalted into philosophy, and we see how little the ordinary appearances of existence concerned Blok. As for a Platonist or a Christian mystic, the sensuous world was a barrier between him and reality, but the reality which he demanded was not a logical whole. It was revealed intermittently, and especially through art. Its excitement informed the poet's work ; it gave the exalted experience of creation. Whatever this power might be, Blok knew that it was real, and he did not trouble to define it, though he drew important conclusions from its existence. He quoted with approval Gogol's words that art " can from life ravish the unravishable " and added in commentary :

Words like these make plain what art is, what it is akin to, what it is capable of ; it is the voice of nature's elements, the elemental force. In this lies its function, and its meaning, and its sole purpose ; everything else is a superstructure built over it, the work of civilisation's fussy hands.

[1] *The Collapse of Humanism* (1919). Trs. I. Berlin.

Like Mallarmé with his belief in a silent music above the audible, like Rilke with his Orpheus, Blok deduced from the existence of poetry a transcendental order which lay behind art and was responsible for it. He was not concerned merely with art or only to be an artist. The revelation of creative power was more to him than the actual writing of poetry ; the inspiration was greater than what it inspired. Nor did he confine his speculations to the regions where this touched poetry. He saw it as a supreme power in life, struggling with those settled habits and forms which he called " civilisation ". He felt that his world had lost contact with the Spirit of Music and was caught in the bonds of an obsolete system. With a logic characteristic of himself and of his race, he saw that what mattered most in the creative life was precisely the power to create. It was this that held his own life together and gave a meaning to it. Instead of dismissing it as inexplicable or reducing it to a place among other states of the spirit, he concluded that it was all that mattered for himself and for everyone. It was the only true reality. The old duality which he found between his visions and his sense of fact was solved through this conclusion. What mattered for him was the creative life, the Spirit of Music. He knew this not from theory but from intimate experience. And what was true of himself must naturally be true of others.

Above all he saw this struggle and this solution in Russia where men were nearer to Nature than in Western Europe and the chains of " civilisation " were less strong. In the ideal of Russia he found something to attract his mystical devotion, to unify his many interests and to provide him with a substitute for the ideal which he had lost with the Beautiful Lady. He had himself been quick to see this, and in 1910, in discussing the position of Symbolism in Russia, he wrote, " we raise to the mast the flag of our native land ". Russia was the focus of his emotions and gave unity to the diverse activities of his imaginative life. He could grasp their full significance because they were attached to a principle. Though the teaching of the Orthodox Church had ceased to have a dominating influence on him, he found in its myths images for suffering and purification, in its ritual symbols of worship and sacrifice. But its insistent ethical claims meant little to him and its limited freedom was not adequate to his vast emotional needs. He wanted something transcendental to hold his devotion, something with the promise and the possibility of an unreckonable revelation. As a young man he had expected the incalculable, and this expectation had not really left him. He was still a reader of signs, which he interpreted in the light of his poetic inspiration. Russia called for his powers and his service ; it was something vague and yet sufficiently concrete, something which could be the object of devoted love and yet deserve his mordant irony and carping blame. In it he found a mysterious being, cruel and lovable, ideal and yet perfectly real, known in the countryside which he loved, in the multitudes whom he championed, in the religion which gave him his symbols of suffering and sacrifice, of guilt and redemption. Russia revived the feelings which he had had for the Beautiful Lady, but it had more reality and stirred all his feelings from hatred and contempt to love and devoted service.

The great Russian poets have in their different ways sung of their country. Of all European countries it is the one which most wins devotion, pity and anger from its sons. Alexei Tolstoy praised it for its natural setting, with its wolves and eagles and nightingales, its winds and steppes and storms; Tyutchev saw that behind its despised poverty it had a special claim to honour because it was a holy land where Christ himself had walked. Blok covered this range from devotion to the Russian scene to passionate care for the Russian soul. For him his country was an object of love, not abstract but intensely personal, and he felt all a lover's moods of distrust, contempt, pride and hope. His own feelings are shown in a poem which in 1910 he addressed to her, the hard imperialist Russia, and asks if she is tired of him. He mocks her for failing in her proud ambitions :

Boats, yes, and towns upon rivers they hew for you;
— Where are the shrines of the Emperor's Town ?
Hawks and wild swans on the steppes rose and flew for you. . . .
Out of the steppes a black mist settles down.

Over the White Sea and over the Black again,
Black when the nights are and white are the days,
Wildly dumb faces' reflections come back again,
Eyes of the Tartars with flames are ablaze.

Gentle and lasting the sky's red is gleaming then,
Night upon night over armies below. . . .
Why do you charm me so, mirage of dreaming, then ?
Why do you play with my free spirit so ?

Blok contrasts the conquering, militant, ambitious Russia of his time with the Russia of song and of dreams. He chooses his symbols with great force and aptness. The Russia of Siberia and its conqueror Ermak, of military roads from Finland to the south, has sent its soldiers like wild birds over the steppes but has failed in its age-old ambition to conquer Constantinople. Against this Blok sets the beauty of the landscape, the infinite spaces of the Russian sky, fit image of an ideal character, and he complains that this imperial spirit is a cruel mockery of him who understands what Russia really is and who almost wishes to have done with her because of her darkened soul.

Love and anger were combined in Blok's feelings about Russia, love of the ideal and anger with the real. Some lines written in 1914 show the savage contempt of which he was capable. He mocks the Russian character which passes between extremes of pious devotion and moral squalor, which sins without shame and without thought, and then, heavy with drink, abases itself in church, comes home to commit some petty act of dishonesty or to make its squalid calculations of profit and loss before a sacred picture, and slumbers, bestially, in a deep feather-bed. Yet though he despises this character with a sarcastic insight, and has no illusions about it, he still loves it. The fierce denunciation ends with a declaration of love, that in spite of everything Russia is the dearest thing in the world to him. He really saw his country as a person, marked its characteristics as if they were human qualities, and felt like a lover feels about the faults of his mistress whom he cannot but love.

In his love for his country Blok showed what can only be called a prophetic vision. He knew her so well that he was able to foresee what was coming to her. In the last years of the Tsarist régime it may well have been clear to many that things could not last for long as they were, and that vast changes were ahead. Blok saw changes both far and near. In *New America* (1913) he foretold without irony or disgust the future mechanisation and industrialisation of Russia. In it he proclaimed that the real Russia was not in the snows and woods and steppes, not in the candles and prayers of the Church, not in the memories of ancient feuds and raids, but in the new factories of the workmen. Instead of Turkish flags on the steppes he saw chimneys and hooters; endless, windy distances broken by mills with workmen's dwellings around them. Coal was to be a subterranean Messiah, a Tsar, a betrothed. The vision might frighten others, but it did not frighten Blok. He listened calmly for the new voice that would come from the stone, the salt and the ore. On the empty spaces he saw a new star burning, his Russia, his bride, a new America to him. His very title is significant. He looked to the New World to redeem the Old. For this redemption he was prepared to sacrifice much of imaginative value and poetical beauty, the Oriental finery and glamour, the vestiges of Tartars and Turks and Varangians, which had for centuries coloured the Russian scene. This new Russia both was and was not what she had always been. She wore a new face and called up strange visions. But she was none the less the object of his love.

This was one vision of the future. There was another, more menacing, more gloomy. Just as in *A Voice from the Chorus* Blok foresaw some vast cosmic catastrophe, so in other poems he foresaw the time of tribulation that was in store for his country. In *On the Field of Kulikovo* (1908) he dreams of the future in a place haunted by memories of an old battle in which the Russians had defeated the Tartars. In a melancholy scene among yellow cliffs and quiet waters, he feels with intense sadness the sorrows of his country, and premonitions are forced on him by the gathering storm-clouds, the blood-red sunset, the horse galloping over the plain. At midnight the apprehension is intensified by the cry of swans and the hard white stone. He hears voices telling him to prepare for war. With the dawn the voices fade, but he still feels that a great conflagration is in store for Russia, and though the mists fall over the marshes, he remembers the noises of battle which he has heard and knows that this is the beginning of some great revolution and that the time has almost come. Even at this date Blok, with uncanny insight, felt that his country's ancient doom of bloodshed was soon to reassert itself. His feelings were mixed. In this coming hour he felt something fascinating and full of fate, but he knew that it called for great responsibilities and for prayer.

When war came in 1914, Blok's feelings were curiously simplified. The time of testing which he had foretold was near. The apocalypse for which he had waited would come through blood and destruction. But for the war itself he felt little but hostility. He was not impressed by the patriotic slogans which praised it and saw in it the end of that civilisation which began with the Renaissance and was pre-eminently humanistic in outlook. He had long felt that this civilisation was in its death-throes, and in the declaration of war he saw a sign that the old world was at an end. His objection was that the war was hostile to the real forces of life and that " by its deliberately anti-musical assent to this war civilisation signed its own death-warrant ". But he did not proclaim how right he was. His poetry found a new strength through the horror and the pity which he felt for purposeless and useless destruction. He saw the battalions marching with songs and gay banners to be slaughtered on the Galician plains; he felt with acute sorrow the contrast between the hurrahs of to-day and the deaths of to-morrow. When the slaughter continued and no real result came, Blok grew more gloomy and distrustful and wrote with short and savage words of the dumbness and emptiness everywhere in the world. The years were burning all to ashes, and from old days of war and liberty there was a reflection of blood on everyone's lips. But despite the deaf ears, despite the vultures circling over the graves, he felt that the Kingdom of God was at hand. He would turn to Russia and proclaim his faithfulness to her in the night of war, where, amid the songs of soldiers, over the deadly snow, shone the star of Bethlehem, bright image of his love for her. He clung to his ideal, to his belief in some immediate and overwhelming revelation. The war was a sign of dread events to come, and for these he waited more in hope than in fear.

In this time of waiting he was liable to attacks of black despair. In one mysterious poem he says that he is cold and dry, that he has finished with kind words and friendship. In the wild world about him he sees no light ; his soul has been burned up and shrivelled ; at such a time it is best to wear an iron mask against the insanity abroad. In another place he cries out against the useless prolongation of the war, and presents a simple scene where a vulture wheels over a lonely field and a mother weeps in a hut for her dead son. He complains that though villages are aflame and revolt has broken out, Russia is still worn and red with weeping, — how long must mothers weep and vultures wheel ? Though his trust in the future sustained him, he found the time of waiting hard to bear. He felt no magic in the call to defend a system in which he did not believe ; his nature was ravaged by the hideous slaughter of his countrymen ; his attempts to escape into regions of fancy and delight were not a complete anodyne. The excitements of battle and the hysterical pleasures of war-time were far removed from his ideal joy. He felt himself torn between a cowardly resignation and a summons to something tremendous. In this mood he wrote of himself :

> Wild wind batters
> Window squares,
> The hinged shutters
> Rudely tears.

> Hour of Mass on Easter morn,
> Bells far distant, bells forlorn,
> Deafness, darkness, everywhere ;
> Only guest a wind in scorn
> Rattles on the barrier.

> Through the windows, — void and black ;
> In the darkness footsteps crack.
> There the ice-bound flood breaks free,
> There a Bride awaits for me.

> How to vile sleep not surrender?
> How drive off that guest from here?
> Not give up my love so tender
> To the cursèd stranger's care?

> How not throw the world away ?
> Not despair of everything,
> If my only guest's a wind,
> Nothing but a wild black wind
> On my household battering ?

> Why, wind, batter
> Window square ?
> The hinged shutter
> Rudely tear ?

He felt that his great hour had come and that he was not ready or brave enough to face it.

In March 1917 the Revolution came, and when it was succeeded by the Second Revolution in November, Blok felt that his hopes were realised and his whole nature satisfied. His aunt records his behaviour at the time :

It seemed to him that the old world was really destroyed and that in its place must appear something new and beautiful. He went about, young, cheerful, fresh, with shining eyes, listening to that revolutionary music in the noise of the old world's collapse which, on his own testimony, sounded unceasingly in his ears.

In the Revolution Blok saw a new and vastly important manifestation of the Spirit of Music. He believed that all important movements in human history were due to it, that it inspired the Renaissance as it inspired the beginnings of Christianity. But in the nineteenth century, he thought, it had been lost. The Humanism of the Renaissance had ceased to count as a vital force. Its place had been taken by a new power, vast and vivifying, the development of the masses. What began in France, what inspired Goethe and Schiller, even Wagner, had found its full expression in Russia with the Revolution. Making a distinction between the real life of the spirit, which he called culture, and its dead formalisation, which he called civilisation, Blok thought that the time had come for Western civilisation to collapse, and he believed that he heard it falling. He thought that it would soon be succeeded by the real and lively culture of the masses, released from the moribund traces of an effete humanism and in perfect harmony with the Spirit of Music. He proclaimed the change in dithyrambic words :

The great bell of anti-humanism peals over the earth ; the world purifies itself, casting off its old garments ; man grows closer to the elemental in nature — he grows more musical.

He saw the birth of a mighty new movement and believed that he foresaw its results. Instead of the old type of man, ethical, political and humane, would come man the artist. He who kept in touch with the spirit would produce life more abundantly and " live greedily in the new epoch of whirlwinds and storms to which mankind is irresistibly advancing ". Blok, in fact, thought that the experience which created everything that mattered in his own life would be communicated freely to others, and that the world, freed from its old habits and trammels, would live at the pitch which he himself had found in his moments of creative exaltation. In the angry, reckless, revolutionary crowds he saw poets in the grip of inspiration, makers of a new world, artists shaping the rough material of life to new and marvellous designs.

In a note found after his death Blok recorded that at no period in his life had he been so continually inspired as in January 1918. The fruits of this inspiration appeared in his longest, most important poem, *The Twelve*, which is said to have been written in a single night, was at once acclaimed as a masterpiece, recited nightly before enraptured crowds, and translated into many languages. It is quite unlike anything else that he had written, and bears the marks of sustained and inspired creation. Its method is quite new. There is a backbone of narrative, but the poem is entirely symbolical. The rhythms vary from sharp incisive octosyllabic couplets to free verse and verse modelled on the songs of streets and factories. The language is often conversational, sometimes slang, but extraordinarily melodious and powerful. The rhymes are often irregular, even dissonant, but the delicate discords are well suited to this brief epic of a falling world. The plot is simple ; the characters are few ; the setting is in Petrograd in winter. Hints of the time appear in references to Austrian rifles, Kerensky's paper money, the Red Guard, the Constituent Assembly. The poem lacks Blok's more splendid imagery. All is reduced to suit the framework of narrative. The method is simple and remarkably effective. With a real scene and apparently real people Blok suggests that both scene and people are symbolical of something much greater outside themselves. The fate almost of the whole world, certainly of all Russia, is involved. This was Blok's vision of the Russian Revolution, his conception of what it really meant.

The Twelve begins with description. It is a dark evening with snow falling. Across the streets hangs a great placard with the words

All power to the Constituent Assembly !

Across the scene pass various typical figures, an old woman " like a hen ", a writer, a fat priest with a great cross swinging on his belly, a tramp, a lady in a lambskin coat. The figures fade and only voices are heard, talking about committees and debates, about love, about money. It is an ordinary night of the Revolutionary winter. But each figure is a type, and the night is a symbol of the deadness of the old world in which the characteristic figures are entirely absorbed in their own petty and paltry interests. They do not understand what is happening or what lies in store for them. They have a kind of comic pathos, when the old woman wonders how many socks could be made out of the great placard, or the fine lady slips in the

snow, or the priest sidles along.   This life is without meaning.
The essential note is struck at the end of the first section in the
menacing words :

> Hate, sorrowful hate,
>   Seethes in the heart. . . .
> Black hate, holy hate. . . .

The black hate is like the black sky.   In the darkness lurks a
power that will change or destroy everything.   The wild wind
too is like it.   It is an incalculable power, which plays with
everyone and everything :

> The wild wind hurts,
> Is mad and gay ;
> It blows the skirts,
> Mows the passers-by,
> Shakes, quakes and makes fly
> The great placard away :
> " All power to the Constituent Assembly."

The wind is a symbol of the force that is at work sweeping
away the ineffective, chattering people and their hopes.
On this scene enter twelve soldiers, members of the Red
Army.   They are like an embodiment of the wind :

> The wind strolls, the snow dances ;
> A party of twelve men advances.

They go smoking their cheroots and firing their rifles to left
and right.   They are convicts and the chief characters of the
poem.   Their talk is of a girl Katya who has gone off with one
of their comrades, Vanya.   Suddenly the pair drive past in a
smart carriage.   Vanya, dressed in a military overcoat, twists
his moustaches and smiles and shows his pearly teeth to
Katya.   The Twelve mock them after they have passed, and
recall with brutal frankness what they know about the girl and
her lovers, the fine clothes that she wore, the officer who loved
her and who has been killed.   The mockery is cruel, but there
is an element of admiration in it :

> Katya, on your neck a gash
> From my knife that does not heal ;
> Underneath your breast a slash,
> Katya, left another weal.

> Well, well, dance for me !
> Your fine legs are good to see.

When the carriage passes again, the Twelve open fire. Vanya escapes, but Katya is killed. The Twelve seem not to care :

> But where is Katya, where ? Dead . . . dead . . .
> Shot by a bullet through the head.
>
> Do you like that, Katya ? Not a sound.
> Lie, carrion, there upon the ground.

But this mood is soon succeeded by another. One of the Twelve is overcome with guilt and remorse, recalls the drunken summer nights which he spent with the dead girl, her eyes like a cat's in the dark. But even he soon forgets his grief in the excitement of looting the town's cellars. On the Twelve go through the night in the blinding snow, mocking their Saviour, past the bourgeois who stands at the corner with his nose tucked in his old fur coat. A starving mongrel follows them and, though they threaten it with their bayonets, takes no notice. In front of them a red flag waves and advances. They cannot see who is carrying it. They threaten and shoot, but without effect. The echo of their shots rings between the houses. Then without warning comes the astonishing end :

> On they march with sovereign tread,
> With a starving dog behind,
> With a blood-red flag ahead, —
> In the storm where none can see,
> From the rifle bullets free,
> Gently walking through the snow,
> Where the pearly snow-flakes blow,
> Marches rose-crowned in the van
> Jesus Christ, the Son of Man.

With that the poem closes.

The Twelve is a symbolical poem of the Revolution. The Twelve are the Russian people. The poet says as much when he closes the eleventh section with the words

> On, working people, on !

But Blok makes no attempt to make his revolutionary people noble or attractive. They are typical Russians as he had come to see them. They scratch their heads and chew sunflower seeds. They are criminals devoured by base lust and murderous jealousy and tormented by guilt. Their chief motive is hate. They cry out for freedom, but it is freedom without Christ. Their desire is to make the bourgeois despair by causing a universal conflagration. Yet though they do not know what they are doing or where they are going, they follow, despite themselves, a divine leader. The remarkable part which Blok gives to Christ has caused some misunderstanding. On the poem's first publication some even thought that it was a satire on Bolshevism, others that it glorified the slaughter of the bourgeoisie. Blok's Christ is simply a symbol of the Spirit of Music, of the new life and strength which he felt in the air. Despite themselves the revolutionary people are being led to a glorious destiny, to a transformation of the world. Their bestiality and brutality are of no account in such a change. The end will show that the means are right. And the figure of Christ has a special significance. Blok has come to see him as a symbol of redemption through suffering and blood. He stands now for that salvation which is coming to Russia through slaughter. The world will be changed and redeemed in blood.

The episode of Katya and Vanya has its place in this scheme. Vanya is a mere traitor who has joined the other side, and there is nothing to be said for him. But Katya is different. She symbolises old ties and affections which have their bestial side but have still some hold on the heart. She is killed by mistake in a moment of wild frenzy. Her death naturally awakes remorse and bows down her killer. But in times like this old affections and pleasures must be sacrificed, nor does it matter what motive prompts their destruction. Through her blood the new world will be made. That is why the Twelve soon forget her. We feel the madness that she stirs in the blood, the dark passions she arouses, the soul-destroying pleasure that she gives. She represents the old sensual appetites of the Russians, their abundant, luxurious, brutal sexuality. There may be regret for her death, but it has to be. The memory of it is soon lost, first in the thought of drink, then in the Russian mood of empty boredom. Just as Blok himself had in the past felt a remarkable sense of strength and peace when he was rid of his loves, so he makes the Twelve feel a kind of deliverance with Katya's death. In spite of themselves, they are free to go to their invisible goal. The revolution is not of man's making. It is a change in the government of the world.

No less significant are the bourgeois and the mangy cur. The two are closely connected, are in effect one. They stand together at the cross-roads, — symbol of the crisis in their destinies, — and bear some resemblance to one another. And both are like the old disappearing world :

> The old world, like a homeless mongrel,
> Stands by, with tail between its legs.

So when the dog follows the Twelve and refuses to be driven off by their threats, it is a type of the bourgeois society which has in spite of itself to follow the Revolution. Cold and homeless, it has nowhere else to go. In it too strange unintelligible powers are at work. The bourgeois and the dog are types of that " civilisation " which Blok decried. To be transformed into something new and to enter into " culture ", they must become one with the masses. He saw that these masses might be barbarian, and says that " it is no paradox to say that the barbarian masses turned out to be the preservers of culture ". So in his poem these dying forces find a strange attraction in the new movement and cannot leave it, though it despises and threatens them. The strange following dog has a better insight than the aimless figures of the opening scene with their endless talk, futile complaints and petty mishaps.

The Twelve is the climax of Blok's poetry. In it his poetical ideas find their final form. The old symbols, such as snow and night, which he had once used for his own emotional life, are extended to a vast scale. The Spirit of Music, which he found in his own creative moments, takes on a cosmic activity and significance. His peculiar notions of redemption through blood are applied from himself to his country. The Revolution was an answer to his prayer, to his insistent demand for some enormous and fearful event to change the world. His Twelve are the Russian people as he had long seen them, squalid and brutal and purposeless but none the less instruments of an extraordinary destiny. The claims and shames of the flesh which he himself had known and felt so strongly were seen at last to be part of a system which was dying before the onslaught of a new spirit. With humorous irony Blok even portrayed the pathetic and futile rôle of the writer in such a catastrophe, when among the figures of the opening he sets one not unlike himself :

Who is that with hair fluttering,
Under his voice muttering,
— We are betrayed !
Russia exists no more. —
Writing must be his trade.

For himself, he was ready to go where the Revolution led. It meant the sundering of many ties, the contempt and anger of old friends. He did not flinch. This was the revelation for which he had asked. He was not going to forsake it.

The religious air of *The Twelve* is perhaps a little deceptive. Blok certainly did not think that the Revolution was going to bring a revival of Christian faith and virtues. But the poem is undeniably and rigorously mystical. It deals with powers for which there are no exact names and whose character can only be apprehended through some kind of symbols. It sounds strange to Western European ears, but it was not so strange to Russia in 1918. Russian poets and novelists had long used the figures and even the central figure of Christianity to express their own ideas, which were often not Christian and certainly not orthodox. The Christian religion provided Blok with his central belief of redemption through blood and suffering. In 1910 he wrote a poem in which he described his life as alternating between long hesitations and moments of illumination in which he felt that he must make a sacrifice and yield his blood. He closed it saying :

Time passes by. Remembering ;
I cried, " I am no bond-slave, — no ! "
Let fall the flower-embroidered sling.
Gush forth, blood, and make red the snow !

There the sacrifice of his own blood was somehow an act of self-deliverance, of self-assertion. In his own sufferings, Blok, like other Russians, saw himself as undergoing the agonies of the Cross. Quite early he had in *Autumn Love* pictured himself as crucified and waiting for Christ to deliver him. In blood and agony he saw redemption, and he naturally used the traditional symbols of Christianity for them. So when he came to write of the rebirth of Russia, he used them again in his figure of the guiding Christ. Just as he believed that his own sufferings were a preparation and a prelude to some great event, so in Russia's agony he saw a similar process and used similar imagery for it. His Christ was a reality to him as a type of a new creative spirit and a force which leads men in new directions. His friend Bely also wrote a poem on the Revolution and called it *Christ is Risen*. But neither he nor Blok really attempted to connect the Revolution with Christianity. Both were concerned with visions of a very different kind.

The *Twelve* was followed at a short interval by *The Scythians*, in which Blok reverted to a more formal and stately manner of writing. It has not the fire and force of *The Twelve*, but it was Blok's last poem and has its own interest. It is a solemn appeal to Western Europe not to desert Russia in her need. The need was indeed great. The Revolution had won many enemies at home and abroad, and Russia, bled white by the war, was now confronted with blockade, starvation, invasion and civil war. Men of the time turned their thoughts away from Europe and imagined a Russia which should have an independent existence between Europe and Asia. Blok appeals to Europe and also threatens it. He calls for a halt before the mysterious future :

> Oh, pause, old world, while life still beats in you,
> Oh, weary one, oh, worn, oh, wise !
> Halt here, as once did Oedipus
> Before the Sphinx's enigmatic eyes.[1]

He warns the West that it has disregarded the signs of wrath to come, the earthquakes of Lisbon and Messina which had always possessed for him a prophetic significance. Then he threatens that if Russia is scorned, she will stand aside in the coming struggle between East and West and no longer be a barrier against the Mongol hordes. He makes his last appeal for friendship :

> Come unto us, from the black ways of war,
> Come to our peaceful arms and rest.
> Comrades, while it is not too late,
> Sheathe the old sword. May brotherhood be blest.[1]

He spoke to deaf ears. For the next twenty years Russia was to live in isolation.

With *The Twelve* and *The Scythians* Blok ended his poetical life. For three and a half years he lived on, protected by his great name and by the good offices of Maxim Gorky, who found him a post under the new government. He worked hard, editing, translating, writing a history of the first revolu-

[1] Trs. B. Deutsch and A. Yarmolinsky.

tion, careful, dispassionate, dry, but hardly any poetry. He started work again at his autobiographical poem *Retaliation*, but gave it up. Something had gone out of him. He was not yet forty, and his creative life was finished. Perhaps like Shakespeare when he retired to Stratford, or like Rimbaud when he left Verlaine for a life of vagrant commerce, he had exhausted his power to write. Perhaps his body felt at last all the strain that he had put on it and avenged itself on him. He was ill ; he was extremely depressed. He seems to have lost faith in himself, in the Revolution, in life. Gorky has left a terrible picture of him in his last days, bursting from his habitual silence into a denunciation of the intellect : " The thing is that we have become too clever to believe in God and not strong enough to believe in ourselves. . . . The brain, the brain. . . . It is monstrously developed. It is a swelling like a goitre." Yet even in this he said what he had said before, when in *Artist* he claimed that the reason kills the soul. He had known this to happen in himself ; he now believed that it was happening in the world. The Revolution, which seemed to bring so magnificent a promise of new life, had failed him as the Beautiful Lady had failed him. Reality once again had not risen to the height of his vision. The slow process of organisation which had to follow the great excitements of 1917 was of no spiritual interest to Blok. He lived in another world, and the contrast between it and reality filled him with despair. He died in Moscow at the age of forty-one in the hot summer of 1921, sitting upright on his chair and keeping the silence which he had kept for many days. A vast procession filed through the sultry room as he lay unrecognisable on the bed, where, because of his pain, he had not lain for weeks.

More than any Russian poet, more than any European poet of his time, Blok gives the impression of being literally inspired. The extraordinary originality of his poetry, its endless surprises and startling strength, its inexhaustible music, seem to have been given to him by some power outside himself and to owe little to painstaking workmanship. Even its occasional oddities, its turns of phrase or imagery which surprise by their quaintness, support the impression. Blok believed that a poet must trust in his visions and write in accordance with them. He was a mystic, a seer. The experience which he found in poetic creation was the fundamental reality to him. But like other mystics, he had a curiously vivid insight and prescience into the world about him. He saw signs where others saw only accidents ; his prophecies were fulfilled with singular accuracy. It was his personal destiny to die in the belief that he had been wrong, that the Revolution had cheated him. But his forecasts of a " New America ", of war, of Russia cut off from Europe and strengthened by vast changes, were near enough to the truth. We may not understand or accept the mysterious processes by which he came to foresee these events, but we must admit that he was right. But his prophecy was only incidental to his poetry. He believed that a poet must write out his intuition, his emotional and imaginative experiences, that he must rid himself of the deceptive processes of logic and dialectic. To this belief he remained faithful to the last, and his words to Gorky were his dying defence of it. His poetry stands by its truth to his visions and to his feelings. It is a powerful record of a nature which felt deeply and saw clearly many secrets of the heart and soul. He was entirely faithful to his standards, and his poetry is always poetry, powerful to recreate in his hearers that almost audible music which he knew when inspiration descended on him and he lived outside time in a region of unspeakable joy.

VI

WILLIAM BUTLER YEATS
1865-1939

English poetry has on the whole kept itself free from theories. Even bold theorists like Wordsworth have often written their best in defiance of their professed aims. With this lack of theorising there has sometimes gone a lack of interest in the technicalities of verse, a tendency to leave the poet to his untutored Muse. Even this has usually been a blessing. It is well that neither Blake nor Shelley was taught his craft in an academy or made to believe that verse which broke conventional rules was necessarily bad. The English poet is left to look after himself and is judged instinctively by the appeal which his work makes. It was therefore unlikely that the French Symbolists would found a real school in England. But in the last years of the nineteenth century English poetry was in so strange a state that something like such a school came into existence. The 'nineties were years of crisis and change. The great Victorian poets had disappeared. Swinburne lived on at Putney, but he had ceased to count. Browning, Arnold, Tennyson, the Rossettis, Morris were in the grave. It was as if the stage had been cleared for some new figure to replace the great departed, but none appeared. The Victorians, used to a secure succession of great men, looked for an heir to Tennyson, but failed to find one. There rose instead a small group of poets, some of considerable promise, most of real talent and genuine devotion to their art. The removal of the demi-gods had cleared the air : poetry was once again an open question. The faults of Tennyson were dragged into the light, and from the force of reaction came the beginnings of a new age.

In retrospect the 'nineties look perhaps like a time when the confidence of expectations was equalled by the magnitude of the general failure. The names which stirred such hopes and such controversy may seem to have left little of absolute value. It is easy to claim that much of the work looks precious and that real talent is often spoiled by mannerism and affectation. It is easy to decry this age, but its failure was not so great as is commonly thought. The 'nineties were doubly unfortunate. Some of the most promising poets died before their promise could be fulfilled, while those who survived and matured are no longer connected with the 'nineties. Dowson and Johnson were frustrated in their development, while Yeats and Housman are seldom related to their beginnings. The 'nineties lie under the shadow of unfulfilled promise, but in spite of certain weaknesses and failures they cleared away the ruins of " that which once was great ", the encumbrance of the masterful and dominating poetry written by the leading Victorians. They felt themselves called to bring poetry back to its natural self and to make it possible for the poet to re-assert his personality. Their situation in the first respect was like that of the French poets who had grown up under the titanic shadow of Hugo. The great Victorians, believing that they were prophets, had included in poetry many elements which would ordinarily be more suited to prose. From their high shrines they made pronouncements on intractable themes such as the conflict of science and religion, the expansion of the British Empire, the place of God in the moral life. The view that poetry is a kind of sermon was equally dangerous for the public and for the poet. Tennyson sometimes wasted delicate gifts on problems which never touched his heart ; Browning was liable to insert a lecture into his most dramatic idylls ; even Swinburne and Patmore thought at intervals that they must guide the public mind. Against this powerful didacticism the pre-Raphaelites had fought a gallant battle, but their work was only a diversion. The great men who preached had won popularity. Reaction against what had become a tyranny was inevitable, and with the youthful claims of the 'nineties the revolution began.

It is one thing to rid poetry of its impurities, and in this the men of the 'nineties were, according to their lights, successful. It is another thing to restore the poet's true personality, to clear it of the poses and false airs which had been forced on it by regard for a devoted public. The failures of Tennyson were ultimately a failure in sincerity. We now know that even in *In Memoriam* he expressed a faith which was stronger than what he often felt, that the hysterical purity of *Idylls of the King* was countered in actual life by a robust coarseness. Tennyson was doubtless honest in what he wrote, but his conception of the poet's position deluded him. He put neither his whole self nor his real self into his poetry, and the loss is great. In his time the poet was a public character who felt that he had national obligations and was to some extent moved to say things because he felt that he ought. So great was the poet's prestige, so much was expected from him, that it was extremely hard for him to be himself. When, like Gerard Hopkins, he tried the experiment, he felt that he was a lonely eccentric and that no one could understand what he was trying to do. Nor were the contributors to *The Yellow Book* entirely free from this influence. They did not indeed regard the poet as a political figure, but they failed to see how important it was for him to be himself. Not all were so theatrical as Wilde with his self-conscious gestures and rhetorical exaggerations. But all were more or less imbued with the belief that the poet must present himself in a certain light and that it was more important for him to write well than to write what he really believed. Obsessed with the importance of technique and the notion of " Art for Art's sake ", they were, in spite of everything, " literary ". Though they wrote about the public-house and the brothel, they saw them through a romantic haze. For this reason their poetry is largely an escape from life and shows its romantic affinities. Even in *The Ballad of Reading Gaol* Wilde failed to free himself of his literary associations and mixed the real poetry of a grim experience with the false verbiage of his earlier work.

In England, then, the problem was both to rid poetry of its prosaic elements and to give it a greater sincerity and truth. In the second task most poets of the 'nineties failed. The work of A. E. Housman has elements of rhetoric and exaggeration, and neither Johnson nor Dowson saw what was really required of them. They reinstated craftsmanship in verse and they gave the emotions a prominent place, but otherwise they brought little new. In so far as they owed anything to France, it was to Baudelaire and Verlaine, and it was little more than a preference for some subjects and a dislike of others. Of the broad issues raised by the Symbolists they had little knowledge. It looked as if English poetry after a return to its lyrical traditions was going to continue as before, uninfluenced by French example. And to a large extent this happened. The Elizabethan grace of Robert

Bridges, the flowery Catholic art of Francis Thompson, had profited by the return to purer ideals, but neither exemplified new methods from France. Thomas Hardy wrote *The Dynasts* without regard to the polish demanded by the age, and delineated cosmic visions in a rustic home-made style. The 'nineties had done their work. It remained for poetry to revive. The English tradition was strong, and there seemed little likelihood that foreign influences would displace it.

In effect this promise was realised. For though Symbolism was to find one of its most distinguished exponents in a man who wrote in the English language, he was not an Englishman and was never fully acclimatised. By his origins, his background, his character, William Butler Yeats stood outside the English tradition. Despite his early association with men of the Rhymers' Club and *The Yellow Book* he preserved something alien and remote. His Irish upbringing had given him an independence from established English ideas and a mental outlook impossible in England. Brought up largely in the west of Ireland, he had in early childhood absorbed the beliefs of an unspoiled peasantry and lived in an atmosphere uncontaminated by science. In that world personality was still as important as it had been in the eighteenth century, and a man was entitled to be unlike his fellows. The inhabitants were nearly all either landowners or peasants. The first kept some of the culture and interests which belonged to their forebears; the latter, beyond the reach of newspapers and largely illiterate, took a lively pleasure in words and in stories. Yeats' father was an artist of the highest tolerance and wisdom. In an unspoiled landscape among unsophisticated people Yeats grew to manhood unlike the Wykehamist Johnson or the cosmopolitan Wilde. From the beginning he carried the marks of a stranger in his accent, in his ceremonious manners, in the richness of his vocabulary and the dignity of his speech. Risen from such beginnings, despite some affinities with the pre-Raphaelites, Yeats could never quite have been an Englishman, and when he took to writing poetry and to theorising about it as an Irishman might, he looked outside England where theory does not flourish and found what he needed in France.

In his first years of creative activity Yeats combined a mood of other-worldliness derived from Celtic legends with an external, descriptive manner that recalls William Morris and to a less extent Keats. In *The Wanderings of Oisin* (1889) there was a bright promise of poetry to come, and even at this date Yeats had written poems like *The Stolen Child* and *To an Isle in the Water* which made his name and have remained connected with it in popular esteem. But from this romantic dreaming verse no one could have foretold that Yeats would develop into a strong personality. He seemed to have rid himself of individual characteristics and to have sunk himself in scenes of fairy life. Even the melancholy which pervaded this and his next volume, *The Countess Cathleen* (1893), seemed more like the reflection of some universal Celtic despair than the personal feelings of a young poet. At this period Yeats looked like a good pupil of William Morris, a poet of escape, the singer of music " in the deep heart's core ", but not in any way typical of new movements or new ideals. He might well have stayed in this manner and repeated the success which he won with *The Lake Isle of Innisfree* if he had not come to London and heard the call of new ideas in the air. Though, like all his generation, he knew Pater's *Renaissance* and owed something to it, though he was the friend of Wilde and Dowson and Johnson and shared their belief in Art for Art's sake and in the importance of technique, the impulse which set him in a new direction came from France. Through his friend, Arthur Symons, Yeats met Mallarmé, and through Symons' translations he came to know something of Symbolism and its aims. He was entranced by Hérodiade's address to " some Sibyl who is her Nurse and it may be the moon also ". The theory and its examples occupied his mind and altered his style. Under its influence he wrote *The Wind among the Reeds* (1899) and *The Shadowy Waters* (1900). He wrote almost deliberately on a theory and abandoned the ease and simplicity of his first style for another more elaborated and studied. The change did not entirely please his friends and admirers. Lionel Johnson complained that he wrote " hopelessly in the would-be austere and hieratic manner ", but to Symons, the propagandist of Symbolism in England, Yeats was " the chief representative of that movement in our country ". Encouraged by this enthusiasm and feeling that he was in the only movement that was " saying new things ", Yeats adapted what he conceived to be Mallarmé's doctrine to suit his own views and wrote poetry accordingly. As he had little knowledge of French, he

learned of the theory through its interpreters, and his natural
bent suited it to his own ideas. The theory, as he expounded
it, was new, though its origins were recognisable.

In two essays, *Symbolism in Painting* and *The Symbolism
of Poetry*, Yeats willingly accepts the view that symbols are
essential to poetry and lays down his general principles :

> All Art that is not mere story-telling or mere portraiture is
> symbolic, and has the purpose of those symbolic talismans which
> mediaeval magicians made with complex colours and forms, and
> bade their patients ponder over daily, and guard with holy
> secrecy ; for it entangles, in complex colours and forms, a part
> of the Divine essence.

In this there is something of Mallarmé, but it has been
transposed to another sphere. Yeats does not regard poetry
as complete in itself, with its own ritual and its own meaning.
He sees it as part of a larger experience, as a means of communication with the spiritual world which lies behind the
visible. For him the poet is almost a medium, an interpreter
of the unseen, and his poetry is the record of the revelations
given to him. The notion, formulated here, was to play an
increasingly greater part in Yeats' work and to account for
some of the stranger elements in it. The man who had been
brought up among folk-tales and magical legends was curiously
confirmed in his beliefs when he met the new theories from
France. They supplied him with reasons for his own view of
art and encouraged him to pursue the hieratic manner which
he desired. He could go on as he wished, fortified by the
conviction that he was acting as a poet should.

After this Yeats has some original remarks about the use of
symbols. He distinguishes, as Mallarmé did not, between
two kinds of symbolism, the symbolism of sounds and the
symbolism of ideas. The first class contains emotional
symbols :

> All sounds, all colours, all forms, either because of their pre-
> ordained energies or because of long association, evoke indefinable
> and yet precise emotions, or, as I prefer to think, call down among
> us certain disembodied powers, whose footsteps over our hearts
> we call emotions, and when sound, and colour, and form are in
> a musical relation, a beautiful relation to one another, they become
> as it were one sound, one colour, one form, and evoke an emotion
> that is made out of their distinct evocations and yet is one emotion.

Here too, if we omit the spiritualist metaphysics, there is much of Mallarmé and a certain amount of Baudelaire, but unlike them Yeats limits the use of symbols to the expression of emotions. Mallarmé was not concerned with these but with pure aesthetic experience. But Yeats, closer to ordinary life despite his magical airs, isolates the emotions as a special field for symbols. The second class of symbols is that of ideas, and of this Yeats says :

There are intellectual symbols, symbols that evoke ideas alone, or ideas mingled with emotions. . . . If I say " white " or " purple " in an ordinary line of poetry, they evoke emotions so exclusively that I cannot say why they move me ; but if I bring them into the same sentence with such obvious intellectual symbols as a cross or a crown of thorns, I think of purity or sovereignty. Furthermore, innumerable meanings, which are held to " white " or to " purple " by bonds of subtle suggestion, alike in the emotions and in the intellect, move visibly through my mind, and move invisibly beyond the threshold of sleep casting lights and shadows of an indefinable wisdom on what had seemed before, it may be, but sterility and noisy violence.

In spite of the metaphors the sense of this is clear. Yeats recognises that words call up associations, and though he has his own opinion of what such a process implies, his account of it is true to experience. But his theory is largely his own. Mallarmé would not have allowed that symbols in poetry could be evocative only of ideas. He believed in an idealism " which (similarly as in fugues, in sonatas) rejects the natural materials and, as brutal, a direct thought ordering them ; to retain no more than suggestion ". Yeats does not go so far. He maintains that a symbol may stand for an idea and play a corresponding part in poetry. At the outset he rejects the drastic view which excludes as much thought as possible from verse. He sees that ideas have a function in it which must be recognised.

Having formulated his theory Yeats asks what changes must be expected in consequence, and he answers :

A return to the way of our fathers, a casting-out of descriptions of nature for the sake of nature, of the moral law for the sake of the moral law, a casting-out of all anecdotes and of that brooding over scientific opinion that so often extinguished the central flame

WILLIAM BUTLER YEATS

in Tennyson, and of that vehemence that would make us do or
not do certain things.

The main idea is true to Symbolist doctrine. Valéry says :

L'histoire, la science, ni la morale ne gagnent point à être
exposées dans le langage de l'âme. La poésie didactique, le poème
historique ou l'épique, quoique illustrées et consacrées par les
plus grands poètes, combinent étrangement les données de la
connaissance discursive ou empirique, avec les créations de l'être
intime et les puissances de l'émotion.

The list of forbidden themes is almost identical. Both Yeats
and Valéry are anxious to avoid the omnivorous capacity of
their immediate predecessors, but Yeats is less rigorous than
Valéry and offers what is almost a compromise. He makes the
important reservation " for the sake of ", and that alters the
situation. The themes are intractable and difficult, but they
need not necessarily and always be excluded. If they are
subjected to a real poetical end, then perhaps they may be
admitted. The young Irishman seems to have seen that
politics at least could not be entirely omitted from poetry.
Yeats has his vision of what this new poetry will be. It
will be marked by a return to imagination, to the state between
waking and dreaming; it will cast out energetic rhythms and
seek " wavering, meditative, organic, rhythms " ; it will pay
great attention to technique and employ, if they are necessary,
even obscure and ungrammatical forms, but it must have
" the perfection that escapes analysis, the subtleties that have
a new meaning every day ". Poetry is to be a record of a state
of trance, and if it is to be a true record, it must take endless
pains to secure its effect by the right rhythm and the right
associations ; for otherwise the state of trance is broken.
This theory partly re-states some of the fundamental principles of lyric poetry, partly introduces the revolutionary
notion that a poem is a charm or instrument of enchantment.
Yeats finds the Symbolist doctrine to his taste not only because its high standards appeal to his artistic sense but
because its mystical claims appeal to something mystical in
him. But his mysticism is of a special kind. It is not aesthetic
rapture, not pure vision, not creative ecstasy, but a belief in
powers behind the visible world, powers that are evoked from
dream and trance. For Yeats poetry is a communication with
spirits, with an unseen order of things, and the poet is he who

conducts the passage from one order to another and finds words for these mysterious messages.

The practical effect of this theory may be seen in the volumes of poetry which Yeats published at the end of the last century. The first impression which *The Wind among the Reeds* makes on a reader familiar with Yeats' early verse is of a greater internal richness reached through a restriction of subject. Except for one or two ballads it is almost completely concerned with the poet's emotions. The Irish mythology familiarised by *The Wanderings of Oisin* is no longer used to tell a story but has become part of the poet's intimate experience and is subordinated to his moods. The volume is practically a collection of love-poems, but, instead of direct statement, imagery, borrowed from Celtic legend, clothes events in such a way as to make them almost a continuation of Irish lore. An experience that might in other words have been familiar is presented as something strange and ancient. At first sight the poems are difficult because Celtic mythology is not the stock-in-trade of every reading man, but it can be mastered, and now much of its first obscurity has been dispelled. And by drawing his imagery almost from a single source Yeats has solved a problem inherent in the Symbolist position. His symbols are all taken from a common stock and mutually related. He even adds explanatory notes, and where he does not, the meaning can be elucidated from sources not impossibly out of reach. There is not in Yeats, as in Mallarmé, a residue of unintelligible matter. This Symbolism creates an impression of mystery, of remoteness, of kinship to ancient and strange forces. It relates present events to remote antecedents and sets the poet's love in a timeless, legendary world. But there is nothing in it which cannot be understood.

Yeats' normal method is to take some figure or creature of legend and through it to express some state of mind of his own. In the first edition he appears in different characters, as Aedh, Hanrahan or Michael Robartes according to the part that he plays, but in later editions these characters are reduced to " he ". The crises in his soul are depicted through legend. When he wishes to get away from ordinary life and feels the fierce fascination of dreams, the influence that shakes him is figured in the Sidhe, the fairy people who travel in the wind and seduce men from their habitual lives. Or when he wishes for the end of the world, his beloved becomes the " white deer with no horns " and he himself " a hound with one red ear ", animals who represent forces of desire, and the coming destruction is figured in the " boar without bristles ", an old image of death. The imaginative value of such imagery is hard to assess. It imparts an air of remoteness, even of majesty, but at times it makes the poems too elaborate to be musical. The welter of strange images is an obstacle to a perfect unity of impression. No doubt for the poet, steeped in such legend, they are the right mirror of his moods, but they come from a world so distant that they leave a blurred impression as if the poems were written in an imperfectly intelligible language. They are too intellectual and not sufficiently associative. We grasp their meaning, but do not catch all their echoes. The effect of mystery is certainly secured, but we are not always convinced that we wish to penetrate it.

This criticism applies only to those poems where the images are so accumulated that the sensibility faints before them. In others Yeats has mastered his manner and produces new impressive effects. In *The Song of Wandering Aengus* he takes the story of a poet who saw a divine being and spent his life searching for her. The subject is old and traditional, but Yeats gives a new meaning and a new magic to it :

> Though I am old with wandering
> Through hollow lands and hilly lands,
> I will find out where she has gone,
> And kiss her lips and take her hands ;
> And walk along long dappled grass,
> And pluck till time and times are done
> The silver apples of the moon,
> The golden apples of the sun.

The image of the wandering bard has its own interest, but it has a symbolical importance because it suits Yeats with his desires for hidden and mysterious forces and may be applied to all who have such desires. Anyone can incorporate it into his own experience, because it is entirely intelligible and sustained by a rhythm which keeps it on the level of song. The individual bard becomes a symbol of a universal longing which is all the clearer for being presented in a vivid, concrete, particular case. Behind it we may hear echoes of the song which William Morris makes the Nymph sing to Hylas :

I know a little garden close
Set thick with lily and red rose,
Where I would wander if I might
From dewy dawn to dewy night. . . .

The roots of Yeats' poem are in the Romantic tradition, but he has changed the whole purpose of such poetry by making it symbolical of himself and of others.

A counterpart to this poem may be seen in *The Happy Townland.* There is a similar foundation in folk-lore, this time in the Irish notion that certain men are " away ", entirely absorbed in the search for an Earthly Paradise which is hidden behind the appearances of the visible world. The rhythm of Morris gives place to something more like that of folk-song. It is wilder and stranger than the more formal rhythm of the earlier poem. The call to this new existence with its promise of happiness and abundance is figured in the little red fox of fable, and the elements conspire to help him :

The little fox he murmured,
" O what of the world's bane ? "
The sun was laughing sweetly,
The moon plucked at my rein ;
But the little red fox murmured,
" O do not pluck at his rein,
He is riding to the townland
That is the world's bane."

The folk-tale behind this implies the existence of two worlds, one of which is quite ordinary, the other full of beauty and excitement. This second is " the townland " and naturally it is " the world's bane ", for he who knows of it and seeks it loses all interest in his work and surroundings. The poem stresses the discord between these two orders, and the old notion in it symbolises a similar discord in the poet, whose search for a transcendental or spiritual world interferes with his customary duties and gives him a distaste for ordinary things. And what is true of the poet is true of all who seek for a more solid satisfaction in dream or fancy than they find in life. The very strangeness of the symbols makes the discord clearer, and the haunting, lilting tune gives its tone and temper.

The symbolism of these two poems is both emotional and intellectual. The images are delightful in themselves and stand for ideas which can best be grasped through images.

In other cases Yeats' symbolism is more emotional than intellectual, especially when he writes about the Rose. He explains that the Rose is the symbol of spiritual love and supreme beauty, and to this extent it is intellectual. But such a notion is too comprehensive to be clear to the mind, and in Yeats' poetry the Rose produces an effect which is mainly emotional. It stands for something exalted and pure and it calls for impassioned allegiance. It is therefore a natural symbol for love, and Yeats writes of

> Your image that blossoms a rose in the deeps of my heart.

It is, too, some vaguer form of blessedness such as is seen by the seer in *The Blessed*. But its full range and significance are revealed in *The Secret Rose*. In the opening lines,

> Far off, most secret and inviolate Rose,
> Enfold me in my hour of hours ; where those
> Who sought thee in the Holy Sepulchre
> Or in the wine vat, dwell beyond the stir
> And tumult of defeated dreams,

the symbol is of something too vast and too exalted for ordinary words, something which can only be expressed in metaphor. But as it proceeds, the poem passes through religious emblems, Christian and Druid, to famous figures of Irish history who have made great sacrifices, and we realise that the Rose is manifested in Ireland. The poem ends with a prophecy of her deliverance :

> I, too, await
> The hour of thy great wind of love and hate.
> When shall the stars be blown about the sky,
> Like the sparks blown out of a smithy, and die ?
> Surely thine hour has come, thy great wind blows,
> Far off, most secret, and inviolate Rose ?

The ideal Ireland of the poet's hope is identified with this high object of reverence and desire, and in the identification the idea of Ireland is exalted and purified. It is seen as an example of a universal power, and the qualities of that power belong to it.

The claim of this method is that it allows the poet to deal with subjects which ordinary speech must leave vague. Such subjects play a large part in all aesthetic experience and are the stuff of which mysteries are made. To define them more closely would be to rob them of some essential characteristics ; to express them in ordinary abstractions would be entirely inadequate for anyone who feels their real character. They can only be revealed in symbols, and for them the Symbolist method is essential. Just as Mallarmé conveyed the distance and impersonality of his Absolute through the symbol of the azure sky, so Yeats conveys a different absolute of beauty and majesty through the Rose. Its meaning may seem to change with its context, but that is because of the variety which it possesses in itself and because it enters into many forms and is manifested in many ways. It exists at a level where precise definition is impossible and it finds a greater precision of meaning according to the clarity of the context in which it is placed. But in every context it keeps its own air and atmosphere, its claim to devotion and honour.

Some chance remarks of Yeats, however, indicate that he did not always follow his theory quite in this way. There are places where he suggests that a poem may now mean one thing, now another, that its clearness to the sensitive mind is not constant. This is not to say, what is obviously true, that a poem will not always have the same effect on the same reader, still less on different readers. Yeats refers to the intellectual use of symbols and assumes that their intelligible meaning may vary. This is not true of the poems which we have examined. The meaning of the symbols is clear and fairly constant. Nor is this claim made for them. But in his note on *The Cap and Bells* Yeats implies a different theory. After saying that he dreamed this story exactly as he has written it, he adds :

The poem has always meant a great deal to me, though as is the way with symbolic poems, it has not always meant quite the same thing. Blake would have said " the authors are in eternity ", and I am quite sure they can only be questioned in dreams.

Here is no simple question of technique. Yeats here regards poetry as a kind of magic, and a new question is posed. *The Cap and Bells* is a fascinating, delightful poem, but it has no intellectual meaning like the *Song of Wandering Aengus* nor even an emotionally intelligible meaning like the poems about the Rose. The soul " in a straight blue garment " and the heart " in a red and quivering garment " are images that bring delight but must inevitably mean one thing to one man and another thing to another. The symbols are used almost entirely for their emotional power and are not related to an intelligible core. And yet the poem is unquestionably charming and undeniably a poem. It creates a world unlike any of ordinary experience, and the colours that are in a sense meaningless affect the imagination. It is far removed from the poetry which treats of common life, and belongs to an order where familiar objects have an unfamiliar significance. So long as the poem delights and provides its rhythmical effect, it has done its work and even given its " meaning ". But this is not what Yeats claims for it. For him the " meaning " is the message conveyed through the dream, the information which, when interpreted as a cipher, it gives about the life of the spirit. Even for him it has more than one such " meaning ". The method employed is certainly symbolical, but Yeats is not content that the poem should be emotionally and aesthetically satisfying. He has related it to a special scheme of existence and found in it clues to secrets outside ordinary knowledge.

In *The Wind among the Reeds* Yeats adapted the Symbolist method to his own views and uses. It suited an important element in his nature, his deep trust in dreams and visions, in the mysterious and the occult. It suited his belief that the poet is a kind of medium between spirits and men, a seer who interprets clues to the mysteries of life. Yet despite his whole-hearted acceptance of Symbolism, as an artist he was not entirely content with the manner which he found through it. His masculine intelligence demanded a more concrete and vigorous style, a greater precision and force. In *The Seven Woods* (1904) such poems as *Adam's Curse* show that he had begun to get closer to fact. But the most formative influence on him in these years was the stage, and can be seen in the remarkable poetical dramas which he wrote between 1900 and 1906. He wished to be a national poet and to create an Irish theatre. He seems to have felt that through the drama he might become more objective and " bring a less dream-burdened will " into his verse.

In time he was to do this, but not quite yet. His first plays are cast in a world of legend and fairy. In them he is still a Symbolist. The dramatic form might at first sight seem ill adapted both for the Symbolist style and the Symbolist temperament. The drama allows no time for its listeners to ponder over difficulties. It must secure its impression at once and it must be clear. The Symbolists reasserted the poet's personality, and in drama this is irrelevant and even a hindrance. On the other hand dramatic expression was dear to them. Mallarmé conceived his *Igitur* as a drama, and *Hérodiade* is cast in dramatic form. The most popular manifestation of Symbolism was the dramatic art of Maeterlinck, in which the characters have no personality but are symbols of the poet's dreams. It is from this tradition that Yeats' drama arose.

In its first stages Yeats' drama must be regarded as an extension of his lyrical poetry. Experiences too complex to be cast into lyrical verse may be put into plays without losing their essentially lyrical character. When Yeats published *The Shadowy Waters* in 1900, it was quite unsuited to the stage. Later he saw this and adapted it. In its first form it suffered from more than its lack of action ; the exquisitely elaborated speech, curtailed and pruned later, is not the speech of men and women but of the poet. Each character speaks with similar cadences and equally abundant metaphor. All is maintained in the same atmosphere of dreaming inactivity and has the air of meditation rather than of action. The slow rich accents fall from the Sailors as from the lovers Forgael and Dectora ; there is no character but seems at any moment likely to be merged in another. The truth is that the poem was not conceived as a drama but as a poem in dramatic form, and the interest centres not on the characters and their actions but on the expression of certain emotions, especially love. In the symbolical expression of love *The Shadowy Waters* is Yeats' most sustained performance. In it the method of *The Wind among the Reeds* is used on a larger scale with more continuous effect and with greater coherence of design. It is a vision of romantic love, and like all Yeats' visions it is related by him to the world of invisible essences which he finds about him, especially in sleep. In the Dedication he explains what the play means to him :

> I have not eyes like those enchanted eyes,
> Yet dreamed that beings happier than men
> Moved round me in the shadows, and at night
> My dreams were cloven by voices and by fires ;
> And the images I have woven in this story
> Of Forgael and Dectora and the empty waters
> Moved round me in the voices and the fires.

This is the world of which Yeats dreamed when he sank himself in Irish fables and used their figures for his symbols. He now projects his emotions into legendary characters, but they do not live on their own, they are " images ", aspects of himself, using his language and his familiar thoughts. He calls the work a " story ", and it is certainly more that than a drama. Its critical moments are not created by the events but by the emotions expressed. The beauty is of speech and sentiment ; character and crisis have little importance. The tone of dreaming ecstasy, of withdrawal into an ideal world of dream, is marvellously sustained, but it is not dramatic. The beauty of *The Shadowy Waters* is really lyrical. Even the magical close relies for its effect on the emotions and ideas which it evokes, not on the situation of the characters :

> O flower of the branch, O bird among the leaves,
> O silver fish that my two hands have taken
> Out of the running stream, O morning star —
> Trembling in the blue heavens like a white fawn
> Upon the misty border of the wood,—
> Bend lower that I may cover you with my hair,
> For we will gaze upon this world no longer.

It hardly matters who says this. It is the speech of the poet to his love, and as such we read and remember it.

The Shadowy Waters is the crown of the poetry which Yeats wrote under the example of Mallarmé as Symons explained it to him. In it the method of *Hérodiade* is carried to a highly personal conclusion, hardly in authentic drama but at least in dramatic lyric according to Symbolist rules. It is the poem of the poet's ideal love, of all such love as he understands it. His other plays of this period are not quite like this. They were meant to be acted and were acted. In them Yeats moved slowly to a more objective kind of drama and to a different manner of poetry. In each perhaps there are traces of Symbolist influence. In *The King's Threshold* (1904) the subject of the dishonoured and unrepentant poet must be drawn from Yeats' own thoughts about himself and his position as an artist. In *On Baile's Strand* (1905) the passionate warrior Cuchulain is a type of the independent high-spirited man who had always some place in Yeats' picture of himself, and in *Deirdre* (1906) he reverts to his drama of an ideal love. But what distinguishes these plays from *The*

Shadowy Waters is that the language is less dream-laden and more suited to the action. There is a new note when in *On Baile's Strand* Cuchulain draws his sword and says,

> This mutterer, this old whistler, this sand-piper,
> This edge that's greyer than the tide, this mouse
> That's gnawing at the timbers of the world,
> This, this — Boy, I would meet them all in arms
> If I'd a son like you.

This lives with its own life. It is not a reflection of the poet's mood. Or again, when in the same play at the beginning and end a Fool and a Blind Man talk prose, they give some of the variety of tone which Shakespeare gives on a far greater scale and to a far richer effect when he combines prose and verse.

In these plays Yeats believed that he was following the tradition of English poetical drama and writing as Shelley wrote *The Cenci*. It is true that *Deirdre* has moved a long way from Maeterlinck and has a truly dramatic situation. But there are qualities in Yeats' dramas which separate them not in degree but in kind from English poetical drama, and these qualities are due to Yeats himself and to his literary situation. It is impossible to feel that the world of these plays is comparable to that of *The Cenci*, let alone to that of *Macbeth*. On all of them there is a peculiar stamp of the poet's personality. It is not merely that Yeats is far less skilful than Shakespeare at hiding his own likes and dislikes or that he does not create a wide range of characters. It is that his personality is so strong that it leaves its mark on everything that he writes. It comes out in the choice of subjects and in the limitation of the action to very plain and clear-cut issues, but most in the extremely personal rhythm of the verse, which makes us feel that the poet, and not his characters, is speaking. The verse has the premeditated grandeur, the completeness and eloquence of a poet who enjoys a fullness of expression and does not care for broken sentences and half-stifled cries, who likes elaborate words and rich imagery and will not sacrifice rhythm to the exigencies of a dramatic situation. It is in some ways the world of Villiers' *Axël*, where the issues of life and death are discussed with rotund fullness and everything is raised to the same pitch of rhetoric. Yeats' style is not rhetoric but it is rhetorical. It is meant to be declaimed, and though drama may be written on these lines, it is not impersonal nor the most dramatic kind of drama.

These plays differ in another respect from Shakespearean drama and even from *The Cenci*. Yeats is so thoroughly a poet, so loyal to his conception of poetry for poetry's sake, that he hardly varies his tone throughout. The persons speak with his voice and with his intensity. The result is that they are not characters in any dramatic sense. They are not even types. They are creatures of the imagination who speak poetically about matters of great and universal import. They have more affinity to lyric than to drama. Now it is true that in the highest moments of all great poetical drama the personality of the character does not count so much as his situation, which is typical of a tragic human destiny, and that at such moments individuality is merged in poetry. Yeats is capable of such effects as this. There is real tragic nobility in such lines as his Deirdre speaks when she knows that she and her lover are to die :

> And praise the double sunset, for naught's lacking,
> But a good end to the long, cloudy day.

But the whole play is pitched at this level and almost in this tone. As a dramatist Yeats did not interest himself in building up the action and the characters, in leading from one tone to another, from ordinary events to a tragic end. No doubt he felt that this was not a poet's business and that poetical drama must throughout be poetry. In his own way he still sought " pure poetry " and provided it in his plays. Poetical drama cannot be " pure poetry " if it is to be dramatic, and Yeats' plays are after all more poetry than drama. None the less in his development they mark an important stage. Just because he had to face a public with them and to make his meaning concise and clear, he was forced to trim and pare his language, to make it more forcible and effective, to be more objective in his presentation of people and events.

The fruits of this activity were remarkable. When in 1910 Yeats published the slim volume of *The Green Helmet*, his whole manner and outlook had changed. The elaboration, the mythology, the vagueness, the wavering rhythms, have disappeared, and in their place are simplicity, directness, plain vivid imagery, terse and concentrated rhythms. Yeats has remodelled his style and forged a powerful instrument which seems to owe nothing to his earlier work. The change coincided with a period of great strain and effort in his life, with the years which saw the death of Synge and the angry controversy with the Dublin Corporation about Hugh Lane's pictures. These events drew Yeats out of himself and made him a politician and a pamphleteer, but they do not entirely account for the change in his style. There were strong influences at work to change the artist no less than the man. The manner which he had invented from folk-tale and legend, all the vagueness and dreaminess associated with " the Celtic twilight ", had been borrowed and debased by a crowd of imitators. Yeats found himself classed with men of vastly inferior talent. The imagery which had meant so much to him became the means for his humiliation, and he turned away from it in horror. His bitterness is described in *A Coat* :

> I made my song a coat
> Covered with embroideries
> Out of old mythologies
> From heel to throat ;
> But the fools caught it,
> Wore it in the world's eyes
> As though they'd wrought it.
> Song, let them take it,
> For there's more enterprise
> In walking naked.

Henceforward he would dispense with his trappings and let his poetry go forth unadorned. And with the trappings had gone, for a time at least, something else, the trust in a world of dreams, the conviction that the poet is a seer, the antinomy between vision and reality. The new Yeats had changed something else than his style.

In *Responsibilities* (1914), *The Wild Swans at Coole* (1917) and *Michael Robartes* (1920) the fruits of the change were manifest in all their strength. Yeats had found a new power of plain statement and wrote with directness about familiar and elementary passions. He had explored deeper into himself, widened the range of his poetry and increased its variety. The roots of the change can best be seen in his love-poetry. So far back as *The Seven Woods* a poem like *The Folly of Being Comforted* showed how Yeats could, if he chose, be perfectly simple and straightforward. In *The Green Helmet* simplicity has become the rule. In middle age Yeats felt, as most men do, that his time for passion was nearly over, and he looked back with pride, with regret, with sorrow, but without repentance, on the great love of his life. Maud Gonne, who had inspired all his early love-poetry, was also reaching middle life. She was a famous figure in politics, an advanced nationalist, revolutionary and rebel. Yeats saw her as she was and remembered what she had been. She was still the ideal of his dreams ; he was still amazed, delighted and appalled by her. This confusion of emotions inspired him. The first splendid signs appear in *No Second Troy* :

> Why should I blame her that she filled my days
> With misery, or that she would of late
> Have taught to ignorant men most violent ways,
> Or hurled the little streets upon the great,
> Had they but courage equal to desire ?
> What could have made her peaceful with a mind
> That nobleness made simple as a fire,
> With beauty like a tightened bow, a kind
> That is not natural in an age like this,
> Being high and solitary and most stern ?
> Why, what could she have done being what she is ?
> Was there another Troy for her to burn ?

Then follow the magnificent series of poems in which Yeats looks back on all that this woman once was to him. His only adequate symbol for her is Helen of Troy ; for like Helen she is beyond praise or comment. Such is the theme of *When Helen Lived*. Such is the spirit behind *That the Night Come* with its comparison of her to a great king :

> She lived in storm and strife,
> Her soul had such desire
> For what proud death may bring
> That it could not endure
> The common good of life,
> But lived as 'twere a king
> That packed his marriage day
> With banneret and pennon,
> Trumpet and kettledrum,
> And the outrageous cannon,
> To bundle time away
> That the night come.

The concentration of this poetry, its occasional conversational words like " bundle ", its sudden and startling similes and metaphors coming with such effect after the plainest of plain statements, its great skill in construction and handling of stops, are something new in English. It has been compared with Dante, and there is truth in the comparison. For it has Dante's terse passion and occasional acridity, his unexpected bursts into simile and his tense concentration of thought. It can be gay in *His Phoenix*, meditative in *Her Praise*, deeply touching in *Fallen Majesty*. In each case the metre and the verbal melody respond exactly to the mood, from the almost popular tune of

> I knew a phoenix in my youth so let them have their day.

to the halting, hesitant rhythm of

> The lineaments, a heart that laughter has made sweet,
> These, these remain, but I record what's gone. A crowd
> Will gather and not know it walks the very street
> Whereon a thing once walked that seemed a burning cloud.

There is still some of the old majesty here, but it is clear and firm. The words come from common life and have all its strength and roots. The rhythm exalts them into high poetry.

Yeats' new manner coincided with some change in himself. Flung by circumstances into action and controversy, he found himself stirred by new themes and responded finely to them. Amongst these was politics, a subject tabooed by the Symbolists and all but denied by Yeats in his youth. It is true that at times he had written of a mystical Ireland and that he saw himself as an Irish poet. But current issues had not entered into his verse. But now he wrote poetry about a matter which might seem to be of a purely transitory interest, the refusal of the Dublin Corporation to accept the French pictures of Sir Hugh Lane. The dark passions which this aroused seem distant enough to-day. The complacent provincialism of the authorities, the campaign of calumny and misrepresentation which they instituted, the welter of ignorant and self-satisfied judgments which they evoked, have joined other inglorious chapters of Irish history. And yet the five poems which Yeats wrote about the quarrel are as fresh as any great poetry. They have passed beyond the transitory interest of their occasion and joined those passages of Dante where he declaims against the weakness and treachery of his beloved Florence. Yeats shows conclusively that the Symbolists were wrong when they thought politics an impossible subject for poetry. These poems are aflame with passion, and through it a subject which might have been of no poetical interest is made moving and important. The temporary quarrel is shown to be a field where vast issues are at stake,— the whole spiritual life of a nation and the turpitude or grandeur of the protagonists in the struggle. These timeless matters are the poet's property if he chooses to use them, and for Yeats the affair of the pictures concerned the noblest and the basest in man. His subject is not the special point at issue but the low motives displayed and the high courage which fought against them. In *To a Friend whose Work has come to Nothing* the original occasion was Lady Gregory's untiring efforts to secure the pictures for Ireland. It is a personal poem written to her, a poem of consolation and of praise :

> Now all the truth is out,
> Be secret and take defeat
> From any brazen throat,
> For how can you compete,
> Being honour bred, with one
> Who, were it proved he lies,
> Were neither shamed in his own
> Nor in his neighbours' eyes ?
> Bred to a harder thing
> Than Triumph, turn away
> And like a laughing string
> Whereon mad fingers play
> Amid a place of stone,
> Be secret and exult,
> Because of all things known
> That is most difficult.

The poet passes beyond Lady Gregory and honours all those who have worked hard to no purpose and are able to take defeat without complaint.

The Lane controversy broke the limitations which Yeats had placed on his art and turned him from an exquisite into a powerful poet. Scorn, pride and disgust had found no place in his earlier verse. But now they came into it and bridged the gap between his old vision of Ireland and his present knowledge of it. This poetry is in some respects that of a man who has been dreaming and finds reality different from his dreams. It recalls Blok's ironical poetry when he ceased to believe in his visions. For Yeats the " secret Rose " has been turned into an angry and quarrelsome crowd with no interest beyond its pocket. No wonder that he wrote

> Was it for this the wild geese spread
> The grey wing upon every tide ;
> For this that all that blood was shed,
> For this Edward FitzGerald died,
> And Robert Emmet and Wolfe Tone,
> All that delirium of the brave ;
> Romantic Ireland's dead and gone,
> It's with O'Leary in the grave.

The words all come from common speech, yet how great is the
effect which the medical word " delirium " makes among the
plain monosyllables. Instead of Conchubar and Cuchulain
a new mythology and martyrology come to the fore with the
heroes of '98, whose names are repeated at every Irish political
meeting and to whom Yeats gives a new dignity. And to
them he adds his own old friend O'Leary who was so true
an idealist that he said, " There are things a man must not
do to save a nation ". The language and the names recall
political life and suggest that Yeats is talking politics. But
every word carries its full weight. He moves in a real world,
but that has only made his poetry more forceful. The harsh
crudities to which he has awoken are best expressed in this
way.

The political excitements of these years paled into insig-
nificance before what was to follow. The Dublin Rebellion of
Easter 1916 is believed, despite its immediate failure, to have
been the beginning of modern Ireland. The selfless sacrifice
of its leaders undeniably made a deep impression on the Irish
people and prepared the way for great changes. Yeats was in
England when it happened. With the rebels' aims he had no
great sympathy. His ideal of Ireland was more spiritual than
political, and he disapproved of the useless shedding of blood.
But among the rebels were some very dear to him, some too
whom he detested. He might have stood aside in mournful
arrogance or proclaimed the futility of the whole affair, but
his feelings were too full for that. He wrote of it not as a
politician but as a man who felt that it had changed his life by
removing that scorn in which he had dealt too freely :

> Being certain that they and I
> But lived where motley is worn :
> All changed, changed utterly :
> A terrible beauty is born.

His emotions are naturally mixed, and the poem gives the whole gamut of them : wonder, exaltation, pity, forgiveness, hope, resignation. It keeps strictly and exactly to fact. The chief characters are described as they were in life : the Countess Markiewicz who spent her days " in ignorant good will ", the schoolmaster Pearse and his friend Connolly, the " drunken vainglorious lout " MacBride. The scene is Dublin with its " eighteenth-century houses " and men going to counter or desk. Suddenly all this " casual comedy " is changed into the reality of tragedy.

The poem is intensely intimate and personal. Yeats says exactly what he felt about the rebellion and even expresses his central doubt, that men who act like this may find their hearts turned to stone. He elaborates the idea in the third section in the wonderful image of the stone in the living stream. Life passes over it, but it remains unchanged and unmoved. Yet even this doubt is not absolute. Yeats passes from it to the hope that good may come. It is perhaps only a hope, yet it is what he feels. And more even than hope he feels the duty of hushed reverence over the dead :

> We know their dream ; enough
> To know they dreamed and are dead ;
> And what if excess of love
> Bewildered them till they died ?
> I write it out in a verse —
> MacDonagh and MacBride
> And Connolly and Pearse
> Now and in time to be,
> Wherever green is worn,
> Are changed, changed utterly :
> A terrible beauty is born.

He who had recently written of Lord Edward and Wolfe Tone now added new martyrs to his list. He uses the methods of popular national poetry. Yet there is nothing cheap or temporary in this. It is too personal, too deeply felt. It shows the overwhelming effect which the rebellion had on Yeats, and shows it so sincerely, so directly, that its rhythms haunt the memory.

In his other poems on the rebellion Yeats shows a similar truth and a grasp of reality which we might not have expected from him. In *Sixteen Dead Men* he knows that once the Irish leaders had been shot all hopes of peaceful settlement with

Great Britain were finished. No logic can outweigh the
argument of martyrdom. In *The Rose Tree* he presents in a
kind of ballad a dialogue between Pearse and Connolly and
shows how well he understood the motives which led to an act
which seemed foredoomed to failure. Pearse argues that
Ireland can only be revived and regenerated through blood :

> " But where can we draw water,"
> Said Pearse to Connolly,
> " When all the wells are parched away ?
> O plain as plain can be
> There's nothing but our own red blood
> Can make a right Rose Tree."

The notion that a country must be redeemed by blood is
familiar from George and Blok. Yeats does not perhaps
himself accept it, but he knows that the rebels did, and he
knows what it means. He himself is still at some distance
from them, but he understands, even admires, them. The
rebellion was not of his making, but he is its greatest poet
because he sees it with the impartial but understanding eyes
of one who knows all its characters as they really were and
judges them not by abstract standards of right and wrong but
by the human heart.

The shock of circumstance had brought Yeats out of his
dreams and shaken his absorption in that other world behind
the visible which had been the mainspring of his activity.
Indeed in 1916 it seemed as if Yeats had really ceased to care
for dreams and spirits, so great was the effect of events in
Ireland on him. To his old mythological manner he never
returned. It had served its purpose and been flung aside.
But he had not really abandoned his belief in a spiritual world
or ceased to be a Symbolist. His poetry had found new
worlds to conquer. He had put far more of his everyday self
into it. But whereas before the antithesis had been between
his poetry and his ordinary life, between his dreams and his
usual self, it now appeared actually in his work between those
poems which dealt with politics and love and those which
dealt with another world of spirits and magic. He had been
interested in spiritualism from his childhood, when one of his
uncles had practised it. He had found food for it in many
popular stories of ghosts and demons. He was not in any
sense a Christian, but like others of his time he needed some

supernatural basis for his beliefs. For a while he had been satisfied with a vague world of beauty behind the real. Now that this had receded, he tried to satisfy himself by other means. When he married in 1917, he found that his wife was a medium, and with her he conducted many experiments and believed that he was in touch with spirits. His orderly, critical mind tried to reduce these phenomena to order, to find in them a system of life. The conclusions were given in his extraordinary book, *A Vision*, first published in 1925. The book attempts to give a theory of the varieties of human types, of the changes of history and of the transformations of the soul here and hereafter, and relates these to a " Great Wheel " which somehow corresponds to the changes of the moon. Yeats attached great importance to this book and took trouble to rewrite it. Yet despite passages of insight and beauty, it presents a deterministic system so contrary to experience that we wonder if he really believed in it, and why. At the end of it he almost suggests that he does not, and that, after all, his system may only be a set of symbols like another. *A Vision* is undeniably disquieting.

Stern young critics have claimed that in presenting this body of belief to the world Yeats was not sincere, that he even wished to make himself interesting by advancing a gospel so far removed from common thought. But surely this is to treat him as if he were a philosopher or a scientist who forms his views through argument or experiment and is careful to make them consistent. *A Vision* is something quite different. In it Yeats tries to systematise various spiritualistic experiences which seem important to him and have affected his life. He admits that he does not fully understand all that they mean. What matters is his conviction that there must be something in them. He had lived too long among dreams and super-natural phenomena to deny the worth of all this. He naturally tried to make sense of it. If in the end he was still uncertain of his conclusions, that is to his credit. He was a poet, and his task was to give in the most expressive form what meant most to him. It happened that this had come through spiritualistic séances. It inspired much of his poetry, but for the public it needed explanation. *A Vision* provides a background ; what matters is the poetry.

For the first time an English poet of mature powers and great eminence wrote about spiritualistic experiences, about ghosts and necromancy. Sometimes Yeats' themes are not merely unfamiliar to religious or scientific opinion but are actually hostile to them. We might expect such poems to be impossibly esoteric, full of meanings which we cannot grasp or feelings which we cannot share. But actually we cannot but surrender to Yeats' power. He compels us to think that, no matter how wrong he may be to believe in all this, it is undeniably exciting and, maintained at his level of concentration and mystery, belongs to aesthetic delight and to poetry. In *Presences* he tells of ghosts who have haunted him because he has written about " returned and yet unrequited love ". But these ghosts are not horrible or even absurd. They are real phantoms, unearthly and yet in some strange way human :

> They stood in the door and stood between
> My great wood lectern and the fire
> Till I could hear their hearts beating.

They do nothing, say nothing, perhaps have no significance. What matters is their presence with the poet in his room. Far stranger and yet none the less impressive for an element of the ludicrous in it is the refrain of *The Apparitions* :

> Fifteen apparitions have I seen ;
> The worst a coat upon a coat-hanger.

In *All Souls' Night* the theme is a séance, a calling-up of departed spirits. The poet, with a glass of wine in front of him, is in a kind of ecstasy in the silence of the night. He concentrates his powers on his task, and the first verse creates the magnificent half-intoxicated moment :

> Midnight has come and the great Christ Church Bell,
> And many a lesser bell, sound through the room ;
> And it is All Souls' Night,
> And two long glasses brimmed with muscatel
> Bubble upon the table. A ghost may come ;
> For it is a ghost's right,
> His element is so fine
> Being sharpened by his death,
> To drink from the wine-breath
> While our gross palates drink from the whole wine.

Then as the ghosts are named, the tone changes, and Yeats shows all his usual candour and irony about their characters.

Despite its strange setting this is a real event. We can understand it and feel its magic.

Yeats' unusual beliefs penetrated into many departments
of life. In *The Double Vision of Michael Robartes* he gives two
visions of great importance to his theories. In the first he sees
a mechanistic system operating through the universe and
displays it in words which show all its inhuman power :

> Constrained, arraigned, baffled, bent and unbent
> By these wire-jointed jaws and limbs of wood,
> Themselves obedient,
> Knowing not evil and good ;
>
> Obedient to some hidden magical breath.
> They do not even feel, so abstract are they,
> So dead beyond our death,
> Triumph that we obey.

In the second vision he sees not the powers behind life but the
forces that count for most in it. Between a Sphinx and a
Buddha, types of withdrawn and complete contemplation, a
girl dances. In her way she too is entirely self-absorbed, and
all three are equally types of that completion which needs
nothing outside itself. This ideal, not utterly unlike Rilke's
Angel, is also Yeats' ideal. As a thinker he might compare
himself to Buddha or the Sphinx, as an artist to the dancing
girl. The mysterious presentation and the hermetic language
hide a truth which we must all recognise, that certain types of
completeness, whether in thought or in action, fill us with
amazement and almost with despair. Yeats, torn between
visions and reality, between abstract speculation and poetic
creation, sees that each has its own perfection and needs no
help from the others.

This apocalyptic poetry may appeal to different moods.
The beautiful song in *The Sad Shepherd* is based on the notion
that the dead grow young again, and is Yeats' memorial to his
friend Robert Gregory. It is a strange consolation to those
who have felt his loss. But despite its strangeness it is more
effective than most conventional solaces. It is only a fancy,
and presented as a fancy, but the poet suggests that perhaps
it is true, and if it is true, there is undeniable charm in this
conception of the dead man

> Jaunting, journeying
> To his own dayspring.

The poem was written to one of Yeats' dearest friends and shows how deeply his occult beliefs were woven into the fabric of his thought. In moments of grief and loss he turned to them. At times indeed they are so closely interwoven that we hardly notice their strangeness. Of his many poems to Maud Gonne not the least beautiful is *The New Faces*, written when both she and he have grown old :

> If you that have grown old, were the first dead,
> Neither catalpa tree nor scented lime
> Shall hear my living feet, nor would I tread
> Where we wrought that shall break the teeth of time.
> Let the new faces play what tricks they will
> In the old rooms ; night can outbalance day,
> Our shadows rove the garden gravel still,
> The living seem more shadowy than they.

In another poet this might be fancy ; in Yeats it is what he believed. He felt sure that the dead haunt those places where in life they have known their greatest and grandest moments. In his hands the notion that love is stronger than death takes a special form, and because he is entirely sincere and natural about it, his poem is not in the least strange. It is a declaration of abiding love.

Of a different kind is *The Second Coming*, a prophetic poem which carries an intensity of fear and horror. Inspired by the anarchy of the world, by the increase of bloodshed and the destruction of belief, Yeats has a vision. We need not believe that he actually saw it. It rises from the mood of doubt and despair, from the sense of coming disaster, which is true enough to all human hearts. Onto his apprehensive gaze it comes :

> Surely some revelation is at hand ;
> Surely the Second Coming is at hand.
> The Second Coming ! Hardly are those words out
> When a vast image out of Spiritus Mundi
> Troubles my sight : somewhere in sands of the desert
> A shape with lion body and the head of a man,
> A gaze blank and pitiless as the sun,
> Is moving its slow thighs, while all about it
> Reel shadows of the indignant desert birds.
> The darkness drops again ; but now I know
> That twenty centuries of stony sleep
> Were vexed to nightmare by a rocking cradle,
> And what rough beast, its hour come round at last,
> Slouches towards Bethlehem to be born ?

The mention of Spiritus Mundi and the suggestion of the Wheel through which history repeats itself come from Yeats' philosophy. But they are fused into the vision and the poem. Like George and Blok, Yeats has his moment of insight into a formidable future. But unlike them, he neither fears nor desires it. He simply sees it and knows that it is extremely strange. He keeps his prophet's detachment, but none the less the poem is full of an extraordinary sense of something portentous. The measured verse, the repeated phrases, the simple and terribly effective images, convey this moment of concentrated and amazed vision. Nor is this merely his own experience. There are few who have not felt some undeciphered evil coming on the world and cannot find here an echo of their own apprehensions.

From this kind of mysticism Yeats moved to the study of philosophy. He was not by nature a logician and he preferred the way of the heart to the way of the mind. But he could not keep himself from reading philosophers and finding something in them to suit his own opinions. He was not like Bridges who in *The Testament of Beauty* built a system on traditional lines. He was wilful in his treatment of theories. In his desire to find a truly subjective system he read Berkeley, but his version of him leaves out the mind of God which sustains the universe when we are not perceiving it. To Yeats philosophy meant not hard, abstract thought but discursive meditation about the universe, and especially about the state of pure contemplation as it is known to Buddhists and all who have found bliss in the annihilation of the flesh. In such trance-like joy there is usually an element of mystical vision, such as Parmenides or Plotinus knew in the vision of the One. Yeats himself seems never to have known this, but he admired it and desired it, believing that it could be found through intellectual effort. But he only desired this as a second-best because he felt that he was growing too old to be a poet :

> It seems that I must bid the Muse go pack,
> Choose Plato and Plotinus for a friend,
> Until imagination, ear and eye,
> Can be content with argument and deal
> With abstract things. . . .

In the chaos of his times and the advance of years he imagined an intellectual solitude in which he would find a mystic's joy. He symbolised this longing and this change in *Sailing to*

Byzantium, and his reason is that he is too old for the ordinary world. He wishes to be like the sages in the gold mosaic of a wall, gathered

> Into the artifice of eternity.

Yet even here the word "artifice" suggests that for Yeats this eternity is something that the poet makes for himself, a triumph of his art.

The fact is that this Absolute of which Yeats dreamed is only half the picture. He never knew it or found it. It was something abstract and ordered, against which he set the changing disorder of his and other men's lives. If his Soul desired it, his Self did not. In *A Dialogue of Self and Soul* the conflict is tense and clear. The Soul says

> I summon to the winding ancient stair ;
> Set all your mind upon the steep ascent,
> Upon the broken, crumbling battlement,
> Upon the breathless starlit air,
> Upon the star that marks the hidden pole ;
> Fix every wandering thought upon
> That quarter where all thought is done :
> Who can distinguish darkness from the soul ?

The ascent to abstract thought, expressed in language that almost recalls St. John of the Cross, is answered by the Self, which pleads for life as it is with all its ignominies and enmities, its ignorance and frustrations :

> I am content to live it all again,
> And yet again, if it be life to pitch
> Into the frog-spawn of a blind man's ditch. . . .

The same conclusion is reached in *Vacillation*, where the Soul and, this time, the Heart debate and the poet throws over the mystics, Von Hügel and the rest, with a noble precedent before him :

> Homer is my example and his unchristened heart.

Despite his desire for intellectual peace, Yeats knew that it was not for him and that his task was to continue in the world of desire.

In such moments he naturally wondered whether perhaps even as a poet he might not find some state akin to the mystic's contemplation. In *Sailing to Byzantium* he imagines that he may become a kind of mechanical golden bird :

> Once out of nature I shall never take
> My bodily form from any natural thing,
> But such a form as Grecian goldsmiths make
> Of hammered gold and gold enamelling
> To keep a drowsy emperor awake ;
> Or set upon a golden bough to sing
> To lords and ladies of Byzantium
> Of what is past or passing or to come,

and he returns to the image in *Byzantium* as an escape from

> The fury and the mire of human veins.

To be a poet and not to suffer all that it entails is a natural desire in an ageing man. It has something in it akin to Mallarmé's conception of the poet who is only himself when he is dead, and to Rilke's belief that song means the loss of personality in some unity vaster than anything we know. Yet for Yeats this was an unattainable ideal. He did not even, like Blok, know the timeless ecstasy of creation. Once perhaps voices had spoken to him, but now he had to work to be a poet. Faced with a choice between an unrealisable ideal and a real world which had for long sustained him, he played with metaphysical notions of escape and even at moments believed that he might make his own destiny. But in the end his common sense triumphed. He accepted his lot, his earthly condition with all its limitations.

A conflict of this kind is by no means artificial or abstract. It may well penetrate into apparently common events and give them a special significance and make them the start for profound meditations. In *Among School Children* Yeats gives a special, remarkable case of his middle state between soul and body. He is now " a sixty-year-old smiling public man " and, no doubt as a Senator, inspects a school kept by nuns. As he looks at the girls, he remembers his beloved who must once have been such a child, and he thinks of her as she now is :

> Her present image floats into the mind —
> Did Quattrocento finger fashion it
> Hollow of cheek as though it drank the wind
> And took a mess of shadows for its meat ?

From her he turns to himself and concludes that it is

> Better to smile on all that smile, and show
> There is a comfortable kind of old scarecrow.

He asks of what use is beauty now, for all beauty is tied up

with the body and destined to decay with it. The philosophers are all wrong. Their experience bears no relation to these facts :

> World-famous golden-thighed Pythagoras
> Fingered upon a fiddle-stick or strings
> What a star sang and careless Muses heard :
> Old clothes upon old sticks to scare a bird.

Even the divine beauty which the nuns worship is displayed in images and copied from perishable things. Yet the conclusion is not despair but its opposite, a proclamation that the body must not be bruised to pleasure the Soul (which is for Yeats that which seeks abstraction), and that what matters is the instinctive joy of life symbolised by the chestnut-tree in blossom and the body swayed to music. Philosophy may hold out consolations to the poet, but in the end he rejects them and goes back to life.

In this splendid poem Yeats' mature method shows all its strength. The situation is real, even realistic, with the children studying history and the " kind old nun in a white hood ". The poet's thoughts follow a natural course. He passes from the present scene to memory, back to thoughts of the present and thence to meditation on what it all means. All takes place in his mind, and of this the poem tells. It has therefore a kind of symbolism quite unlike Yeats' earlier mythological symbolism. The chestnut-tree and the dancing body are symbols which stand for complex ideas and yet are full of life and significance. The poem is characteristic of Yeats' later symbolism. Though he had given up his old mythical methods and though he often wrote without any symbols at all, they were still necessary to him when his subject was at all intricate or abstruse. In fact he had never abandoned them. In his starkest days he had dramatised his own ideal love as that of Paris for Helen or of Solomon for Sheba. He had distinguished between logic and intuition by the symbols of the hawk, with its direct swoop to kill, and the butterfly which hovers from flower to flower. In *Meditations in Time of Civil War* he saw " phantoms of the heart's fullness " as unicorns with ladies on their backs. In his own circumstances he made symbols of what he saw about him, the old tower in which he lived, the winding staircase in it, the Japanese sword which lay on his table, the streams flowing underground from one place to another. The tower stood

differently for the aspirations of the intellect and the soul, for the self's assertiveness, for the modern nation " dead at the top ". The staircase stands for the intricate process by which the self ascends, the sword for action, the underground streams for the spiritual forces which make for new life. The symbols may vary in their contexts, but their meaning is always clear. They save much explanation, and they give a concrete form to ideas that would otherwise be dim.

More characteristic of Yeats is the mythology which he made out of people. Till old age he kept his legendary figures, the characters of history and poetry, who symbolised ideals for him. But he supplemented them with others from his own friends. The process began in his reveries over his own lost youth, over the friends who were dead when he was still in the prime of life. His first mention of Synge is of this kind :

> And that enquiring man John Synge comes next
> That dying chose the living world for text
> And never could have rested in the tomb
> But that, long travelling, he had come
> Towards nightfall upon certain set apart
> In a most desolate stony place,
> Towards nightfall upon a race
> Passionate and simple like his heart.

What Yeats valued in Synge was his naturalness, his nearness to common life. Of this he made him a type, a symbol. So with his other friends and acquaintances. Just as in *A Vision* each section of reality has its special and appropriate human type, so in Yeats' poetry different characters stand for different kinds of existence. He creates a mythology, even a hagiology, from philosophers and statesmen, patriots and mystics. In Berkeley and Parnell, in O'Leary and Florence Emery who went to teach in India

> Hidden from eyesight to the unnoticed end,

in many others who stood for principles which he valued, Yeats reveals his view of life, his likes and admirations. In most of them there is a proud independence, an integrity of character which refuses to be deluded or browbeaten. Most came from the Anglo-Irish class to which Yeats belonged :

> The people of Burke and of Grattan
> Who gave though free to refuse.

This was a new kind of Symbolism. Mallarmé was little

concerned with human beings until they had passed into eternity. But Yeats, with his great feeling for the concrete and his sharp insight into human nature, came to see the universe as largely a matter of human types. He tried to arrange and classify them, to impart order to their disparate variety. But he knew them as individuals, even if they stood for the many fates that may fall to man. In consequence his treatment of them is singularly sharp and clear, as if it were a matter of ordinary human relations. Even the most strange conflicts of the soul may be reduced to the differences between opposing types of men. The struggle between Soul and Body is that between Von Hügel and Homer, the perpetual struggles of Irish politics are nothing but the differences between those who are like Parnell and those who are not. Sometimes the method is a little too simple. The human beings represent too much. But on the whole this new kind of poetry is extraordinarily expressive. It gives to the great issues of existence the quality of some intimate and intensely felt relation.

The struggle between Soul and Self, between mind and heart, which had long occupied Yeats, was solved in his old age. The Self won. Yeats was still conscious of the mystical background to life, but what interested him most was life itself. He came nearer to it, was content to enjoy it. The result was a loosening in his style, an ever closer approximation to the language of every day, to old refrains and rhythms of ballads, to the simplest and most natural topics. In his *Last Poems* there is not even the stern majestic utterance of his mature work. He has flung the whole of himself into them and found at last a complete expression of his abundant complex nature. He is no longer torn by the conflict in himself between the man and the poet ; he no longer wears what he calls a " Mask " to present himself to the world. The old age which he had dreaded as the end of poetry brought a greater power to create and a freedom from all hindrances. Yeats even came to glory in it, to wish to be " a foolish, passionate man ". Perhaps the old Oedipus of Sophocles' play *Oedipus at Colonus*, which Yeats translated, influenced him. For it contains a terrifying study of a daemonic old man. It agrees with Yeats' own prayer for himself :

> Grant me an old man's frenzy,
> Myself must I remake
> Till I am Timon and Lear

Or that William Blake
Who beat upon the wall
Till Truth obeyed his call.

It was truth, uninhibited and unrestrained, that Yeats now
desired. It made him extremely frank even about the most
delicate things. He shocked some of his friends by his outspoken language on sex ; and answered them in *The Spur* :

You think it horrible that lust and rage
Should dance attention upon my old age ;
They were not such a plague when I was young ;
What else have I to spur me into song ?

He did not care now what men thought about him or try to
live up to any ideal of what a poet ought to say. He wished to
be himself.

The change to the last style came about 1929. In the
spring of that year Yeats recovered from a dangerous illness
and found himself full of " an uncontrollable energy " which
led to the group of poems *Words for Music Perhaps*. Here are
new easy rhythms of song, refrains which suggest contrasts
and backgrounds, an absolute frankness, and a remarkable
character called Crazy Jane. In her Yeats presents someone
entirely natural who accepts the world and enjoys it, and,
because she is physical and simple, is in touch with truth.
She mocks the Bishop who deplores the loss of her virginity ;
she shows that there is no need to lament passing joy, for " all
things remain in God " ; she accepts hate as a part of life.
She stands for what Yeats has become. His chief desire is to
take life as it is and to enjoy it, and the range of this enjoyment
is large. It includes an unashamed pleasure in sex, and it
includes humour, which is in turn savage, imaginative and
frankly absurd. It is easy for him to make fun of established
butts like statesmen or John Bull, but now he even laughs at
himself. In *High Talk* he makes fun of those who have great
pretensions and seems to place himself in their company. In
The Statesman's Holiday he, who had treated himself seriously
as a Senator and sat on pompous committees, flings aside all
his pretences and sees himself as a genial figure of fun, dirty
and disreputable :

With boys and girls about him,
With any sort of clothes,
With a hat out of fashion,
With old patched shoes,

215

With a ragged bandit cloak,
With an eye like a hawk,
With a stiff straight back,
With a strutting turkey walk,
With a bag full of pennies,
With a monkey on a chain,
With a great cock's feather,
With a foul old tune.
Tall dames go walking in grass-green Avalon.

The final refrain, so splendidly incongruous with what has gone before, gives the contrast between the poet as he now mockingly sees himself and what he was years before when he lived among imaginary princesses in realms of faery.

What counts in this last poetry is its zest. Yeats, over seventy, found pleasure where before he had found responsibility. He was now free from all obligations and could be frankly and enjoyably himself. The old age which he had dreaded brought an enhanced vitality and freedom. He could strike out right and left, assume any air he chose, indulge his innate love of malice and mockery. He had at last put into his poetry the qualities which had for long been prominent in his conversation. In a scurrilous passage of *A Story-Teller's Holiday* George Moore reports a rumour that Yeats had retired from life in the belief " that the poet should apply himself as soon as his poetry is written to the weaving of a ' Poetic Personality ' ". Moore wrote of 1916 when Yeats was at the height of his powers, and the rumour can have had little base in fact. But there is such a thing as a poetic personality, and Yeats possessed it in a high degree. He judged and saw things in a peculiarly individual way with all a poet's insight. But only in his last years did this personality really fill his verse. He now wrote out of his full being, not merely out of his more serious self. Not that the new playful or mocking spirit overwhelmed the old seriousness. In *The Municipal Gallery Revisited* he looks back on his friends, and his own life. He is proud to have known these people who really did something to make modern Ireland, and hopes that his friendship with them will be remembered to his credit. His self-mockery had not reduced his natural and proper pride in what he had done.

Yeats, now as always, made a virtue of pride. It has been held against him, and the politically conscious who are unable to judge a man until they have fixed a party-label on him, have condemned him for his authoritarian sympathies. It is true that at intervals Yeats flirted with political ideas and fancied that he might play some impressive part in public life. He was even impressed by the antics of D'Annunzio and curious about the influence of Stefan George. In this aberration there was an element of ambition, pardonable enough, to be more honoured and recognised than he was. Yeats had his share of vanity and liked to think that he had made his mark on the world. His failure in politics and his final disgust with them did not prevent him from wishing to be acclaimed by the crowd. Actually he was quite unfitted for the compromises and stratagems of political life. If he felt at all, he felt strongly, and then nothing could hold him from saying in the most trenchant manner what he believed. In Catholic Ireland he spoke up boldly and eloquently for divorce and against the censorship of books, and failed in both cases. He might believe that an authoritarian government would give him the honours that he desired, but practice proved the opposite. He was far too independent, far too conscious of the freedom which the poet needs, ever to acquiesce in any such system. And though in his poetry he sometimes seems careless or cynical about brutality and bloodshed, that is only because in his last years he was so honest about himself that if he had such feelings, as most men at times will, he felt impelled to say so. They were part of his recklessness, his zest for saying exactly what he felt.

On the other hand Yeats seriously and constantly stood for an aristocratic ideal. He imagined a society of cultivated landowners and inspired peasants. He had, as he believed, found it in his youth in Ireland. The peasants had provided him with a mass of vivid stories and beliefs ; the aristocracy, represented by Lady Gregory, had turned these stories into art and created the Abbey Theatre. Like Villiers de l'Isle Adam, he liked to think that he himself was of noble stock. His dislike of any middle class in this scheme of things was intensified by the controversy about the Lane pictures and remained with him. Yeats' scheme of society was imaginary. Even in the Ireland of his youth few of the country gentlemen would have understood him or his ideals. His best support came from the small and highly cultivated professional class which produced Wilde and Synge and Yeats himself. Yeats' belief in aristocracy may have been based on illusions but it meant much to him. What he really admired were the old virtues of independence, magnanimity, courage, devotion. They are hardly the virtues of ordinary bourgeois life, which allows little scope for their display. But they are the traditional virtues of nobility. Yeats was singularly unable to submit to restraint or to endure opposition. He must at all costs have his own way. Therefore he pictured a perfect society in which everyone was as noble as he liked to think himself. He stood for something valuable in his affirmation of personality ; any theory of government to which he may have attached it is of little importance in comparison.

Yeats' career is an instructive commentary on Symbolist doctrine. He was well fitted to welcome it, and through it he found his first real style. Even when he was brought down to reality and abandoned his earlier manner, he was still to a large extent a Symbolist ; he still dealt with subtle and intangible matters behind the immediately visible world ; he still saw the artist as a superior being who is almost necessarily out of tune with his times. But what marks him off from other poets of his training is that through Symbolism he found a way to create an extremely lively and concrete poetry about himself. He worked hard to rid his verse of all vagueness and looseness. What he lost in mystery he gained in power. To otherwise commonplace events he brought a wonder and significance, a vitality and enjoyment, which made them extraordinarily vivid and real. He attached great importance to the emotions, and since he was himself highly emotional and even passionate, he tried, with consummate success, to make poetry of them. Even in his most abstract themes there is a great intensity of feeling. He flung all of himself into his verse, till it contained the many qualities of his exuberant and abundant personality. At the one end is what takes place

> In a foul rag-and-bone shop of the heart,

at the other the absolute satisfaction which he found when his faculties were freely at work :

> So great a sweetness flows into the breast
> We must laugh and we must sing,
> We are blest by everything,
> Everything we look upon is blest.

VII
CONCLUSION

No one, not even Aristotle, has found a satisfactory definition of poetry. We all think that we know what it is, but soon
find that our idea of it is not shared by our contemporaries, let
alone by the great critics of the past. Each definition seems
both to include and to exclude too much. The fact is that the
theory and practice of poetry differ from age to age. It lives
by change and is constantly renewed by the introduction of
new standards and new technique. What satisfies one period
cannot satisfy another. On a long view the conception of
poetry seems to oscillate between two extremes, between
instruction and magic. Boileau said proudly

> Et mon vers, bien ou mal, dit toujours quelque chose.

He excites the derision of those who search for " pure poetry ",
but his attitude was usual for two centuries and is inherent in
any form of classicism. At the other extreme is the romantic
notion that poetry does not state but create, not inform but
produce an effect. Such is Coleridge's wish :

> Could I revive within me
> Her symphony and song,
> To such a deep delight 'twould win me,
> That with music loud and long
> I would build that dome in air,
> That sunny dome ; those caves of ice !

No less it lies behind Mallarmé's belief that poetry makes a
change in the world :

> Une agitation solennelle par l'air
> De paroles, pourpre ivre et grand calice clair.

Between these extremes many compromises are possible.
The greatest poets, Homer, Dante, Shakespeare, have both
informed and created, have been both teachers and magicians.
They were fortunate in their times which expected a poet to be
a repository of wisdom and to have a special insight into life.
The modern poet is less lucky. Much of his inherited task

has been taken from him by science. The astronomer, the geographer, the psychologist are thought to know more about their subjects than ever he can. Even in ethics he must compete against the priest, the moral philosopher and the journalist. He is not expected and not allowed to claim his old rights. He must be simply a poet, and what that means the public does not know nor very much care. By a natural process the poet has reverted to the old magical conception of his work and has become again a kind of shaman whose success lies in the hypnotic excitement which he can produce in others. He may at moments show a startling insight into the human soul or give expression to what lies hidden in many hearts, but his chief business, his distinctive function, is to lay an enchantment, to make an impression, an effect.

Mallarmé was fully conscious of this limitation of the poet's sphere and made a virtue of it. He believed that it was a great advantage because it forced him to be only a poet, to concentrate on his real task, to write pure poetry. His own verse has much of the quality of incantation. The thought in it, the mere meaning, emerges gradually after the magic has done its work. He creates in his readers a complex state in which understanding plays only a small part. His successors have followed him, but not all the way. They have on the whole abandoned the search for pure poetry and found that in practice it is impossible to lay down what subjects are poetical and what are not. They have increased the amount of intelligible matter in their verse and have even condescended to argue and explain. They have not sought for the ideal page, for the silence more expressive than song. They accept the fact that words have meanings and that poetry must be understood. But they have none the less kept to the magical view of it. They aim at moving hearts and stirring imaginations. Even when they have become teachers like George or prophets like Blok, their messages are based on their conception of poetry. It is poetry which is to change the world, the spirit of song or of music which is to create new societies. They have thus found a place for themselves and solved the discord which the original Symbolists felt between themselves and the public. The poet, it is now felt, can do something that other men cannot do. He can give a special kind of life through his art ; he can show what things really mean in their associations and relations. Through the feelings and the imagination he creates an effect which science never can. The scientist is the mere expositor, the poet the man of action.

The magical conception of poetry has taken different forms. When Henri Bremond said that poetry was like prayer, he touched on something near the truth about the post-Symbolists. For not only is their poetry an incantation ; it is based on the belief that the poet is in touch with some superior order of things and that his art is the ritual by which this is brought down to men. Rilke's theory of death and transformation, George's cult of Maximin, Blok's Spirit of Music, Yeats' spiritualism, are all attempts to make a religion out of the creative process which lies behind poetry, to find in its dynamic manifestations a power at work in the whole universe. Even Valéry's acceptance of poetry as something unique and inexplicable and his unceasing surprise that such a thing can exist are an admission that there is a mystery somewhere. In the Middle Ages, even in the time of Milton, the Christian cosmogony explained poetry as it explained everything else. But this explanation has ceased to count. The poets of the 'nineties needed some other object for their faith, some other principle to explain and support their devotion. They found their own special answers, and these have given them strength and confidence in themselves. They have felt at home in their work and in the world. But the strangeness of their solutions has detracted from their influence. It is their central ideas which the average man finds impossible to accept. We might argue that if poetry is a kind of magic, its theory can hardly be rational. But none the less it is possible to accept the premiss without the conclusion and to hold that poetry is indeed mysterious but that its existence does not justify beliefs so odd as these. Valéry seems nearer to the common view when he accepts the mystery but erects no theory on it. And in fact it is from the beliefs, not from the poetry, that the younger generation has revolted. In their own kind of mysticism the post-Symbolists have left no successors. The new poets explain their work by quite different theories.

The magical view of poetry gives a special place to the poet. He is once again the " Vates ", the instrument of unseen powers who work by superhuman methods. He is no longer a man among other men or expected to think the common thoughts of his time. In consequence he is free, as he has seldom been, to be himself, to develop his individuality and private tastes. The aristocratic and autocratic tendencies of George and Yeats are as much a reflection of this as are Blok's obedience to his emotions and Rilke's refusal to identify himself with any country or movement or school. All feel that they must follow their own inclinations and be free to do what they choose ; otherwise their powers would be hampered. And this independence is, by tacit consent, allowed to them. They are even respected for it. It is because they are unlike other men and have a peculiarly personal view of life that they are listened to. What counts is the uniqueness of their work. The cult of the self may sometimes bring disadvantages to their art. George's desire to impose his own will on the world led him to an unpoetical didacticism ; Rilke's solitary communion with his sensibility made some of his work morbid. But these losses are compensated by far greater gains. Because the poet is free to be himself, he can make his art conform to his own ideas without sacrificing anything to public opinion ; he can mature his gifts and find by experiment what new possibilities can be realised ; he can concentrate on his technique until it really satisfies him. At a time when many writers spoiled their work by writing down to the public mind, the poets kept themselves intact.

This independence does not mean that the poets lived in an ivory tower. The aesthetic seclusion of Huysmans and Villiers de l'Isle Adam was replaced by a robust appetite for life. The poets began with fine dreams and an exquisite sensitivity which shrank from the coarse impacts of reality. But their abundant natures felt restricted by this ascetic cult of the Beautiful and drove them to closer contact with common things and stronger emotions. Yeats and George looked down from their heights to the political issues of their time ; Blok flung himself tempestuously into his ideal revolution ; Rilke, who had retired deep into himself, found there a new vision of the universe which gave significance to many apparently trivial things ; even Valéry, detached and analytical, wrote his best poetry about the most simple subjects. When they extended their range, their early apprenticeship served them well. They knew their business too well to adapt their private feelings to a vague general emotion. They kept their personal view of events and avoided the false simplification and false emphasis which are the besetting faults of those who write for a large public. They showed that political themes as such are not alien to poetry, that what matters is the treatment of them. If this is in accordance with the poet's best art, they can yield their own poetical effects.

The return of the poet's personality brought remarkable results for poetry. The eminent Romantics had spoken much about themselves, but their self-revelations have a touch of unreality, of staginess. They know too well how they would wish the world to see them. Their comments and confessions are not always convincing. Even when, like Shelley, they are undeniably sincere, we still wonder if they really understand, or are interested in, themselves. Victor Hugo was so conscious of his greatness that he could not but conform to his ideal of what a poet ought to be and impart a portentous solemnity to thoughts which are sometimes not even serious. The Parnassians, on the other hand, sank their personalities in an objective art. Their inner histories and their opinions play little part in their poetry. Even their sensibility is usually restricted to what the eye can see. But the Symbolists and their successors found a way to speak about themselves which was at once sincere and impressive. In this they undoubtedly owed much to Baudelaire. The man who wrote

Hypocrite lecteur, — mon semblable, — mon frère !

had no illusions about himself or his readers. He takes them into his confidence because they share his faults. This is a candour with which the old high conception of the poet had no contact. Mallarmé imparted a new tone of intimacy to it when he spoke of his inmost desires in words quite free of exaggeration and with his exquisite tact showed exactly what they meant to him. The post-Symbolists developed this to a high degree. They wrote boldly and sincerely about themselves. In most cases the struggle to achieve this was hard. They had to pass through preliminary stages, to dramatise themselves as historical or mythical characters, to display their feelings indirectly through symbols. But in the end they found how to present their full selves. We know and value them for being what they are and for their candour in speaking about it.

This is a success for their poetry and for nothing else. The personality that counts is not that picked up from memoirs or letters or stray remarks but that known fully and faithfully from verse. These poets are extremely candid. Not all are so outspoken as Yeats, who can keep his dignity and our interest in such lines as :

> I thought him half a lunatic, half knave,
> And told him so, but friendship never ends.

But nearly all have presented full records of their feelings in most directions. Blok's great emotional range, George's personal approach to great issues, Rilke's nervous analysis of his discontents, are different manifestations of the common impulse to bring back the poet's self to poetry. Even Valéry's art, which seems remote and Olympian, is entirely based on his own conflicts and excitements and would not exist if he did not know himself thoroughly and possess the ability to say in verse what his complex states are and mean. The psychological insight displayed by the great novelists of the nineteenth century touched the poets and enabled them at least to know themselves. This knowledge was all the easier because when they grew to manhood the value of the individual had not been seriously challenged. The new creeds and movements which were later to shake it so ferociously had not yet gained a hold. The poet, sure of himself and of his place, thought it right to speak about them. In himself he had an inexhaustible source of subjects. He puts them at our disposal, and in him we see much of ourselves.

Through this self-knowledge poetry has gained new fields which more than compensate for the loss of others which had outlived their interest or been annexed to prose. Sometimes the new matter is of a peculiar kind, like Yeats' spiritualism or Rilke's psychology of the self. But usually it is drawn from the common stock of experience and needed only genius to bring it out. • Yeats, for instance, has created an almost new kind of poetry about his friends by making them at once entirely real and yet symbolical of various destinies. They are his saints, his martyrs, his examples of success and failure, of the varied human scene. In his own way George has done much the same, when he addresses his friends on points of intimate interest and makes them see themselves as important cases in the spiritual history of man. The whole range of Valéry's matter is new. He typifies in his own conflicts the general conflict between knowledge and the emotions, between the mind and the body. Such a conflict was sharpened by the scientific outlook of the nineteenth century and has to be solved for himself by almost every civilised man. Valéry is not merely conscious of it but fully conversant with it in many forms. In his poetry at least he has solved it and given an answer to Rimbaud's desperate denial : " Il faut être absolument moderne. Point de cantiques : tenir le pas gagné." Even the discontents which Rilke voices so poignantly are a kind of modern sickness, the fruits of a ripe individualism. We cannot imagine them before the twentieth century. They are the poetical counterpart of the scientific activities of Freud and Jung. In their choice of new subjects these poets owe much to elements in themselves which had hitherto been neglected or imperfectly transformed into art. Even the extraordinary candour of Blok has the imprint of modernity. Not even in Russia would an earlier poet have told the truth with such complete frankness.

Of course if we compare the post-Symbolists with later poets, they may well appear old-fashioned. It could hardly be otherwise and brings no discredit. Nor is it merely that they did not hold doctrines which are now fashionable or that their central ideas have failed to make a wide appeal. It is rather that the sphere in which they work is different and determined by limits which are no longer recognised. The change can be seen in the entirely different spirit in which older and younger poets treat the eminently modern theme of machinery. For George and Valéry it does not exist. They say nothing about it and presumably think it of no importance so far as poetry is concerned. The others are conscious of it, but very much in their own way. When Yeats wrote *An Irish Airman foresees his Death* the subject of flying had to be considered, but all that matters is the purely human interest of the airman who knows that he will die :

> A lonely impulse of delight
> Drove to this tumult in the clouds.

The mere machine is of no importance, has no romance, no appeal. Before this, in 1910–1912, Blok had written a poem *Aviator*. Unlike Yeats, he is by no means indifferent to the actual machine and is even fascinated by its monstrous shape like a sea-monster, the music of its propellers, its copper engines. But he too is chiefly interested in the man in it. He asks what his reasons can be for so insane an adventure which means certain death, and wonders if it is some strange self-denial or anticipation of war to come. For him, as for Yeats, the real question concerns not the machine but the human being in it. This was the attitude of poets at a time when Kipling preached the virtues of machinery and progressively transferred his admiration from men to animals and from animals to railway engines and steamships. Unlike him, they did not feel that machines were more noble and more interesting than men. Kipling may have been closer to the common feelings of the time and more prophetic of what was to come, but the poets did not share his growing hatred of humanity and his consequent worship of the inanimate. If they had to choose between men and machines, they chose men. To Rilke the mechanisation of life was a menace. He saw the dangers which machinery might bring to the spirit :

> Sieh, die Maschine :
> Wie sie sich wälzt und rächt
> Und uns entstellt und schwächt.[1]

He had his answer to the threat. Machinery is no menace if we control it and make it our instrument instead of becoming its :

> Alles Erworbne bedroht die Maschine, solange
> Sie sich erdreistet, im Geist, statt im Gehorchen, zu sein.[2]

What matters for him is the spirit which controls and transforms, which can make even machinery part of itself. The post-Symbolists were at one with him. They found no romance in mechanisation. That has been left to those who lack belief in the human self.

The case of machines is significant of much in the post-Symbolists' work. Unlike their successors, they believed that poetry is concerned with Beauty. This was their ideal, their gospel. They accepted it without question and allowed it to guide their work. Their position undoubtedly involves an ambiguity. If they meant merely that it is important to write

[1] Machinery, observe it :
Rolling itself in rage,
Spoiling our heritage.
(Trs. J. B. Leishman)

[2] The machine is only a menace to all our human endeavour
So long as it dares to exist in thought instead of in thrall.
(Trs. J. B. Leishman)

well, no one can quarrel with them. And in effect this is what they meant. For them the Beautiful was the principle that informed their art. But if they meant that the poet chooses his themes from what is generally recognised as beautiful, it is another matter. They might then be rightly criticised for hampering free creation by a convention or a theory. The assumption that the stuff of poetry must be confined to a recognised list of beautiful subjects can only mean that poets are unable to break fresh ground. Of this the post-Symbolists show no sign. Their themes are sometimes by common standards painful or even disagreeable. They knew their task too well to be tied by any such convention. None the less if we compare them with some modern poets, their work certainly lies in different limits. It has an air of dignity which has since been rejected. The followers of Jules Laforgue and Guillaume Apollinaire deal with more ordinary themes in a much more conversational way. Yeats and Blok may draw imagery from common life, but the world as they see it is not the common world. The difference is undeniable. The moderns have invented a poetry of the commonplace. For their changed outlook they have found a modern style. In their realistic rhythms and everyday subjects they have moved a long way from the older generation which, with its religious or oracular view of art, cannot but keep an air of aloofness. It believed that it was different from other men and was proud to be so. The modern realists are the poets of the multitude. Their thoughts run on common topics and in common words. Once again poetry has had to change her character that she may keep her youth.

Because these poets write about themselves, they are often and indeed usually subjective. The unity of a poem is secured not by a theme or a setting but by the poet's mind, in which everything takes place. Valéry's *Le Cimetière Marin* and Yeats' *Among School Children* are composed on the same principle. In both there seems to be an external setting, the cemetery by the sea or the schoolroom, but this is seen through the poet and exists in his sensations. The visible phenomena are in him ; the crisis takes place in him and concerns him personally ; the great universal questions arise from his private history and situation. There is no clear distinction between the poet and the external world. Both are merged in him. The method is very different from such a poem as

Shelley's *Stanzas written in Dejection*, where the waves and the sunlight, the whole scene in the Bay of Naples, are quite exterior to the poet and almost mock him by their severance from him. Rilke carried this subjectivity even further than Valéry or Yeats. His last poetry exists in the conviction that everything gets its right value through being absorbed into us and transformed. Even George makes the past live only because it has a present value and shows in a clear form the permanent aims of the spirit. All the post-Symbolists have a kind of philosophy in which the phenomenal world exists in the poet and gets its interest through his apprehension of it. This view owes little to professional philosophy. It is a natural result of the rediscovered self and of the failure of old systems to satisfy modern needs. The independent, external world, which science presupposes, is for many reasons unsatisfactory. It demands too great a distinction between things and our awareness of them. The poets, with clearer insight, know that everything that is theirs is somehow in them and that their work starts from this. It may be related to some greater system, and this in their different ways they have tried to discover; but what matters is, after all, the given, the sensations and feelings which the poet has. For poetry this is a great advantage. The experience which the poet has and puts into verse is infinitely complex and individual. Scientific objectivity simplifies it into unrecognisable abstractions. It cannot be reduced to order on these lines. It must be presented as the poet sees and feels it. Philosophers may argue whether art is concerned with the universal or the particular. For most men it is concerned with both. It presents in a markedly individual way what many must know and recognise as real.

All art has its limitations. Success in one direction is gained by neglect in another. The Symbolists and their successors set out with a clear view of what poetry ought to be. They modified it greatly with the years, and yet they still kept to some of the main tenets ; its mystical grandeur, its aloofness, its element of music. By concentrating on these points they missed opportunities which later poets have seized, especially that creation of poetry from the most ordinary words and things which has since come to the fore. Their high standards of technique almost forbade any attempt to reduce the language of poetry to that of speech, or to use slang except for some strange ulterior purpose, as Blok uses it in *The Twelve*. If they condescend to this, they still keep their distance. So too their respect for verbal harmony precluded them from the more staccato effects of modern verse. Even their occasional *vers libre* has its own dignity. Their plainest words have a noble and measured tread, a due respect for " la musique avant toute chose ". There is perhaps a special music in the jazz orchestra or in senseless exclamations, and no doubt this will play its part in poetry. But the inheritors of Mallarmé imagined more solemn and more regular harmonies. At times they could burst into song, but their song, ravishing as it often is, has never the authentic Elizabethan grace. The poetry of their age owed too much to Wagner for that. It is too packed, too orchestrated, for direct outbursts. It keeps a hieratic quality even when it is wildest and most unpremeditated. But because it keeps these solemn qualities, it is always fully laden and extremely expressive. Each word does its work, each line has its strength. It fulfils, as more improvised poetry cannot, Keats' desire " to load every rift with ore ". The desire to make poetry like music had at least the result of making it sonorous and expressive. The rhythm varies enormously even in the works of a single poet, but it is always functional and adds incalculably to the main effect. There are many kinds of music which it does not attempt, but within its own choice it does what it sets out to do. This poetry is the work of men who had a clear and exacting conception of what poetry ought to be, and to this their art conforms.

The danger of the aesthetic approach to life is that by concentrating on beautiful objects it loses a taste for ordinary things and may even be pained or disgusted by them. In the last resort it leads to a passive melancholy, a refusal or inability to face experience as it comes. These poets were not like this. There was nothing in them of Des Esseintes or Sebastian van Storck. Despite their different personalities and diverse metaphysics, all found an intense excitement in living. Even Rilke's cult of death became a conviction that everything should be a subject for praise if we look at it in the right way; George's worship of Maximin was a strong protest against any negative or puritanical creed; Blok's delight in the collapse of the old world was founded in his trust that an infinitely more exciting world was being born in its place. All stood for an increased awareness, an enhanced vitality. They wished to extract the most vivid possible experience from what happened to them. Their times were certainly hard. The twentieth century has brought poets into touch with facts far more brutal than their immediate predecessors ever knew. But the greater the disaster, the greater the chance for the poet :

Tison de gloire, sang par écume, or, tempête !

Out of the blood and storm he has won glory. The post-Symbolists have had the confidence to assert human values in the face of meaningless circumstance and to rise to a tragic grandeur. From the griefs and burdens of mankind they have extracted a noble exaltation. Despite their yearnings for other worlds, their feet were firmly set on the earth. Their desire for transcendental orders of experience is no denial of the here and now. It bears no relation to Plato's distrust of the senses or Christian antinomies of soul and body. Indeed these mystical backgrounds give significance to life by relating its multiple phenomena to a single scheme. The Ideal, remote and intangible, is known only through its sensible instances. These are what count. Even the poet's own joy in creation, which seems so unlike other human activities, is intimately dependent on what his senses give him. His theories, his mystical exaltation, his sense of another, more real world, end paradoxically by making him attach more value to the sensations and appearances which constitute his daily life. They sharpen his insight and make him find charm and significance in much that others dismiss as trivial or fail altogether to notice. The claim of the post-Symbolists is largely that their imaginative art has thrown a new enchanting light on themes which might seem stale or exhausted and on quite familiar events. But they have done more than this. They have delved into the increased and complex consciousness of civilised man and found in it mysteries whose real nature can never be conveyed through the abstract methods of science, whose worth for human life can only be expressed through symbol and suggestion. They have proved that in the modern world there is still a place for poetry because it does something that nothing else can do.

INDEX

Apollinaire, G., 227

Bachofen, H., 107
Balmont, C., 145, 146
Baudelaire, C., 1, 2, 3, 6, 7, 30, 44, 145, 182, 223
Bely, A., 147, 148, 177
Blake, W., 5, 15, 180
Blok, A., 144-179, 201, 204, 209, 211, 220, 221, 222, 224, 225, 226, 229
Boileau, N., 219
Bremond, H., 221
Bridges, R., 183, 209
Browning, R., 2, 181
Bryusov, V., 69, 145, 146

Carducci, G., 44
Claudel, P., 17
Coleridge, S. T., 29, 219

D'Annunzio, G., 217
Dante, 5, 46, 108, 125, 200, 219
Dickens, C., 144
Dostoyevsky, F., 144
Dowson, E., 4, 181, 182, 184
Du Bellay, J., 15

Eliot, T. S., 47, 74

Flaubert, G., 12

George, S., 58, 98-143, 160, 204, 209, 217, 220, 221, 222, 224, 225, 228, 229
Goethe, J. W. v., 44, 45, 107, 109, 125, 145, 148, 170
Gogol, N., 163
Gorky, M., 177, 178, 179
Gourmont, R. de, 13
Gregory, Lady, 201, 217

Hardy, T., 67, 183
Heredia, J. M. de, 2, 8, 67, 105
Hofmannsthal, H. v., 58, 108
Hölderlin, F., 107
Homer, 31, 210, 219

Hopkins, G. M., 4, 15, 182
Horace, 15
Housman, A. E., 32, 181, 182
Hugo, V., 1, 8, 60, 133, 223
Huysmans, J. K., 12, 13, 222

Jammes, F., 17
Johnson, L., 4, 181, 182, 183, 184

Keats, J., 184, 229
Kipling, R., 226
Klein, K. A., 99

Laforgue, J., 227
Leconte de Lisle, 8, 60
Lenau, N., 115
Lermontov, M., 144, 161
Lucretius, 19

Maeterlinck, M., 194, 196
Mallarmé, S., 1-16, 17-19, 21, 22, 28, 29, 33, 34, 36, 38, 54, 60, 76, 89, 98, 99, 100, 101, 103, 114, 116, 164, 184, 185, 186, 192, 194, 195, 211, 213, 223
Milton, J., 6, 36, 126, 221
Moore, G., 216
Moréas, J., 17, 113
Mörike, E., 115
Morris, W., 183, 184, 189, 190
Musset, A. de, 133

Nietzsche, F., 107, 125, 126

Pater, W., 3, 4, 13, 14, 184
Pindar, 132
Plato, 5, 124, 131
Poe, E. A., 12, 89, 133, 145
Pushkin, A., 1, 144, 156, 161

Regnier, H. de, 17
Rilke, R. M., 56-97, 98, 103, 116, 164, 211, 221, 222, 224, 225, 226
Rimbaud, A., 178, 225
Rodin, A., 57, 58, 59
Rossetti, D. G., 3, 4

231

Schiller, F., 170
Shakespeare, W., 95, 133, 178, 196, 219
Shelley, P. B., 29, 30, 35, 180, 223, 228
Sologub, F., 145
Solovyev, V., 146
Sophocles, 214
Stendhal, 144
Symons, A., 184, 195
Synge, J. M., 198, 213, 217

Tennyson, A., 2, 8, 180, 181
Theognis, 124
Thompson, F., 183
Tolstoy, A., 165
Tolstoy, L., 144
Tyutchev, N., 165

Valéry, P., 9, 14, 17-55, 57, 73, 92, 96, 99, 104, 112, 118, 147, 187, 221, 222, 224, 225, 227, 228, 229
Vergil, 23, 69
Verlaine, P., 1, 2, 3, 7, 99, 145, 156, 182
Villiers de l'Isle Adam, 12, 13, 99, 196, 217, 223

Wagner, R., 8, 9, 12, 170
Wilde, O., 3, 13, 102, 182, 183, 184, 217
Wordsworth, W., 15, 43, 180

Yeats, W. B., 43, 155, 180-218, 221, 222, 224, 225, 226, 227, 228

Zola, E., 2

THE END

Printed in Great Britain by R. & R. CLARK, LIMITED, *Edinburgh*